LITERATURE AND CULTURE

IN MODERN BRITAIN

Volume One: 1900–1929

Literature and Culture in Modern Britain

Series Editors:
Clive Bloom, Principal Lecturer in the Faculty of Humanities, Middlesex University
Gary Day, teaches English Literature at University College Cardiff
Brian Docherty, Poet and Lecturer with the Workers Education Institute

Forthcoming volumes:
Literature and Culture in Modern Britain, Volume Two: 1930–1955
Literature and Culture in Modern Britain, Volume Three: 1956–1992

Literature and Culture in Modern Britain

Volume One: 1900-1929

Edited by Clive Bloom

Longman
London and New York

Longman Group UK Limited,
Longman House, Burnt Mill,
Harlow, Essex CM20 2JE, England
and Associated Companies throughout the world.

Published in the United States of America by Longman Publishing,
New York

© Longman Group UK Limited 1993

First published 1993

ISBN 0 582 07549 1 CSD
ISBN 0 582 07548 3 PPR

British Library Cataloguing-in-Publication Data

A catalogue record for this book is available from the British Library

Library of Congress Cataloging-in-Publication Data

Literature and culture in modern Britain / edited by Clive Bloom.
  p.   cm.
  Includes bibliographical references and index.
  Contents: v. 1. 1900–1929
  ISBN 0-582-07549-1. – ISBN 0-582-07548-3 (pbk.)
  1. English literature – 20th century – History and criticism.
2. Great Britain – Popular culture – History – 20th century.
3. Great Britain – Civilization – 20th century. I. Bloom, Clive.
PR471.L5   1993
820.9'0091 – dc20   93–932
                                                        CIP

Set by 14B in 10/12 pt Bembo

Produced by Longman Singapore Publishers (Pte) Ltd.
Printed in Singapore

Contents

Series Preface

LITERATURE AND CULTURE IN MODERN BRITAIN

As literary and cultural studies expand into new areas of enquiry, the aim
of this three-volume sequence is to give the reader an intertextual cultural
history of modern Britain, one in which literary, cultural and historical
processes are intimately connected. It is a history in which literature is
neither seen as a mere reflection of social forces nor as separate from such
forces, but rather as a participating and moulding factor in the history of
perception in this country over the century.

List of Contributors

Clive Bloom teaches at Middlesex University.

Robert Chaplin is a teacher in London.

Lez Cooke teaches at Staffordshire University.

Gary Day teaches at University College, Cardiff.

Robert Giddings teaches at Bournemouth University.

Michael Hayes teaches at the University of Central Lancashire.

John Morris teaches at Brunel University.

Brian Morton is a freelance writer and music journalist.

Nicholas Rance teaches at Middlesex University.

Jim Reilly teaches at London University and the Open University.

Michael Woolf is Director of the Council on International Educational Exchange, London.

Chronology

YEAR	LITERARY EVENTS	OTHER CULTURAL EVENTS	POLITICAL AND OTHER EVENTS
1900	Conrad, *Lord Jim* Yeats, 'The symbolism of poetry' Death of Oscar Wilde	Death of Arthur Sullivan	Relief of Mafeking
1901	Alfred Dreyfus publishes his story in the UK		Death of Queen Victoria Accession of Edward VII
1902	A.E.W. Mason, *The Four Feathers* Conrad, *Heart of Darkness* Beatrix Potter, *Peter Rabbit,* H.G. Wells, *First Men in the Moon* Kipling, *Just So Stories* Conan Doyle, *The Hound of the Baskervilles* Bennett, *Anna of the Five Towns*		End of Boer War Education Act

YEAR	LITERARY EVENTS	OTHER CULTURAL EVENTS	POLITICAL AND OTHER EVENTS
1903	Erskine Childers, *The Riddle of the Sands* Shaw, *Man and Superman* Samuel Butler, *The Way of All Flesh* James, *The Ambassadors*	Alfred Harmsworth founds the *Daily Mirror*	First aeroplane flight
1904	Robert Hitchens, *The Garden of Allah* Baron 'Corvo', *Hadrian VII* Conrad, *Nostromo* James, *The Golden Bowl*		
1905	Edgar Wallace, *The Four Just Men* Conan Doyle, *The Return of Sherlock Holmes* Baroness Orczy, *The Scarlet Pimpernel* Wilde, *De Profundis*	Alfred Harmsworth becomes Lord Northcliffe	
1906	Baden Powell, *Boy Scouts: a suggestion* Galsworthy, *A Man of Property* Shaw, *The Doctor's Dilemna*		Liberal government elected
1907	Forster, *A Room with a View* Bennett, *The Old Wives' Tale* Death of 'Ouida' (Marie Louise de la Rainée)	Northcliffe buys *The Times*	

YEAR	LITERARY EVENTS	OTHER CULTURAL EVENTS	POLITICAL AND OTHER EVENTS
	Kipling wins Nobel Prize Synge, *The Playboy of the Western World*		
1908	Kenneth Graham, *The Wind in the Willows*		Old Age Pensions Act
1909	Death of Swinburne Death of George Meredith Wells, *Tono-Bungay*		Blériot flies the English Channel 'People's Budget'
1910	Jeffrey Farnol, *The Broad Highway* Forster, *Howard's End* Yeats, *The Green Helmet*	Death of Florence Nightingale Trial and execution of Crippen First post impressionist exhibition	Death of Edward VII Accession of George V Crisis over House of Lords
1911	G.K. Chesterton, *The Innocence of Father Brown* Katherine Mansfield, *In a German Pension* Conrad, *Under Western Eyes* John Masefield, 'Everlasting Mercy' Galsworthy, *Strife* Copyright bill		National Insurance Act Suffragette riots
1912	First Georgian anthology		Strikes by miners and dockers Ulster opposition to Home Rule
1913	Sax Rohmer, *The Mystery of Dr Fu-Manchu*	Bertrand Russell and A.N. Whitehead, *Principia Mathematica*	Lords reject Home Rule Bill

YEAR	LITERARY EVENTS	OTHER CULTURAL EVENTS	POLITICAL AND OTHER EVENTS
	Lawrence, *Sons and Lovers*		
1914	Joyce, *Dubliners* J.M. Barrie, *The Admirable Chrighton* Shaw, *Pygmalion* Forster, *Maurice* (completed but not published)	The *Daily Mirror* achieves circulation of 1,200,000	Army officers defy government over Home Rule Suffragette riots; Mary Richardson slashes *The Rokeby Venus* First World War begins
1915	Lawrence *The Rainbow* John Buchan, *The Thirty-Nine Steps* Rupert Brooke, *Grantchester* and 'War Sonnets' published Death of Rupert Brooke Somerset Maughan, *Of Human Bondage* Death of Julian Grenfell Ford Maddox Ford, *The Good Soldier*		
1916	John Buchan, *The Power House* Joyce, *A Portrait of the Artist as a Young Man* Shaw, *Androcles and the Lion* Death of Henry James	Beaverbrook buys majority share in the *Daily Express*	First Battle of the Somme Easter Rising, Dublin

YEAR	LITERARY EVENTS	OTHER CULTURAL EVENTS	POLITICAL AND OTHER EVENTS
1917	'Bartimeus', *The Long Trick* Edgar Rice Burroughs, *Tarzan of the Apes* T.S. Eliot, *Prufrock and Other Observations*		Russian Revolution
1918	Arthur Waley, *170 Chinese Poems* Death of Wilfred Owen		End of First World War Representation of the People Act
1919	Yeats, *The Wild Swans at Coole* H.L. Mencken, *The American Language* T.S. Eliot, 'Tradition and the individual talent'		
1920	Agatha Christie, *The Mysterious Affair at Styles* 'Sapper', *Bulldog Drummond* T.S. Eliot, *The Sacred Wood* Wilfred Owen, *Poems* Shaw, *Heartbreak House* Lawrence, *Women in Love*		'Black and Tans' recruited
1921	E.M. Hull, *The Shadow of the East* Aldous Huxley, *Crome Yellow*		Irish Free State established
1922	'Sapper', *The Black Gang*	Trial of Edith Thompson	

YEAR	LITERARY EVENTS	OTHER CULTURAL EVENTS	POLITICAL AND OTHER EVENTS
	T.S. Eliot, *The Waste Land*		
	Last Georgian anthology		
	Joyce, *Ulysses*		
1923	Arnold Bennet, *Riceyman Steps*	Marie Stopes, *Contraception*	
	Death of Katherine Mansfield	Edith Sitwell and William Walton, *Facade*	
	Aldous Huxley, *Antic Hay*		
	Yeats wins the Nobel Prize		
	E.M. Hull, *The Sheik*		
1924	Mary Webb, *Precious Bane*	T.E. Hulme, *Speculations*	First Labour government
	Margaret Kennedy, *The Constant Nymph*		
	P.C. Wren, *Beau Geste*		
	Forster, *A Passage to India*		
	I.A. Richards, *Principles of Literary Criticism*		
	Shaw, *St Joan*		
	Death of Conrad		
	Death of Edith Nesbit		
1925	Warwick Deeping, *Sorrel and Son*	Bertrand Russell, *ABC of Relativity*	
	Woolf, *Mrs Dalloway*		
	Noel Coward, *Hay Fever*		
	Shaw wins Nobel Prize		

YEAR	LITERARY EVENTS	OTHER CULTURAL EVENTS	POLITICAL AND OTHER EVENTS
1926	Agatha Christie, *The Murder of Roger Ackroyd* A.A. Milne, *Winnie-the-Pooh* Oswald Spengler, *The Decline of the West* (Vol. 1) F. Scott Fitzgerald, *The Great Gatsby*		General Strike
1927	A.A. Milne, *Now we are Six* Dornford Yates, *Blind Corner* Forster, *Aspects of the Novel* Woolf, *To the Lighthouse*	Freud, *The Ego and the Id*	
1928	A.A Milne, *The House at Pooh Corner* Yeats, *The Tower* Spengler, *The Decline of the West* (Vol. 2) Radclyffe Hall, *The Well of Loneliness* Compton MacKenzie, *Extraordinary People* Evelyn Waugh, *Decline and Fall* Aldous Huxley, *Point Counter Point* Lawrence, *Lady Chatterley's Lover* Death of Thomas Hardy		

YEAR	LITERARY EVENTS	OTHER CULTURAL EVENTS	POLITICAL AND OTHER EVENTS
1929	G.K. Chesterton, *The Father Brown Stories* Woolf, *A Room of One's Own* 'Seamark', *The Mystery Maker* W.R. Burnett, *Little Caesar* T.E. Lawrence, *Revolt in the Desert* Robert Graves, *Goodbye to all that* R.C. Sheriff, *Journey's End*		Wall Street Crash

There is scarcely a Liberal sentiment which animated the great Liberal leaders of the past which we do not inherit and defend.

Winston Churchill.
BBC, London, 4 June 1945

History is now at an end ... this History is therefore final.

W.C. Sellar and R.J. Yeatman,
1066 And All That (1930)

As difficult as the task may be, cultural history must at least try to capture the spirit of an age.

Modris Eksteins, *Rites of Spring*

Introduction

Clive Bloom

LITERATURE IN CULTURE

A social history of literature attempts not only to create a context for aesthetics within the wider activities of society but also to give an indication of the way aesthetic activity helps organize communal perception and actively shapes it. Here is a theoretical position which sees art's organization (its formal characteristics) as an expression of social forces and as an *active* social force in itself. Thus art is not static, timeless or sublime but part of the everyday fabric of material existence. Formal questions, questions directed at art's internal organization and awareness of itself, are now seen as processes within a social and historical setting. Art's form exists not only within the limited setting of a strict history of artistic production (a strictly formal aesthetic history), but is a *consequence* of and a contributing factor in the wider history of human perceptions. It is no longer viewed as separate from life (above or beyond the ordinary experiences of life), nor does it any more enjoy, as a consequence of that separation, a discrete history of its own (one untouched and untainted by life). The life of art is now understood as a functioning component of society's overall structure: a component composed of many interconnecting strands which come together within history to form the material and temporal object which is art.

We can sum up the ideas suggested above as follows: a sociology of literature must account for the relationship between history, culture and social relations. For a social history of literature to succeed it must have a working understanding of these three areas. Here, all are given the broadest definition and for our purposes such definitions are merely *pragmatically* placed signposts. Culture is seen as the whole field of production in which historical change occurs (that which is the material of history); social relations, the whole range

1

of relationships within human society from which culture is produced, and in particular those divisions of class which result as a consequence of negotiation, conflict and possible exploitation.

It is obvious that such crude and simple definitions will need close conceptual analysis but for pragmatic purposes they will suit us well enough. The recent liberal revisions in cultural theory still contain the essential elements laid out above, and whilst political Marxist practice is in disarray it has, nevertheless, left us with a highly sophisticated explanatory theory of historical process. Equally, one can ignore Marxism altogether and still accept that group conflict and dynamics give rise to history and culture and that these conflicts and negotiations, in short, these often contradictory activities, are expressed and exemplified in *individual* endeavour. That the individual is tied to history and culture is an inevitability and, unless we resort to complex metaphysics, we should accept that however individuals succeed or fail, they will be expressing (as individuals) the current conditions of their culture. Can an individual transcend society? In a theory of literature which has a true social base one cannot transcend circumstances dictated by a total community which itself is in a continual state of flux and change. The very notion of transcendence itself will be seen as an *idea* born *in* society to express certain social aspirations at a given time and would itself be, therefore, a suitable subject for historical and material analysis. Why, we might ask as historians of ideas, did such an idea gain currency, how did it evolve, and how did it gain expression through individual action?

The *idea* of transcendence belongs to the realm of *perception*: the way individuals, singly or in groups, view their existence and understand their actions. It can be materially situated however, in the arts, objects and practices of a society. In a sociology, no society can exist *apart* from its perceptions (both of itself and others) and therefore a close examination of thought and how it is materially displayed is essential. Art formalizes perception and calls it aesthetic experience. It organizes the perceptual properties inherent in society and materializes them in the *formal* properties of art: perception is then a type of organizing function. To understand how society sees itself we have to negotiate between what a text literally says, what it implies and what it leaves out altogether (but from which silence it actually emerged). This is both a delicate and controversial business and is open to abuse. What the sociologist of literature attempts to uncover is the way the dynamics of history, fired by the conflictual energy of certain groups, will produce artefacts which bear the *unconscious* stamp of that process, a process reworked and added to in every new reading. What is important is *not* the differentiation of various psychological types (characters) as they appear as part of the *context* of a work of literature. Rather, we are interested in the emergence of new and dynamic structures (genres) and why they occur when they do and why these forms and *no* others satisfy various societal needs.

Traditionally, form can be seen as meaning the relationship between what is said and how it is said. A social contextualization goes beyond providing a discussion of the 'internal' components of the art object as if they existed in a vacuum (New Criticism), but is an attempt to place the object as part of a framework in which it is a particularly sensitive barometer of the way people think and live, summing up the contradictions and ambivalences that are the fabric of everyday thought.

Whilst most art objects are the work of one person, they are consumed by the many. Thus we can safely say that individual productions sum up and articulate attitudes inherent in society and that a perceptual analysis will uncover these attitudes and these perceptions and set them in a context governed by historical process rather than the vicissitudes of transcendence and inspiration. Every work of literature and every human artefact will open to such an inquiry. Art's complexity and sophistication, its complex production and consumption is the most eloquent expression of the perceptual systems of a society. Indeed a work of art may express a group's attitudes 'unconsciously' so that only an outsider can point to the way a theme emerged which took root in popular consciousness at a certain time. Recent examples of this type of inquiry have emerged, and disenfranchized groups such as feminists and black study groups have brought to the surface attitudes inherent in 'art' which had hitherto been ignored, dismissed or given another more innocent gloss.

Let us sum up what the preceding paragraphs have suggested. We have said that a social history of literature is the relationship between history, social relations and culture. We are concerned with the *material expression* of these three terms in everyday life (avoiding metaphysical explanations and idealizations) and their relationship (their expression) as consciousness. Moreover, we are interested in the material conditions that produce the interrelationship of the above terms, the material conditions of consciousness itself and the *material expression of consciousness* (art). This material expression, whilst being always offered by individual effort, will nevertheless be understood as a *social* consciousness.

Thus, we are investigating the interrelationship of individuals in society and this will be expressed as a set of social relationships externally expressed (as material objects) and internally processed (as consciousness). Such an investigation forces the critic to consider the complex realm of language and its formative role in perception. These individual relationships will be understood historically, culturally and through class and other social relations. Most importantly, all this will be viewed as a process and not as static. Inevitably the point of so complex and, it should be admitted, so sophisticated an approach is to create models which explain how art's *meaning* is produced, for it is meaning that is the central question here. In a sociology of literature what something means is determined by the processes described in the preceding paragraphs.

Should what has just been explained be in need of practical example, the reader will be well advised to look at two versions of the process. The first comes from George Orwell and is his magnificent contextual analysis of the work of Charles Dickens; the other comes from Roland Barthes and is his deconstruction of the formative strands inherent in the work of Edgar Allan Poe.[1] For those who wish to find out more about the theoretical basis of these ideas a visit to the library or bookshop will reveal works by George Lukács, Walter Benjamin, Lucien Goldman and Pierre Macherey.[2] For those interested in the indigenous Anglo-Marxist tradition and who have already enjoyed George Orwell, Raymond Williams (to whom this writer owes much of the preceding ideas) is an ideal (and *dear!*) exemplar of the sociological viewpoint.[3] Terry Eagleton's advocacy of this attitude has been summed up in a number of books and his work offers the usual entrée to the subject for new students.[4] For a relatively contemporary and practical application of the views expressed here, the works both of the Thames Polytechnic (now the University of Greenwich) group through the journal *Literature and History* and the conference papers of the Sociology of Literature group at Essex University are recommended.[5] Finally, mention must be made of the Lumiere Group, who have comprehensively applied these ideas to the field of popular literature and culture and who are responsible for the present volume and its two companions.[6]

A HISTORICAL PERSPECTIVE: CRISIS OR RENEWAL?

Although it is an attractive way of understanding the movement of history, the idea of epochs can be dangerously misleading. The Britain of 1900 was as different from the Britain of 1914 as that date from 1929. Nevertheless, if we use epoch only as a convenience of periodization then such expanses of time will serve us well. This span of almost thirty years is one both momentous in its cataclysms of taste and perspective and serene in its continuities of ownership and loyalties. A period which begins with the end of Victorianism and ends with the beginning of the modern world – including the rise of organized labour, world conflict, new technological innovation, the aggressive appearance of mass consumption, the giving of votes first to mature women and then to all over 21, the disasters of repeated strikes, the ominous rise of American economic might, European communism and fascism and the domestic collapse of liberal politics under the onslaught of labour – suggests one rich in ambivalence and contradiction!

This is an age broken up not merely by its events but by its perspectives, the expectations of 1900 mutating and maturing into the demands of 1926; the failures of 'Poplarism'* triumphing finally in the Labour victory of 1923; the collapse of consensus liberalism wilting in the glare of demands for equality as a right: in all, the triumphal ascension of welfare socialism, retarded only briefly by world war. B.B. Gilbert was able to observe in 1939 that 'the British state had committed itself to the maintenance of all its citizens according to need as a matter of right without any concurrent political disability'.[7] After 1945 consensus would again reappear, but only after the nationalizing of mines, rail and docks (all demanded prior to 1929), the appearance of the National Health Service and the educational reforms which followed *The Beveridge Report* (1942), now considered as rights given to the British at birth and not privileges to be earned. This astonishing accord between Tory and Socialist, to which even in the 1990s lip service must be offered, was the direct result of the immense confrontation between privilege and impoverishment whose narrative spanned the years discussed in these pages.

One hardly needs to be overtly radical to notice this movement marking the years before and during the Great War, the rising tides of which were cause for comment not merely by the landed aristocrat defending his dwindling power in the clash of Lords and Commons over Lloyd George's social security reforms of 1911, but also by the suffragette force-fed in Brixton, by the docker refusing to load guns for ships bound for White Russia in the early 1920s, by Sir Edward Carson grimly challenging central rule from Ulster, by soldiers massed against workers in Glasgow, parading in Tonypandy or marching on the Somme, or by those exhausted and broken who trudged to the workhouse as of old. In every walk of life, at every stage of our story and in every town and hamlet of the British Isles, a major key to the age was this conflict between the power of ownership and the power of labour. As these mighty forces marshalled, they marshalled in masses. The pragmatic, ad hoc and occasional were outmoded in this conflict and were replaced by the programmed, the permanent and the continuous, such abstractions finding expression in the appearance of state and collective control. Such are the contradictions in victory and defeat. In this light both sides began to give up their ancient and self-understood rights in order to protect themselves and armour themselves against the other. The appearance of a *collective perspective* and a homogenized voice ran through trade unionism, Hollywood films, public broadcasting, suburbanism, scientific management, behavioural sci-

---

*An early 'welfare state' experiment which ended in prison sentences for Labour Councillors in the Borough of Poplar in London.

ence, summer holidays and domestic purchasing – *it was the cultural birth of the controlled collective and mass produced experience.* The state and its slowly growing bureaucratic machinery would attempt to demolish ancient individual privileges by ironically jeopardizing the very privileges of a new type of individuality the state sought to protect. Thus the state and its nameless, faceless bureaucracy was a symptom of the growth of the mass and the subordination of individuals and their freedom to the demands and pressures of the aggregate.

Collectivism protected and redefined the individuality of those it came to stand *substitute* for. Now the individuals would be forced to define their very presence against the abstract and invisible barriers of the new collective. As well as the older loyalties of family, parish and religion amongst others, a new collectivity, corrosive of these older social institutions, was gradually shaping. It came in the form of uniform, urban sprawl, the dominance of mass opinion created through national dailies and radio, chains of shops like Woolworth's with their cheap and standardized goods and in the presence of universal form-filling at the labour exchange and elsewhere. The door-to-door sales-man selling the glamour of American cosmetics and electrical goods, the adverts to improve one's memory and business acumen suggested a freedom at once intoxicating and restraining; a consumer generation was being born which would increasingly measure success by material possessions, possessions which standardized response and actually limited potentially erratic purchasing activity. Freedom would be increasingly constrained by ownership through-out the period, and American goods with their hint of the exotic, Hollywood stars and Californian bathing beauties would provide, through the act of purchase, a mythic landscape of desires. If this process was almost entirely unconscious then it was well, for those who faced the medusa were often gorganized.

The movement towards collectivization progressed steadily through the early twentieth century. Even so the notion of this collective experience was still embryonic. Individual experience was still the measure of perception, politics and progress. It was on the individual level that the abstract movements of the collectivity were played out and thought through. The abstractions of collective organization and control provided pressures only capable of con-crete expression at the level of the individual and his or her immediate surroundings. Squeezed, albeit unconsciously, between the emerging modern welfare state and its opponents and between the dominance of capital and its opponents, the conscious horizons of individualism were ripe for redefinition. It would not be long before forms of individualism once considered eccentric but acceptable would come under suspicion as the aberrations of perversity or the conditioning of the drives. Indeed, from the late nineteenth century onwards, individualism was itself defined as a condition of aberration, and the control and exploration of behaviour went hand in hand with the meaning of individual rights and consciousness.

An age is rarely one of steady progress or steady decline. The period between 1900 and 1929 was no exception to this rule. Implacable forces were gathering to oppose immovable complacencies but these forces kept to their own timetables, sometimes opposing and sometimes upholding the status quo. The rate of demonstrable change in this period certainly does appear dramatic, from its steam and horse-drawn origins to its electronic and oil-fuelled end. But one must be wary of labelling a period of rapid change one of 'crisis', as if crisis and change were synonymous. Change then becomes shorthand for a situation on the brink of disaster. This is clearly not the case in any period, as the rate of change and people's *perception* of that rate of change may be quite different: the pressure is never quite the same at all places nor at all times. Equally, the television-heritage version of the 1900s and 1920s should be avoided. Complacency and crisis went hand in hand.

For the historian George Dangerfield (writing in 1936), the prewar period was running on a timetable towards revolution and anarchy. So it was that from 1912 to 1914 'England was in ... a dangerous state of hysteria'.[8] For Cyril Connolly (looking back from the 1930s) 'the central concept of the nineteen-twenties [was] futility'.[9] More recently Francis Mulhern, referring to these early years, follows Dangerfield when he transfers the fears and pressures of prewar Britain to the postwar peace, hence 'the condition of British society in the 1920s was ... one of crisis ... the effects of this crisis were pervasive.'[10] The period itself had its commentators on both sides: '*The Times* of 19 January 1909 emphasised how contemporary Edwardians "place the golden age behind them, and assume that no generation ever had to deal with evils so great and perplexing as those of the present day" '.[11] In July 1914, *The Times* in consternation over Ulster's defiant attitude commented, 'the country is now confronted with one of the great crises in the history of the British race'.[12] On a less parochial note Havelock Ellis could state in the preface to his 1923 publication *The Dance of Life*,

> it may seem to some that this book reveals the expansive influence of that great classico-mathematical Renaissance in which it is our high privilege to live.[13]

So crisis metamorphoses into renaissance.

For Oswald Spengler the mystery of civilization's 'decline' before World War I was explicable in a theory of rebirth – a kind of Christology of history. In his massive and influential two-volume *The Decline of the West* (first published in German in 1918 and 1922 and which became available in translation in Britain between 1926 and 1928) the sense of ending is a sense of crisis only in so far as it leads to a cleansing in millenarianism. Spengler eulogises:

> But over this surface, too, the great Cultures accomplish their majestic wave-cycles. They appear suddenly, swell in splendid lines, flatten again and vanish, and the face of the waters is once more a sleeping waste.
>
> A Culture is born in the moment when a great soul awakens out of the proto-spirituality of ever-childish humanity, and detaches itself, a form from the formless, a bounded and mortal thing from the boundless and enduring. It blooms on the soil of an exactly-definable landscape, to which plant-wise it remains bound. It dies when this soul has actualized the full sum of its possibilities in the shape of peoples, languages, dogmas, arts, states, sciences, and reverts into the proto-soul. But its living existence, that sequence of great epochs which define and display the stages of fulfilment, is an inner passionate struggle to maintain the Idea against the powers of Chaos without and the unconscious muttering deepdown within.
>
> This – the inward and outward fulfilment, the finality, that awaits every living Culture – is the purport of all the historic 'declines', amongst them that decline of the Classical which we know so well and fully, and another decline, entirely comparable to it in course and duration, which will occupy the first centuries of the coming millennium but is heralded already and sensible in and around us to-day – the decline of the West.[14]

Thus, for Spengler and his mystical-fascist version of history, the decline of the modern age would bring the final glorious battle 'between money and blood' and 'the triumph of the will-to-power' of Nietzsche's *Übermensch*.[15] In such a way civilization's decline is its *promise* of renewal. Hence the critical and crisis-laden, viewed as the workings of a rigid destiny, merged with the complacent and the composed awaiting of a supreme fulfilment.

If 'on the one hand, the Edwardian years have been presented as some kind of golden age: on the other, as an age of accumulating crisis', then so too were the 1920s, at once renaissance and decadence.[16] If for Spengler, as indeed later for A.J.P. Taylor, 'at the beginning of the twentieth century ... there was a feeling of the end of things', then for Havelock Ellis that ending was a new beginning, a new renaissance centred on 'relativity' in human affairs.[17] Such comments aptly demonstrate the inevitable confusions of historical analysis, millenarian wish fulfilment, common nostalgia and the vicissitudes of memory creating an age of crisis *and* complacency, of continuity *and* change.

FROM CRISIS TO THE COLLECTIVE

Under the shadow of relative economic decline, growing militarism and dramatic political readjustment, nevertheless, the Edwardian era was the Indian summer of the richest and most powerful ruling class the world had yet seen. Britain still just held the economic dominance she had won, through leading the industrial revolution … [T]hrough commerce, conquest and colonisation, one quarter of the world's surface flew the British Flag. London was the world's financial and political capital. Yet this vast Empire was governed and owned by an extraordinarily small élite. In 1913 a mere 1% of the adult population of Britain owned more than two thirds of the national wealth.[18]

Edwardian Britain was the most urban nation in the world. The village community had been drained to work the industrial revolution. Three quarters of its people lived in towns and cities, and a mere 7% of its workforce was still in agriculture.[19]

Moreover the end of the Great War saw a Britain with much of its social fabric still intact, change occurring less by revolution than by grudging compromise in the face of an expected revolution.[20] Changes of a profound nature were occurring, however.

A.J.P. Taylor pithily summed these up when he said 'the baby Austin ousted the baby, the nursery gave place to the garage'.[21] These changes were not merely in a decline in the traditional Victorian family towards its modern 'nuclear' successor and the acquisition of the most powerful *personal* product of the industrial age, the motor car, nor in the rise in house building and the spread of the suburbs, but were ones of profound individual perception. The statistics of an age take us part way to the perceptions of that age. So it was that in 1911 three quarters of all workers were in manual industries: the old, heavy industries which formed the basis of Victorian power and prestige. These were in terminal decline. By 1931, although the absolute number of manual workers had risen, their percentage amongst workers of all types had declined by 4 per cent.[22] White collar workers, whose perceptions were *critical* to literature in the period, increased from 18.7 per cent of the working population in 1911 to 23 per cent by 1931, and the increase continued until the late 1930s when over a quarter of the workforce were in the new technological and service sector, mainly gathered in the south.[23] Clerks increased from 4.5 per cent of workers in 1911 to 6.7 in 1931 and retailers like Boots the Chemists could watch a steady increase in sales and a steady rise in new stores. By 1938 Boots had 1,180 stores throughout Britain.[24] Over the period the rise in all types of white collar jobs was over 40 per cent.

Meanwhile, the older industries declined. Between 1920 and 1929 those employed by coal mining slipped by 22 per cent. Indeed, between 1920 and 1938 coal miners declined from 1,083,000 to 675,000.[25] In cotton, the decline left only 302,000 from a 1920 population of 534,000. Shipbuilding almost halved and agriculture lost 400,000 jobs. Such decline was matched by a massive growth in new technological industries. After the adoption of mass production techniques in 1922 by Morris and Austin* the number of

---

*These were still restricted by piece rates, unlike mass production in the United States.

car workers increased to well over half a million. In 1923 the Central Electricity Board established the National Grid and workers in all the utilities (gas and water included) rose from 185,000 towards the 300,000 mark. Most dramatically of all, electrical engineers rose from 171,000 to 326,000. Despite the decline of the older heavy industries and the constant background and threat of poverty (between 17 per cent and 20 per cent of the population were below the poverty line), money wages and their purchasing power rose steadily and between 1920 and 1934 the cost of living fell in contrast to the prewar years.[26] Meanwhile, the power of those in work rose to a point where they felt strong enough to challenge the state, indirectly by challenging groups of employers (often aristocrats turned industrialists) or directly by general strike. Trade union membership grew steadily and had doubled between 1913 and 1920.[27] Those affiliated to the TUC rose also from 2.2 million to 6.5 million.[28]

As unemployment waxed and waned so too the prospects of trade unionism. It must be emphasized that despite the varying fortunes of the trade unions and the never ceasing battle with the employers which the unions often lost; despite all this, such solidarity and determination of purpose gave working people a self-respect and identity previously denied: the more deferential meanings of 'them and us' and 'knowing one's place' were on the decrease. Paradoxically, a sense of working-class identity was emerging in the power of labour, and exemplified by the Labour Party manifesto of 1924 which called for nationalization (state ownership) of rail, mines and power.[29]

And yet, long term unemployment rose during the 1920s, Labour governments seemed powerless to reverse the decisive power of aristocracy (the most powerful of whom were now industrialists) whilst the miners (with their families one tenth of the total population) had been broken by the General Strike of 1926, through the action of the middle classes and the army. By the decade's end Ramsay MacDonald had formed a government with Tories and Liberals, and Labour's immediate prospects, hopes and desires had fallen by the wayside. The progress of Labour would now be won by local compromise and negotiation, with the age of 'direct action' (the belief that trade unions should take political action to change the government) buried by humiliation and disillusion. With the prewar syndicalist aspirations of Tom Mann and others over, big business was back in charge.

The massive forces of aggregation and division met headlong in the struggle of the General Strike. Here the old came against the modern; the manual met the technological and automated; the world of coal and steam fell to the world of chemistry and oil; the worker in the north finally brought down, after a sharp fight and a lingering rearguard action, by the middle classes in the south, their allies the intellectuals of the old universities and the ultimate conservatism of their own leaders. Guarded by soldiers and police, volunteers ferried vital supplies, worked as tram and bus conductors and in a host of other jobs, and marshalled their cars in Hyde Park.[30] This action was class war in its most brutal and obvious form. That 'bolshevism' and 'anarchy' had been defeated gave only scant solace – the injustices of poverty and the demands of working people still existed and grew more urgent throughout the latter years of the decade and into the 1930s. The General Strike enters our mythology as a type of betrayal. Such direct pressure for change (aimless and protean as many of its demands were) returned not through direct action, but through the use in 1928 of a universal vote for all over 21, regardless of wealth or gender, and the return of a Labour government which looked forward to the post-1945 reforms and of the welfare state.[31]

This process of decline and reversal, growth and adoption of the labour movement reflected the wider twists and turns of the period. The coming of war in 1914 had, temporarily, diluted and redirected those urgent political and economic claims that again gathered head after the armistice. Boom gave way to bust and the homecoming heroes found they had not come into their inheritance. Nevertheless, the pressing problems of the prewar years were finding solutions. Ireland, scene of rebellion and civil war had been successfully partitioned in 1921 and its troubles sloughed off; women had, after the horrors of imprisonment and forced feeding, won the right to vote by 1918; the wealth and security of working people were visibly growing; that the General Strike represented, in part, a *moral* protest against the injustices that still existed gave it an importance which outweighed the irresolute politics that backed up its claims. This moral dimension, with the spontaneity of action characteristic of both sides, was to an extent the result of *indignation* at the conditions governing change.

On all levels the aggregation of interests went hand in hand with the feeling of individuals caught up in movements they could little comprehend (or comprehend a little too well), a feeling that things were falling apart even if in fact, they were not: the social fabric made taut but yet hardly cracked. For many, to adopt the phrase from Yeats's apocalyptic poem of 1919, 'The Second Coming', the 'centre could not hold'. The slow (and, yet, accelerating) decline into anarchy which so many saw written in every workers' protest, Irish demand and suffragette outrage was, in fact, a symptom of new *cohesive* attitudes emerging at the time. Such a contradiction was hardly noticed. The reason why anarchy and cohesiveness went together was because the forces of change acted in ways that were not traditional. The greater the pressure towards conformity, centralization and control so too the greater the forces of marginalization, disturbance and division.

The sporadic outbursts of anarchist activity that had disturbed Edwardian streets culminated in the 'siege of Sydney Street' (1911), but by the end of the First World War the shadow of the anarchist had become the spectre of bolshevism – a term so vague as to include free thinking, vegetarianism, free love, modern literature and the like. The term went into the English language for any kind of trouble maker, hence being 'bolshie'. A hysterical refrain found bolshevism behind every labour demand, one member of the Lords suggested:

> The people of this country voted overwhelmingly against Bolshevism at the last election … They certainly did not put the present Government into power to 'bolshevize' British industry.[32]

In order to minimize the risk of revolution, embryonic state and council *centralized* planning would be used, conceding labour demands and at the same time neutralizing equally centralized labour power. Thus the boom in private housing was accompanied by the growth of council housing for 'dangerous and uncontrollable elements!'

> When we talk of expense and cost let us realize that everything is comparative, and let us measure the cost of our housing proposals by the cost of Bolshevism to the country and the cost of revolution … The money we propose to spend on housing is an insurance against Bolshevism and revolution.[33]

Local town council welfare had, indeed, been a solution from the early part of the century. In an ironic meeting of minds the city came to symbolize welfare for both tory advocates of a new paternalist, incorporationist state and their socialist opponents; and according to one Glasgow councillor, the object of the council was 'to provide everything the population required in its passage from the cradle to the grave'.[34]

Such welfare 'concessions' were expediencies, somewhat visionary and somewhat muddled, brought about by pressure from a perceived threat of anarchism and bolshevism. The fear of the bolshevist threat to order was debated too in books whose themes were those of decline: Goldsworthy Lowes Dickinson's *The European Anarchy* and *The International Anarchy*, Elie Halévy's epilogue to the second volume of his *History of the English People in the Nineteenth Century*, which appeared just after the period, and J.R.M. Butler's, *History of England 1815–1918*.[35] Yet bolshevism was also a term of approval, of democracy and of modernity itself, a word for the undermining of a stale and outworn status quo.

That this word bolshevism was a taboo to so many is perhaps indicative of the potential truth in their musings. For Tom Mann, syndicalist and union leader, the fears of the *Daily Mail's* editorial that a 'revolutionary movement'[36] had begun were *gratefully* justified: 'THE GENERAL STRIKE [sic] of national proportions … will be the actual Social and Industrial Revolution,' he declared.[37]

But it was far from merely the Left who threatened and who were themselves falling into anarchic behaviour. The conditions governing parliamentary democracy seemed to be under threat also from the Right. Elements of the women's suffrage movement, for example, reflected the deep, underlying conservatism of their class beneath a radical agenda and violent, direct action. The Pankhursts (despite Sylvia's disaffection to the Left) became more mystical and high Tory as their campaigns went on. Their violent activities were the products of a disenfranchisement of one section of the Right. Throughout the war, Emmeline Pankhurst preached the 'good war' and the suffragettes were among the first women to present men in civilian clothes with the white feather.[38] By the 1920s Christabel had been 'reborn' into mystical Christianity. The refusal of the army to fight in Ireland in 1913 constituted a fundamental threat to liberty – here was 'mutiny' amongst the officer class with Henry Wilson (recalled to active service during the war and shot in 1922 by the IRA) declaring a Protestant partisanship against Home Rule that allied him with the rebellious machinations of the Conservative leader Andrew Bonar Law and the Unionist Sir Edward Carson.[39] Toryism, taking to extra democratic activity (threatened by labour and the middle classes) had come dangerously close to dismissing any form of consensus. The army spent as much time protecting the older northern and Welsh industries for the vested interests of 'law and order' as they did protecting the empire. Little wars across the world were paralleled by the army's action again workers across Britain. The last cavalry charge was in a Welsh valley rather than at Omdurman. In Ireland, the Black and Tans were let loose between 1920 and 1921 as a force of internal mercenaries.

The anarchy of labour, women and Irish nationalists was met by the anarchy of the conservatives, High Tories and middle classes. In the name of law and order workers were locked out, suffragettes 'tortured' in Brixton and civil war declared in Ireland. State violence and growing state secrecy met private disorder. The state took on the activities and attitudes of the anarchists. Thus was *terrorism* born in suffragette arson, syndicalism, Irish and Ulster nationalism.* In the Middle East during the Great War T.E. Lawrence had shown disorganized peoples how to use guerrilla warfare to throw off imperial control. Terrorism and the growth of state control went together: the suffragettes did not want their economic power disturbed, the Lords allowed Lloyd George to tame them in 1911 but not remove them (for Liberals too were unwilling to grant concessions unless by exception rather than rule). Ireland was far away and compromise was ultimately possible, the north of England was too poor and also too far away and too weak to bring fear-bred concessions from the new wealth of the south. The world changed but did not crack open. It cannot be forgotten and needs to

---

*The world 'terrorist' was first used in its modern sense in this period and is used particularly by Joseph Conrad in *The Secret Agent* (1907).

be emphasized that these events *ranged across thirty years* and thirty years is a very long time indeed. Parliament survived and the power of the state grew. Those extra democratic forces which gathered and organized before and after the General Strike brought into view the new world order: the aggregation of the city, the emergence of the high street, the appearance of new industries organized around the production line and scientific management, the use of local welfare and local council controls, the repeated calls for nationalization of major industries and utilities, the actual emergence of big corporations like Imperial Chemicals in 1926, the accelerated growth of national trade unions, the women's vote, Hollywood and radio.

In the art of the period as elsewhere the conditions of the times were reflected and promoted. New complacencies found their place amongst the ruins of old certainties. The arts of the period with modernism in the vanguard were the perceptual space in which the dramas of the age found expression and 'resolution'.

TOWARDS A MASS CULTURE: THE CASE OF LITERATURE

The years running from 1900 to the late 1920s saw the gradual completion of a process of mass production and consumption that was to dramatically accelerate across those years until it became cause for serious discussion during the 1930s amongst an intellectual élite concerned about the 'erosion' of cultural values and the vitality of consumer consumption. In publishing, the old high-polished and plush red-leather gentleman's club atmosphere still prevailed at the level of relationships between authors and their publishers, but slowly increasing was the realization of the possibility of large turnovers governed by increasing levels of literacy: the turning of books into commodities.

To discover the actual figures for increased readerships, let alone interpret their real meaning is something of a nightmare and anyone interested in an inquiry into reading habits and the involvement of various social classes must be advised to proceed with caution. Anyone who undertakes research into the accounts and transactions of the various companies trading at that time will soon find huge gaps appearing in the evidence since pieces of the puzzle will fit together only crudely. Simply put, it is extremely difficult to establish *who* bought particular works within the various price bands in which a particular title appeared. It is equally difficult to unravel particular themes and their impact on sections of readers.

Research will illustrate the extraordinarily difficult problem of matching sales figures to readership patterns (of age and gender and profession) and will only partially illuminate the themes which emerged at the time, and which can be taken as *indicative* of a way of life enjoyed by substantial sections of the general public.

If we turn to the records of the publishing house Hodder and Stoughton (the records of which are kept in the Guildhall Museum, London) we find a history of publishing diversification typical of the time.[40] Though fragmentary and confused, nevertheless, here is evidence of a substantial publishing house moving outward from its nineteenth-century trade which was based on ecclesiastical literature into a substantial interest in popular fiction designed to sell to all levels of society. Whilst popular fiction increased in sales and importance during the thirty years at the beginning of this century, such work as lives of saints, sermons and Bible commentaries continued to sell well, at least until just before the outbreak of the Great War (approximately half our period).

The ledgers show a diverse group of popular authors. Precise figures are difficult to establish, but they do suggest the relative success and popularity of particular titles. As with most publishers of the period, titles would sell at two or three price bands according to the quality of the bindings, illustrations and paper. An author could expect his work to sell in half a crown, one shilling and sixpenny editions (and lower) *simultaneously*, gaining the attention of a wider readership. Such democratization in reading habits, building on Victorian foundations, was led by the demands of market forces and the need (hardly articulated then – especially by gentlemen publishers) to monopolize consumption of printed material. This was the age of Northcliffe, Rothermere and the rise of mass circulation newspapers, and book publishing was itself encouraged by and driven through the insatiable desires of its public. Indeed, at the lowest price range print runs of 40,000 or more were possible and profitable.

Amongst the more expensive books, J.M. Barrie was selling consistently between October 1907 and March 1912 with *Peter Pan*. Frank Baum's *Wizard of Oz*, though not selling as strongly, was earning royalties between 1906 and 1908.[41] Equal to J.M. Barrie's sales, however, was Bell's *Standard Elocutionist*, suggestive of the need felt amongst the trading and lower-middle classes for a guide, on the one hand 'to know one's place' and, on the other, to rise above it. Also on Hodder's list were classics such as *Jane Eyre*, which was binding in small numbers between March 1908 and March 1911. Arnold Bennett's *The Old Wives' Tale* (1908) was selling well, with good anticipation of sales. In the shilling series one could get Hall Caine's *Captain Davy's Honeymoon*, and for sixpence boys could read G. A. Henty's *The Young Buglers*. Other books from this publisher included such adventure tales and romantic novels as H. Rider Haggard's *Red Eve*, Hall Caine's *The Manxman* and *Christian*, Mrs Henry Wood's *Esther Vanhomrigh* and Israel Zangwill's *The King of Schnorrers* which was earning royalties during 1911.

Amongst these popular and romantic novelists was E. Phillips Oppenheim, a now almost forgotten author, yet one of Hodder's best sellers throughout the 1920s, his sales earning the privilege of a ledger to themselves. He was still selling well in 1938 with his thin tales of espionage, detection and romance. His prodigious output is recorded on page after page of one vast (and now) dusty sales ledger. His royalties on books that were variously priced at three shillings and sixpence, a florin and nine pence allowed him a champagne lifestyle on the French Riviera.[42] In the same ledger, sales recorded under 'colonial' editions become simply export copies, reminding us of the growing importance of the world market. Interestingly traditional works of Christian piety, such as Bunyan's *Pilgrim's Progress* and the anonymous *Hours with the Saints*, were doing a roaring trade, equal to some of the other titles between January 1910 and March 1912.

What sales deals were made with American publishers for these authors who were internationally read and enjoyed remains largely a matter for conjecture and speculation. The reputations of E. Phillips Oppenheim and Edgar Wallace (another Hodder author) were made through an Anglo-American reading public. Yet, the intervention of a well placed V-1 rocket (which destroyed the records of one major literary agent who dealt with Hodder), the dumping of hundreds of documents because of a move by another agent in 1987, and the subsequent purchase at auction and stocking of the remaining 350,000 pieces of information from the latter agent by a major American university means that we are unlikely in the short term to find out anything else of value. Decrepitude and the decay of memories as well as the death of the original clerks, authors and agents means that many intriguing questions will remain simply and literally closed books.[43]

Such a cautionary tale argues against hasty generalizations and requires us, where possible, to refuse the generalizations so easily made about art and its themes. It is an almost intractable problem to know on what issues the readership of a half-crown novel concurred with that same novel's readers who bought at sixpence and came from another social class. The fact that a book's themes can be enumerated is not a guide to how much each theme was emphasized amongst different reading (and economic) groups at any one time and this must remain a matter for careful and deliberate investigation: it is the very heart of the relationship between production, consumption and perception.

We can, however, make some general comments as guidelines to inquiry in the knowledge that, though it may be inappropriate to apply certain literary and thematic traits and ideas to any one specific place or time, they are the discernible trends of the aggregate and of the era.

The rise in mass readerships, fuelled by rising literacy, cheap paper and print methods, fast distribution via rail and new motorized transport, new information-carrying media (radio and cinema), the provision of new public libraries and increasing leisure, was equalled not only by the emergence of new themes in poetry and fiction but also the appearance of new genres such as the spy thriller. The dichotomy between serious literature ('high-brow') and entertaining slush ('low-brow') began now to make an appearance.[44] Late-nineteenth-century forms such as the short story (driven by the journal and magazine market) still had a ready market as did novels (usually serialized first in popular magazines). Poetry, too, was still widely read and appreciated, perhaps taken on a bicycle ride in the new Everyman edition, suitable for carrying in jacket pockets. The Georgians could command an unaffected, unselfconscious readership for poetry (of the consolatory sort), as could Ella Wheeler Wilcox later (although whether one can dignify her work as poetry is another matter), and this amongst all literate classes. Alongside the short story, novel and poem was the vast world of journalism (from whence increasing numbers of authors appeared). The dual pressures of journalism and Hollywood were to change the very nature of fiction as the era drew to a close.

Here it is perhaps useful to delineate the aesthetic conditions which governed the period and which ultimately gave rise to the aesthetic of modernism (an aesthetic actually less important to British taste than to the French and Americans from whom it was borrowed). Our period is governed by groupings of authors (through thematic or formal interest rather than mere friendship or partnership). The important writers (though also experimentalists like Conrad) stuck to 'traditional' methods of writing and avoided innovation in form in order to concentrate on either the psychology of bourgeois domesticity or the political and economic inequalities of society. Here we find H.G. Wells and George Bernard Shaw, Henry James and Arnold Bennett, John Galsworthy and E.M. Forster. In popular literature, psychological and social investigation was subordinated to an episodic escapism: an aesthetic of heroic individualism which filled the work of Edgar Wallace, Sydney Horler, Ethel M. Dell, E. Phillips Oppenheim, William Le Queux, John Buchan, Edgar Rice Burroughs, Zane Grey and a myriad of forgotten hopefuls. Historical romance fulfilled at once the demands of the thriller and of the love story and Baroness Orczy and Rafael Sabbatini supplied this mixture throughout the 1920s as did Achmed Abdullah, whose *Thief of Baghdad* was a novelization of one of the great silent movies (1924).* The

---

*Achmed Abdullah was brought up in Russia, educated in Britain and finally lived in the United States.

exotic was supplied by E.M. Hull's *The Sheik* (1923–4), Sax Rohmer's villain, Fu Manchu (who found book form in 1913 having been previously serialized), and the play *Chu Chin Chow* (1916). A much smaller group, whose experimentalism evolved from the early 1900s to the mid 1920s, rejected both serious traditional literature and popular literature, and attempted to formulate a new *international* aesthetic which became known as modernism. Of this group, T.S. Eliot, Hilda Doolittle ('H.D.'), Amy Lowell, Dorothy Richardson, Robert Frost and Ezra Pound were American (albeit some of these were domiciled in Britain), and only James Joyce (an ambivalent Briton), Virginia Woolf and D.H. Lawrence can claim any real status as important British innovators. Of Richard Aldington's work there is now only silence, and there is little but disregard for the work of Percy Wyndham Lewis. That modernism was an alien imposition in Britain remains a suspicion. What cannot be denied is that many of the great literary works of modernism were written *in* English. Modernism begins the process whereby English literature becomes *literatures* written in English (a very different proposition). A final group might be noticed, those whose writings stuck to a post-Christian message, the theosophists, nature junkies, Christian scientists and magicians who ranged across the whole spectrum of writing talent. Here we find W.B. Yeats, the later Arthur Conan Doyle, H. Rider Haggard, the last book by Mark Twain, the consolations of Marie Corelli and Ella Wheeler Wilcox and the race/gender mysticism of D.H. Lawrence.

Behind all of these writers to a greater or lesser extent were the thinkers of a previous century: Marx and revolutionary socialism; Darwin and the social Darwinists; Alphonse Bertillon and the science of racial and criminal types, and William James and the religion of psychology. Newer voices were also present: Einstein and the cosmic 'elsewhere' with its intersection of time and space; Freud and the vicissitudes of the unconscious. Equally strong were the indigenous watery views of the Fabians; the theologies of Madame Blavatsky and the Golden Dawn; the artiness of the arts and crafts and later 'arty and crafty' movements (a Pre-Raphaelitism that never left and that can be detected in all sorts of ruralisms); the English drawing-room version of the war between the sexes, and debates over Free Trade and imperial destiny.

If British literature was informed by these sources and many others it was not particularly driven by them. Many authors combined views at once incompatible and contradictory in one book or over several books. Georgians wrote modernist poems and modernists were anthologized in Georgian collections. Edward Marsh wanted to reward Joyce with a place on the civil list for the lyricism of *Dubliners*, something surely, incompatible with the final evolution of *Finnegans Wake*.[45]

Indeed, *Dubliners* owes as much to Ibsen and British serial-publishing practice as it does to proto-modernism and the evolution of the self-contained novel.[46] Amongst avant-gardists too there was little cohesion. Virginia Woolf disliked Joyce's 'vulgarity' to the point of dismissing him, D.H. Lawrence was contemptuous of Katherine Mansfield and T.S. Eliot found his 'hero' Joyce cool towards him when they met. Despite arguments to the contrary, W.B. Yeats is far less a born-again modernist after his friendship with Ezra Pound than many have argued and Rupert Brooke, the doomed darling of lyric poetry, was quite able to produce a modernist work, as I have argued elsewhere.[47]

This being said, it is no wonder that the rich mixture of possibilities in art that this period has to offer is rarely pure or its constituents easily differentiated. Such a conclusion is hardly surprising for, as we have seen, the period itself reflected contradictory forces and equally varied responses to its possibilities, threats and disappointments. Yet we can still identify a driving preoccupation at *all* levels of literature in forming many of its works and the nature of their production: the tension between the *individual and the collective* (the state, the class, the gender, the union, the race).[48] The use of the spy thriller is, I believe, exemplary in its suggestion of this movement: a world essentially alien, unknowable and neurotic (paranoid), in which individuals are pitched head-long into conflict with forces at once beyond and above their control or understanding.[49]

> The formal origins of the spy genre lay hazily within an amalgamation of the imperial adventure tale and the detective novel. Both forms emerged in their proper state in the last quarter of the nineteenth century and were themselves responses to social pressure. The spy thriller coming early in the twentieth century (in its fully-developed form) was, more than both its predecessors, *the* genre tied to *international* political and social tensions. Indeed, more than any other form the spy thriller responded to a need to represent *covert* activity by state organisations. As Eric Hobsbawm has pointed out, when working people gained the vote the overt political agenda was seen more and more to be subverted by governmental agencies organised to *thwart* given political freedoms. The spy genre records that process in one of the least attenuated forms of fiction. In this sense the spy novel read as a historical record as well as a 'mere' form of entertainment can be highly enlightening.
>
> By the end of the last century the power of the State in all western countries had increased dramatically. The growth of the bourgeois idealogy of autonomous individual freedom (including the right to privacy) was accompanied by an equally bourgeois need for *public* control of all private functions. At this moment the bourgeois state came into being, armed with the legislative and cultural power to regulate all forms of expression (including dissent), either through governmental interference (bureaucratised secret police forces at one end) or through cultural control of the mass circulation of printed material (novels, newspapers and journals).[50]

This *political* conflict runs through the age's literature, but it rarely appears in the literature in its political dimension. The tendency of the art of the period was to *aestheticize* politics and to *psychologize* political content: the individual remained the focus of attention. In the 1930s the opposite tendency occurred, with aesthetic and psychological questions being bound to the demands of either revolutionary socialism or industrial fascism.

Whilst the tendency of aggregation was the dominant dynamic of the period (the tendency to think of and deal with the mass, and the consequences that brought for the individual citizen), it cannot be overemphasized that in the *particularities* of the period's activities this tendency was necessarily subordinate to pressures both more immediate and more pressing, whether they were votes for women or keeping the buses running during the General Strike. In literature this tendency saw expression in a concern amongst middle-class writers for the spiritual crisis going on within a closed circle of characters. The very notion of mass society was unknown and the terms 'community', 'tradition' or even 'family' substituted. Thus the individual was seen to be in a spiritual (that is, psychological) conflict with the community (of other disturbed spirits) and this only indirectly reflected the wider social and political developments of the period in which most aspects were considered subordinate to individual destiny.

Amongst the literate classes this was the age much more of Freud than of Marx, an age of confused liberalism not revolutionary socialism. Political questions became aesthetic problems expressed through a revolution in formal shape and practice. Centre stage was the individual and it was the question of individual destiny that dominated both modernists and popular writers alike. In the literature of modernism this destiny was worked out through the meanderings of the unconscious, whilst in popular fiction it was a matter of fisticuffs. It was individual 'health' that dominated the conceptual framework of the period's literature. The age of Freud was also the age of Havelock Ellis, Marie Stopes and a whole caboodle of eugenicists, racial purists and social Darwinists, such a mixture of ideas being visible throughout the work of 'serious' writers such as D.H. Lawrence as well as popular fictionalists such as 'Sapper' (Herman Cyril McNeile) and Edgar Wallace. Although this was an age concerned with aberration and its expulsion, from the individual as well as from the social (the obsession with white slavers, Chinese warlords, dacoits, Levantines, dagos, Jewish-financier-bolsheviks, racy women and dastardly Germans), it could no longer rely on the ethical certainties of a Victorian Christian moralism.

The age of science and mass society demanded a scientific notion of 'spiritual' health − a notion that would be both moral and reassuringly Anglo-Saxon. From now on morality would be governed not by *purpose* but by *organization*. The most perfectly organized mind would therefore be the most receptive and the most judgemental: in a word the most *moral*. The *balanced* liberal humanist Anglo-Saxon conscience was more organized (that is less 'deranged', 'neurotic' or 'perverse' (a favourite term)) than either the fanatical extremists who preached revolution or the racial subtype barbarian hordes in 'Golders Green' or 'Kentish Town'.[51] In order to rejuvenate an enervated Anglo-Saxon race a message of health had to be preached, a message devoid of overt moralism (such as found in Kipling or Baden-Powell), a message devoid of politics (an aberration of the unwashed), but one deeply concerned with the spirit of the individual (devoid of church doctrine). If perfection of organization was the goal, and the most perfectly organized individual was a spiritually (culturally) superior being, then the question of organization was ultimately an *aesthetic* question. The most perfectly beautiful would now be the most perfectly moral. Hence the elevation of Rupert Brooke as a mythic figure during and beyond the 1920s.

ORDERING SOCIETY, ORDERING LITERATURE: LITERARY CRITICISM

The question of morality, as a style of aesthetic organization, found its spokesmen and -women amongst the newly established modern-literature courses that appeared after the establishment in 1917 of the first modern English course in Cambridge University.[52] It may be no coincidence that the establishment of literary studies as we now know it as the last human 'science' should have had as its 'hidden' dynamic the notion of health, that one of its advocates, the poet T.S. Eliot should have demanded a poetry of 'impersonality', a subordination to 'cultured tradition and an escape from personal emotions' (he had just had a nervous breakdown), or that the first important academic literary analyst should have started life as a psychologist.

I.A. Richards in his concern for a theory of 'communication' as well as 'value' is seminal in his attempt to put literary studies on a formal, that is functional, basis. Following Eliot's 1921 manifesto 'Tradition and the Individual Talent', Richards's own theoretical position was stated in 1924 in *Principles of Literary Criticism*, a work crucial to the formation of literary studies.[53]

It is not my concern here to offer a full account of this important book; nevertheless, it raised issues that related directly to the relationship between aesthetics and modern political and social life. Whilst T.S. Eliot was concerned with the relationship between the artist and the history of art, Richards was concerned with the relationship between the reader and the complexity of each individual work of art (in this case, specifically poetry) and the ideal position of a correct reading: one open to all the possibilities of the poem's meaning. Such a correct reading was further codified in *Practical Criticism* (1929) and in Richards's practical exercises which made up the book's content.[54]

Richards's psychological training had suggested to him that literature was part of the art of communication, and that as such it could be 'objectively' studied. His belief in the ideal scientific exactitude of 'neurology' allied him less with Freud than with Pavlov and behavioural science: communication was action and reaction; art a sophisticated form of that process. Nevertheless, art contained values, ethics and morals which seemed beyond scientific explanation.

Richards circumvented this problem using hints from Eliot. If art was communication and the organization of messages, then the values contained in these messages could not be separate from the messages themselves but were a *condition* of them and an integral part of their organization as meaningful utterances. Meaning was not separable from the message but part of the way the message functioned. Meaning would necessarily be the organization of the message itself, because to separate the meaning from its form would necessarily make it something no longer integral to the very nature of art. It would simply be extraneous, something other than art. Meaning and, therefore, value were *internal* to the system of art, not external (social or political). It posed a question of aesthetics and this question was ultimately one of organization and function, a static rather than purposive question. The better organized a work of art was and the more *integrated*, the more 'healthy' it was and the less it tended towards perversity. Open to all possibilities (as F.R. Leavis would later see it), the great work is fully responded to by only those specially trained individuals who are fully alive and fully 'organized' (i.e. mentally open to all stimuli, but consciously able to sift out the harmful or chaotic).

This is a million miles away from W.B. Yeats's aesthetic of inspiration, magic, transcendence and personal irrationality as laid down in his 'Symbolism and Poetry' of 1900. It is much closer to modernism's concern for authority and the subordination of parts (including character and event) to an artistic whole which is both self-contained, highly formal and conditioned not by a moral message but by the organizational properties of language. This accord between literary values and those of modernism project rather conveniently excluded other modes of expressive form: popular fiction's episodic nature, its elevation of character and incident over total effect and its propagandistic social and racial morals. The overt questions posed about politics and class in popular fiction could be seen to be a debased 'extra literariness' which modernism avoided and which in modernism was subordinate to the over-riding question of aesthetics itself.

For Richards modernist and scientific theory acted as his guides to morality, a morality which could now be reconciled with the objective study of art as supreme communication. Thus the analytic tools defined the area of study. Such a theory provided a model in which subjectivism was banned and in which a community of reading could be established, an order of correctness agreed and objectively verified and aberrant readings dismissed as the perversities of the individual. Aesthetics belonged to an era gone by, but literary criticism seemed to turn this unlikeliest of areas into a realm of scientific endeavour; morality was the organization of the best minds and the cultural 'order' (to use Eliot's word) they benignly imposed. Importantly, Richards's theory was based on the notion of controlled response not aberrant creativity; a theory for readers not creators.

In the work of this significant shaper of cultural thought whose impact on the study of literature still has immense effect and whose ideals held sway well beyond the 1920s, we find an unlikely strand of the tendency towards the control of large numbers and their subordination to circumstances (roles, laws, institutions) beyond their individual control. Only the correct reading would now do. And in this tendency, which subordinated the individual to the mass, we find a strange demon of contradiction. Richards *opposed* his age, its philistine attitudes and haphazard lack of discrimination, and sought in his work to find a space apart from it, yet he fulfilled the demands of his age all the same.

Reading the preface to *Principles of Literary Criticism* we find Richards telling us, dramatically and shockingly, 'a book is a machine'.[55] Yet the urge to renege on the engineered and technological present immediately makes itself felt. Thus, 'this book might better be compared to a *loom* [my italics] on which it is supposed to re-weave some ravelled parts of our civilization'.[56] This important revision contains more than enough hints of William Morris and John Ruskin, with its distinct ruralist penchant and its feeling for the arty crafty handmadeness of the twenties folk lobby. The contradiction in this, the abysmal gulf between the loom and the modern machine, is hardly noticed. For Richards the 'beauty' of art, the morality of its organization, was because it was essentially handmade, crafted and authentic.[57] Driving this contradiction itself was a hidden language of technology, chemistry and automatism. Writing at the time of the invention of the word 'robot' Richards's language of neural bundles (the receptive apparatus of the brain), chemical impulses reacting to the stimulus of art, messages transmitted and received along the lines of wireless transmission, as well as the possibility to 'programme' correct responses, is much more suggestive of the new electrical and chemical industries than of any craft-based rural hand looming. Such nostalgia was not merely the antidote, but the product of a new technological environment determining hidden impulses for art, its values and aesthetic tendencies.

MODERNISM AND THE MASSES

Literary criticism as it emerged in the universities during the 1920s was driven by a need to understand the workings of art, not through the aestheticism of those who still held to the intrinsic beauty of forms, but by a compulsion to put that beauty under the eye of behaviourists and organizational experts. This desire for the exact and the objective had previously driven the art movement from which literary criticism had itself partially sprung: its prophet was T.S. Eliot. Although of necessity committed to analyse *all* literature, literary criticism as a discipline recognized, indeed declared, a partiality for the modern. From the moment that Eliot's *The Waste Land* had been declaimed through a Cambridge megaphone to eager students to the point where, in 1926, F.R. Leavis, then a probationer teaching the only twentieth-century literature course in Cambridge, attempted to get *Ulysses* accepted as a set book, the progress of modernist literature amongst young British intellectuals was assured. From this moment, modernity as represented by the modernists was the only acceptable, legitimate view of the contemporary world.[58]

By 1936, with the ban lifted from *Ulysses*, the general public could find out what the fuss had been about, but modernism as a movement had long since run its course. What came from the varied aesthetic, philosophic and cultural backgrounds of its leading avatars was old and cold, swept away by newer politically aware realisms. The experimenters of 1909 and 1910 had all gone their separate ways by the end of the Great War; some dead, others no longer interested. The appearance in 1930 of *Imagist Anthology*, the year also of D.H. Lawrence's death, marked the end of the era of experimentalism in modernity. Yeats and Joyce still had great works to come, but what these mark in relationship to the main body of experimental modernism is debatable. Is *Finnegans Wake* modernist, modernism's decadence, the first postmodern book or simply Joyce in an artistic dotage? What do we mean when Yeats is described as modernist in the same breath as T.S. Eliot? There were many *modernisms* and their characters are blurred and confused, run together almost accidentally. The campaign that had begun with the Imagist anthologies, the publication of *The Egoist* and the appearance of *Poetry* had been fought and won when in 1933 Eastbourne Technical Evening School put Joyce on the reading list without anybody declaring it would lead to degenerate behaviour amongst the mixed sexed classes to which it would be taught.[59]

Essentially this revolt against English complacency and philistinism (a revolt in the name of a righteous classical élitism) was led by a group of British and American writers under the theoretical spell of French aesthetic philosophy. Their demand: to be truly realistic by *returning* to classical roots long since forgotten or ignored, hence to be more modern by this return to exactitude in form and expression. What classical poetry meant to these writers was a matching of form to function, beauty being in the exactness of the match. No longer would the material (in this case the special language of art) be disguised, but instead *celebrated*. In modernism the form was the message and language had its own adventures. As with the Art Deco steel and concrete skyscrapers of New York or the bright aluminium fighter planes and cross-continental trains, so in literature the *unadorned* material (here words, syntax, grammar) would be celebrated and here it was hoped language would match its subject exactly. Away went misplaced decoration and the hazy 'platitudes' of romanticism. If imagism itself contained internal clichés they went almost unnoticed at the time.

A war of sensibilities had been declared, with anti-humanist classicism and its attendant emphasis on form, order, law and subordination in the ascendant; that these tendencies finally led to fascism, rejectionism, suicide, religious conversion, racialist propaganda, disillusion and a depressing English snobbery was inherent in a movement that was both the product of Victorian liberalism and its gravedigger.[60] The return of classicism and the declaration of its manifest intents meant the necessary rejection of everything 'romantic' and ended appropriately in an aesthetic *fanaticism*. Compromise was not possible (if compromise was the essence of democracy) in a situation where it was felt the salvation of art itself was at issue. The democratic nature of literature died with the imagists' manifesto. The 'availability' of Dickens (whom Leavis later could call no more than 'a great entertainer') had to be suppressed in modernism's refusal to compromise. Yet it was this 'élitism' that liberated artistic form and offered it a dynamism it was felt had been sacrificed to acceptability. Modernism's complexity demanded a highly sophisticated reader; if everybody could not make the climb then so be it.

Modernism's principles, which were in fact rarely found 'unalloyed' or complete in any one writer, can be summarized as an art of metropolitan life which concentrated upon technology (the function of things, rather than mere references to modern objects). In so doing, it elevated form over content in order to subordinate its various parts to the grammar of the totality of form, and by so doing it also elevated a 'mastercode' (in the notion of an ordering *Logos*). Spacial and grammatical organization were now the moral coordinates of art, which replaced the narratalogical *purposive* model of traditional writing. For modernism, science no longer held the ultimate authority; nevertheless *authority*, the authority of text to which man as an animal who uses symbolic language is subordinate, was the key to human endeavour.

Modernism, or at least those movements, alliances and affiliations that characterize it, was always a hybrid affair, always strongly Anglo-American salted with French theory. If it included D.H. Lawrence, Richard Aldington, F.S. Flint and T.E. Hulme in its earliest incarnation and James Joyce, Virginia Woolf and Percy Wyndham Lewis later on, it also included Ezra Pound, T.S. Eliot, Amy Lowell, Hilda Doolittle, Harriet Monroe, Ford Madox Hueffer, John Gould Fletcher and William Carlos Williams amongst its leading advocates. If Virginia Woolf still wrestled with the vestiges of a certain English Pre-Raphaelitism, modernism itself seemed a 'foreign' growth and a strange hothouse flower. The theoretical strength it gained from T.E. Hulme and later Pound and Eliot had little currency amongst the generality of English readers. As Gary Day points out in his chapter on poetry in this volume, during the period it is no longer easy to differentiate and oppose the Imagists and the Georgians. If imagism and its spread into full-blown modernism was seen by its advocates as a radical aesthetic opposition, this did not stop imagist writers fraternizing with the 'enemy' and appearing in non-imagist anthologies. As for the Georgians, now mostly forgotten (no less forgotten than H.D. Richard Aldington or Wyndham Lewis it should be said), their version of literature, with its emphasis on narrative, subordination of form to content, love of decoration, ruralism, cynicism (and emotionalism), syncopated and jazzy effects (especially in Brooke), social concern and subject matter, satiric attitudes and obsession with the 'beauty' of death, was also clearly responding to another version of the then contemporary notion of modern life and how it should be reflected in literature.

CONCLUSION: LITERATURE AND CULTURE

Modernism never produced a Wilfred Owen whose plea is couched in a language which is both democratic and uncompromising (both as to content and as to the integrity of artistic form). In fiction we may generalize the points discussed already. Popular and serious fiction unallied to modernist principles emphasized episodic narrative (good for serialization); teleological and purposive movement (the unveiling of secrets and the unmasking of villains); outward appearance and avoidance of psychology (character *is expressed as action*); elevation of character over plot, and elevation of the central character over the form in which he or she participates. All this, in a bland and accessible language which reinforced the general values of society. This is not the whole story. The serious novels written in this manner emphasized science, social determinism, class confrontation and sexual warfare. The less serious converted these issues into personalized battles: the spy novel, cowboy novelette, romantic love story and detective novel predominated – in a phrase, works of fantasy which reduced the social to the personal.

Modernist fiction to the degree that it infiltrated British culture emphasized the subordination of parts to whole, the suppression of episode, the conversion of character into psychological study and the 'textualizing' of character, through stream of consciousness: psyche and text become one. Thus narrative becomes an inner exploration of psychic forces and the denial of outward (social) presence. With a refusal to engage in political issues, the modernists saw only the domestic and the sexual as relevant (both experienced as inner trauma). The destruction of boundaries between form and content, narrative and motive meant that character and text became synonymous and thus language now *was* mind as it was also *grammar* and thus it became the *form* of inner understanding. The little man replaces the hero – only the *totality* of the text can stop the individual and the world collapsing into fragments. Nothing can be done, all that is left is 'silence, exile and cunning' as the universe 'sneers behind our backs'.[61] In this respect Lawrence marks a middle path between modernism and the Georgian vision and indeed it should be said marks a modernism peculiarly English. Thus literary modernism and popular culture fiction, aesthetic theory and mass entertainment in their complex and contradictory ways respond to the pervasiveness, the democratization and relativism of a dynamic new culture.

NOTES

1. See George Orwell, 'Charles Dickens', in '*The Decline of the English Murder' and Other Essays* (Harmondsworth, 1939; 1988). See also Roland Barthes, 'Textual Analysis of Poe's "Valdemar" ', in Robert Young, *Untying the Text: a Post-Structualist Reader* (Boston, 1981), pp. 133–61.
2. Especially George Lukács, *The Meaning of Contemporary Realism*, trans. John and Necker Mander (London, 1957; 1979); Walter Benjamin, 'The Work of Art in the Age of Mechanical Reproduction', in *Illuminations* (London, 1979), pp. 219–54; Lucien Goldmann, *Towards a Sociology of the Novel*, tr. Alan Sheridan (London, 1964; 1986); Pierre Macherey, *A Theory of Literary Production* (Boston, 1966; 1978).
3. See for example Raymond Williams, *Marxism and Literature* (Oxford, 1978).
4. See for example Terry Eagleton, *Criticism and Ideology* (London, 1978).

5. *Literature and History* was edited by Peter Brooker, Helen Carr, Francis Duke, Peter Humm, Lucy Jeffreys, Jane Maxwell Smith, Roger Richardson, Paul Stigant and Peter Widdowson. Francis Barker, Jay Bernstein and Peter Hulme were the force behind the influential conferences held at Essex University.
6. The Lumiere Group was formed in 1984 by Clive Bloom, Brian Docherty, Jane Gibb and Keith Shand. Clive Bloom and Brian Docherty were later joined by Gary Day.
7. B.B. Gilbert, quoted in Anne Crowther, *British Social Policy 1914–1939* (London, 1988), p. 13.
8. Pseudo-Freudian terminology became current during and after the war.
9. Cyril Connolly, quoted in Randall Stevenson, *The British Novel Since The Thirties: an Introduction* (London, 1986), p. 66.
10. Francis Mulhern, *The Moment of 'Scrutiny'* (London, 1981), p. 7.
11. Donald Read (ed.), *Edwardian England* (London, 1982), pp. 14–15.
12. Ibid., p. 15.
13. Havelock Ellis, *The Dance of Life* (London, 1923), p. ix.
14. Oswald Spengler, *The Decline of the West*, tr. Charles Francis Atkinson (London 1926; 1928; 1959) pp. 106–7.
15. Spengler, vol. 2, pp. 506–7.
16. Read, p. 14.
17. Ibid., p. 1.; also Ellis, p. ix.
18. Paul Thompson and Gina Haskell, *The Edwardians in Photographs* (London, 1979), p. 13.
19. Ibid., p. 52.
20. Noreen Branson, *Britain in the Nineteen Twenties* (London, 1977), p. 2.
21. A.J.P. Taylor quoted in Read, pp. 20–21.
22. Stephen Constantine, *Social Conditions in Britain 1918–1939* (London, 1983), p. 3.
23. Ibid.
24. Ibid., p. 4.
25. Branson, p. 92.
26. Constantine, pp. 19–21.
27. Four million in 1913; five million in 1918; over eight million in 1920.
28. Constantine, p. 14.
29. Branson, p. 250.
30. Over 40 per cent of the drivers who brought their cars to Hyde Park to assist the government were women.
31. Marian Ramelson, *The Petticoat Rebellion: a Century of Struggle for Women's Rights* (London, 1979), p. 169.
32. Branson, p. 25.
33. Ibid., p. 109.
34. Derek Fraser, 'The Edwardian City', in Read, p. 65.
35. Ibid., p. 22.
36. Branson, p. 178.
37. Ibid., p. 179.
38. Ramelson, p. 167.
39. Dangerfield, pp. 97 and 407.
40. I should like to acknowledge the kind permission of Hodder and Stoughton in compiling the following information. All information for this publisher comes from the Guildhall Library, London.

41. See Publishing Ledger Number 12 Fiction '1903' (MS:16, 310 Guildhall Library) which records *The Wizard of Oz's* sales at September 1906. Of 500 bound, 40 were complimentary copies, 212 were sold and 248 were still on hand at 1 April 1907.
42. See MS:16,319 Guildhall Library. For the lives and dubious attitudes of Oppenheim and his contemporaries, see Colin Watson, *Snobbery with Violence* (London, [1971] 1987).
43. Respectively, Pinkers, A.P. Watt and the University of North Carolina at Chapel Hill.
44. Terms invented by H.G. Wells. See Robert Graves and Alan Hodge, *The Long Weekend: Social History of Great Britain 1918–1939* (London, 1940; 1985).
45. Ibid.
46. See Richard Ellman, *James Joyce* (Oxford, 1959; 1982).
47. See Clive Bloom 'The Falling House that never Falls: Rupert Brooke and Literary Taste', in Brian Docherty, *British Poetry in the Twentieth Century* (London, 1993).
48. See George Lukács, p. 21.
49. A figure ranging from the Chaplinesque 'Little Tramp' to the gentleman-adventurer Richard Hannay.
50. See Clive Bloom, *Spy Thrillers: from Buchan to Le Carré* (London, 1991) pp. 1–2. The detective novel itself is founded on the notion of *bewilderment* (of the reader, characters and police) in the face of an irrational action (murder) by a greater force (the murderer) until an equal and bewildering force (the eccentric detective) can restore order.
51. T.S. Eliot, 'A Cooking Egg'.
52. For this history see Mulhern (note 10).
53. I.A. Richards, *Principles of Literary Criticism* (London, 1924; 1976).
54. I.A. Richards, *Practical Criticism: a Study of Literary Judgement* (London, 1929; 1973).
55. *Principles of Literary Criticism*, preface.
56. Ibid.
57. See Benjamin, ibid (note 2).
58. Alistair McCleery, *Times Higher Education Supplement* (13 September 1991), p. 18.
59. Ibid.
60. Glenn Hughes, *Imagism and the Imagists: a Study in Modern Poetry* (Stanford, Calif., 1931) p. 14.
61. James Joyce, *A Portrait of the Artist as a Young Man*; Virginia Woolf, *The Waves*.

CHAPTER ONE

The Poets: Georgians, Imagists and Others

Gary Day

"Drake and Nelson, rural England, fear in a handful of dust"[1]

As Clive Bloom notes in his introduction, the period between 1900 and 1929 saw a shift from an individualist to a collectivist state apparent in the development of monopoly capitalism, the extension of the franchise and new legislation to deal with poverty and unemployment. One consequence of this change was the growth of new discourses of social regulation which addressed the human subject less as a unique individual than as an object for state concern. The subject was no longer an active agent, as in classical laissez-faire economics, but someone to be regulated and administered according to particular forms of knowledge, specifically the sciences of human engineering, often summarized in the phrase 'social Darwinism'.[2]

The subject was now perceived as a citizen, not an individual. The category of the citizen stresses what members of a society have in common, the category of the individual how they differ. The term citizen functions as a norm by which difference becomes deviancy, the term individual, by contrast, allows for and even celebrates difference. With the ascendancy of the term citizen comes a standardized view of the subject expressed in standardized language.

Of course, this transformation was a gradual process and one which still continues. The concept of the individual was not suddenly usurped by that of the citizen, rather they constituted a complex and shifting relationship in which the category of the individual and its attendant structures persisted as a critique within the formations of citizenship and collectivization.

The question this essay addresses is how this relationship manifested itself in the poetry of the period and the part that poetry itself played in that relationship. One immediate point is that modernism, with its emphasis on impersonality, helped to produce the kind of perceptions appropriate to the idea of the citizen, while the more traditionalist verse of the period continued to provide resources and vocabularies appropriate to the idea of the unique individual. However, it is necessary to be cautious about such assertions for Georgian verse could be as modernist as imagist poetry could be traditionalist.

Showing how poetry reflects and shapes society's perceptions of itself is an important way of understanding how poetry functions in society. But it is also important to remember that poetry is *made* to function in a quite specific way by the institutions of criticism such as schools, colleges and universities where it is decided what can actually count as poetry and which criteria are to be used for its appreciation. By these and other means criticism plays a small but not insignificant part in producing and maintaining society's ideological consensus. This process will also be touched on in the course of this essay, and raises the question of whether it is possible to read otherwise and thus free poetry from its normal ideological usage so as to challenge that usage and perhaps generate new readings, offering new perspectives on the present as well as the past.

Before addressing these issues in more detail, however, it is first necessary to give a brief account of poetry prior to 1911 so as to better understand the place of Georgian poetry and the impact of modernism.

POETRY PRIOR TO 1911

The sense of a major cultural shift was expressed in poetry by a number of developments at the turn of the century. The Decadent poets of the 1890s differed from the great Victorian ones in their concern for the elusive nature of experience. Their conception of it was somewhat complex and suggests that the traditional ideological way of authenticating and making sense of experience were no longer adequate. For the Decadent 'all actual experience ha[d] the habit of seeming vicarious'.[3] There was also a concern with being understood, most clearly evident in Dowson's lament 'You would have understood me, had you waited' which points to a problem in intersubjective relations.[4] Experience is pursued, not for itself but for the fruits it yields and there is a desire to charge bodily experiences with profundity. Chiefly there is a consciousness of corruption which is both desired and reviled, 'waters of bitterness, how sweet'.[5] The sense of decadence and corruption is important because it compensates for the absence of meaning in experience by the intensity of experience. Subjectivity is reduced to sensation, which is private and perhaps incommunicable but certainly is the one genuine experience open to the self. Indeed, being oneself becomes a matter of artifice, as Clive Scott remarks of the Decadents:

> Make-up, the music hall milieu with its garish lights, costumes, and other forms of ostentation are at once the *art* of being oneself and the way that, for others, knowledge of a self becomes a series of sensory delights. In this essentially baroque world of fluid roles, identity depends on the particular stimulus one transmits at a given time. [6]

But it is not just in their approach to the problems of subjectivity and experience that the Decadents anticipate modernist verse. One of the prime figures in the Decadent movement, Arthur Symons wrote the influential *The Symbolist Movement In Literature* (1899) which Eliot admitted changed the course of his life.[7] Symbolism valued form over content, it was suggestive rather than straightforward and was based on a belief that reality lay beneath the surface of things and could only be apprehended by the symbol. These related ideas were to have a profound influence on modernist verse: the symbol came to be a focus, a way of organizing and making sense of disparate phenomena, but its significance in the work of say Yeats and Eliot could only be known to the educated few. The symbol thus redefined the relationship between the poet and his public, making verse exclusive and 'élitist.'

Symbolism did not inform Decadent poetry to any great extent but the symbol, with its connotation of privacy and irreducible complexity, was not alien to the Decadent concern with experience. Both Decadence and symbolism represent an ambiguous response to the atrophy of the notion of the individual. On the one hand they are an assertion of the individual in the face of the forces of collectivization but, on the other, they seem to suggest that the individual is an empty category – either sensation or technique, nothing more. Over-refinement and accumulation of adjectives which mark the Decadent style seem a desperate attempt to capture a vanishing essence as indeed does the symbol. The notion of the individual is almost protected by the latter's obscurity. Just at the moment when history wants to dispense with the individual, symbolism pronounces him or her infinitely rich and complex. Thus art can be seen to be trying to maintain an ideological category just as, in other fields, it begins to lose its effectivity.

Both Decadence and symbolism were to influence modernist verse but, around 1911, the poetry with which most people were familiar was a mixture of the pastoral, the romantic and the patriotic. The poet was a bluff, no nonsense type of figure who wrote decent, comprehensible verse which dealt with matters anyone could understand and, in both form and content, that poetry represented a conservative reaction not just to the morbid sensitivity of the Decadents. Poets like Alfred Noyes, Henry Newbolt and William Watson were typical of the period. Their writing was characterized by approval of imperial adventures and a sentimental view of England as essentially a collection of villages when in fact it was becoming progressively and disturbingly urban. These writers confidently presumed to speak on behalf of the public in matters of morality and religion. However, their broad generalities, imprecise diction and traditional poetic forms were essentially a nostalgic assertion of Victorian certainties in an age of rapid change. The imperialism of poems such as Henry Newbolt's 'Drake's Dream' were a confident assertion of the quintessential British voice defying the forces, such as foreign competition and the growth of mass consciousness, that threatened to destroy it. But although this verse gestured to the past it also, paradoxically, belonged to the present and future, for the very public as opposed to the private nature of the poetic voice allied it with movement from an individual to a more collective notion of subjectivity. This did not, however, prevent it from being displaced by Georgian poetry which, while clearly different to imperialist verse in some respects, in others was very similar; both for example showed a preference for the rustic rather than the metropolitan life.

GEORGIAN POETRY

Georgian poetry can be identified most simply as the five volumes of verse which appeared between 1912 and 1922, edited by Edward Marsh and published by Harold Munro at the Poetry Bookshop.[8] At first, Georgian poetry was seen as a healthy reaction to the ornate, specious and didactic verse represented by poets like Noyes. In contrast to them both *Georgian Poetry I* (1911–12) and *Georgian Poetry II* (1914–15) displayed 'poetic realism or truth to life'.[9] The achievement of the Georgians, according to Stead, was 'to confine poetry within the limits of what had actually been experienced'.[10] James Reeves goes further, praising Georgian poetry for its 'natural simplicity, emotional warmth, and moral innocence'[11] and he goes on to say that 'The celebration of England, whether at peace or war, became a principal aim of Georgian poetry'.[12] By the end of the First World War, however, Georgianism was already under attack, though there were still two more volumes to appear. It seemed out of touch with the modern world and Edith Sitwell in particular was merciless in her derision of poets who only seemed to be able to write about sheep. Even allowing for her modernist bias it is hard not to feel some sympathy for her views, vitriolic though they were, when confronted with the following:

> I lingered at a gate and talked
> A little with a lonely lamb

He told me of the great still night
Of starlight
. . .

William Kerr, 'Counting Sheep' (*GP V*, 1920–22)

The faults of Georgian poetry are well known: sloppy sentimentality, facile rhythm and a concern with the trivial and the commonplace.[13] However, to discuss the poetry in this manner is to accept the terms of an aesthetic discourse which trades in value judgements that are by no means as innocent as they seem. For example, is the dismissal of Georgian poetry anything to do with the fact that a number of Georgians, such as Wilford Gibson and James Stephens, had not trod the usual paths of public school and Oxbridge? It is also interesting to note that poets who did, like Robert Graves and Edmund Blunden, rarely have their Georgian past referred to except as something of an embarrassment. In other words, the marginalizing of Georgian poetry is perhaps ideologically motivated. In this context it is worth remembering that Georgian poetry with its gentle celebrations of Englishness was arguably the first popular poetry of the modern age. The first volume sold 15,000 copies, a phenomenal number for a poetry book, prompting W.H. Davies, one of the contributors, to write to Edward Marsh saying 'You have performed a wonder, made poetry pay'.[14]

Critical dismissal of Georgian simplicity in favour of modernist sophistication identifies poetry as a specialist discourse, the preserve of an intellectual élite. Poetry is thus placed out of the reach of the 'ordinary person' but, more than that, the values embedded in the particular poetic discourse of Georgianism are neutralized, making it difficult for them to signify with any effectivity either in poetry or even in politics. A mode of expression is thus removed from popular circulation and so are the values belonging to it. In addition, not only is poetry, for so long associated in the popular mind with self-expression, removed from the people, thus leaving them even fewer forms in which to voice their concerns, but it is also, to reinforce the point, redefined as the very antithesis of self-expression first by the modernist mandarins and later by successive critics. By such means does criticism support the hierarchy of class society; crushing poetry's democratic potential by implicitly suggesting that only those of taste and education can appreciate it, thereby legislating a political superiority by asserting a parallel cultural one.

The hostile reception of Georgian poetry needs to be understood within the context of the broad social, economic and political developments of the time, particularly the growth of international monopoly capitalism. The assault by the modernists on the Georgians is, in part, a reflection of this move away from a national to a more international outlook, precipitated, in the final analysis, by changes in the economic organization of capitalism. Cosmopolitan culture grows as national ones wither and a sense of rootlessness drives out a sense of belonging. On this analysis, Georgianism is an anachronism the moment it appears. But a deeper irony afflicts modernism which, while symptomatic of historically progressive forces, is nevertheless opposed to the changes they bring in their wake. Hence modernism tried to combat the fragmentation of the urban experience by bringing together aspects from different traditions in the hope of lending some coherence, however ironic, to the modern condition.

Setting Georgian poetry within the context of its time not only helps illuminate the relationship between criticism and historical developments, it also throws some light on why Georgian poetry, although anachronistic, continued to be published throughout the period and under discussion in a number of newspapers and magazines, most notably J. C. Squire's *London Mercury*.[15] Clearly, Georgian poetry served some purpose, the key to which may lie in what Reeves calls its 'naturalness of utterance'.[16] This, together with its apparent distrust of rhetoric and grandiose themes, suggests a connection between Georgian poetry and ideological experience, for what characterizes the latter is the very sort of 'simplicity' and 'spontaneity' which characterized Georgian verse.

Ideology has many functions, but perhaps the most important is to produce a subjectivity which is able to reconcile the contradictions of lived experience and so ensure the continuity of the bourgeois state.[17] Significantly, the shift from an individualist to a collectivist state meant that the nature of subjectivity and its production were thrown into crisis. Georgian poetry can perhaps be seen as renewing through *verse* the traditional ideological ways of making sense of the world, ways which come into prominence when challenged by new forms of understanding. Georgian poetry briefly galvanizes a dying ideology, one which produces an individualist subjectivity which understands events as natural rather than historical and one which endeavours to reconcile contradictions in society by displacing them onto the individual's relationship with nature. It is in this context that the notorious pastoralism of Georgian verse can best be understood.

Georgian poetry is consistent with the ideology of individualism; its lyricism recalls familiar and more stable perceptions of the world but ones which will be increasingly marginalized as the collectivist impulse takes concrete form at all levels of state and society. In short, Georgian poetry functions to prop up the ideology of individualism, and its demise has less to do with its aesthetic qualities than with the change from an individualist to a collectivist state. As a result, the 'sense-making apparatus' of Georgian poetry, at least in terms of high culture, was effectively redundant by the 1930s. However, strains of Georgianism continued to flourish in popular poetry as they do today when conceptions of verse are, to some extent, still shaped by the ideas of nature and the self to be found in Georgian poetry.

It is now time to turn to a more detailed inspection of the verse itself, noting the problems involved in trying to revive an individualist voice in an increasingly collectivist age and also to see whether there is any aspect of Georgian poetry which could conceivably be described as modernist.

Critics have compared the presentation of nature in Georgian poetry with its presentation in Wordsworth and so found it lacking. They have attempted to understand it solely within the terms of the romantic tradition rather than in its specific historical context.[18] As a result nature, in Georgian poetry, is seen as a falling away from the Wordsworthian standard rather than as a term in its own right. Nature is made to signify in a number of ways in Georgian poetry. At the simplest level it is there to be described:

> For all that's left of Winter
> Is moisture on the ground.
>
> Lascelles Abercrombie, 'Ryton Firs' (*GP V, 1920–22*)

This straightforward observation suggest a stable relationship between the subject and the world, the former observes the latter in a direct fashion and the world appears both known and knowable. However, the empiricism implicit in this view is challenged when Ralph Hodgson questions whether 'catalogue and pigeon holing' ('Babylon', *GP III*, 1916–17) are adequate ways of organizing experience to the extent that they threaten its full sensuous immediacy. As such, his idea of poetic discourse challenges the new language of taxonomy and classification which was being employed in the production of the citizen as opposed to the individual. One way to preserve this 'felt life' was to remove it from society to nature but, since nature can be mapped like society, it becomes necessary to go a step further and mystify that nature. Nature is thus protected from the encroachments and limitations of empiricism by being mysterious. One way in which it is made so is by being exoticized.[19] A significant proportion of the nature that appears in Georgian poetry belongs to a foreign setting which immediately challenges the cliché that Georgian verse celebrates Englishness.

> It was a deep night, and over Jerusulem's low roofs
> The moon floated, drifting through high vaporous
> Woofs.
>
> Robert Nichols, 'The Tower' (*GP III*, 1916–17, p. 71)

> Far are the shades of Arabia ...
> ... And so dark is that vaulted purple
> Flowers in the forest rise
> And toss into blossom 'gainst the phantom stars
> Pale in the noonday skies.
>
> Walter de la Mare, 'Arabia' (*GP I*, 1911–12)

The exotic gestures towards empire and the kind of sexual freedom that could be enjoyed in the colonies but not at home. Using a mediterranean landscape T. Sturge Moore is able to present his characters in a more erotic manner than if he set his tale in the English countryside. Describing a 'Twelve or thirteen year old boy,' he writes,

> ... His wide brimmed hat of straw was arched
> Over his massed black and abundant curls ...
> ... his curls against his hat
> Bounce up behind. The daintiest thing alive ...
> ... I ... devour him with my eyes.
>
> T. Sturge Moore, 'A Sicilian Idyll' (*GP I*, 1911–12)

But the exotic does more than provide a means of representing a sensuousness marginalized by a new social discourse; it stands opposed to knowledge as a condition of its existence. This may explain why it is not daytime but night-time nature which so often engages Georgian poets. Night is also the time of dreams, another frequent word in Georgian verse, and this too helps to de-realize nature as a physical entity capable of being investigated and known.

At the point that it loses its specific identity and becomes a screen for subjective preoccupations nature in Georgian poetry touches on the Wordsworthian tradition. However, the historical conditions which authenticated Wordsworth's poetic do not apply here and that is why Georgian musings on nature fail to convince:

> O thou mysterious lake, thy spell
> Holds all who round thy fruitful margin dwell ...
> ... Those who among thy waters plunge, arise
> Filled with new wisdom and serenity.
>
> Harold Munro, 'Lake Leman' (*GP I*, 1911–12)

As well as imparting its qualities to humans, nature also supplies them with a vocabulary for their moods and emotions:

> Mist, grief, and stillness everywhere ...
> And in me, too, there is no sound
> Save welling as of tears profound ...
>
> Robert Nichols, 'November' (*GP V*, 1920–22)

Nature, free from the empirical threat, has become the preserve of, and the language for, a besieged subjectivity. Despite this, nature is dangerous:

> Last night a sword, light in the sky
> Flashed a swift terror in the dark.
>
> John Freeman, 'Stone Trees' (*GP III*, 1916–17)

And it is so on two counts. First, if everything has become subjectivity there is nothing to confirm subjectivity. Unless subject can differentiate itself from what it is not, it cannot know specifically what it is. This problem is compounded by another feature of Georgian poetry – its absence of human relations. Very few poems in these volumes take their cue from human interaction and this reflects the fact that the discourse of Georgian poetry has marked itself off from the discourse of the social realm where intersubjective relations were being reorganized. The language of nature only promotes a relationship with nature and not a relationship between subject and subject. Consequently, nature in Georgian poetry is faced with an intolerable burden: it has to function as an object so that subjectivity can know itself *as* subjectivity, but it must also compensate for lost intersubjectivity which it cannot do if it is object. This paradox prevents nature from confirming subjectivity which, with nothing to define itself against, is confronted by its own nothingness. There is no escaping the irony that, in wanting to avoid being known, the subject puts its own survival in jeopardy and hovers on the verge of disappearing before the nature which was to be its salvation.

This crisis of subjectivity manifests itself in a number of poems which question how the subject can be represented if it is to forego the new discourse of representation. Thus John Masefield:

> When I am buried, all my thoughts and acts
> Will be reduced to lists of dates and facts
>
> John Masefield, 'Biography' (*GP I*, 1911–12)

Masefield feels that 'dates and facts' cannot capture the essence which is he and which is expressed through this poem as a sort of 'gleaming', a series of 'bright' or 'golden' moments which escape representation. The irony is that, in attempting to convey a sense of lived experience, Masefield has to resort to those very facts which he denounces as being unable to represent his essence. His response to this impasse is to try and go ever deeper into the self.

> If I could get within this changing I ...
> ... [To] The brain's most folded intertwisted shell ...
>
> John Masefield, untitled sonnet sequence, part III, (*GP II*, 1916–17)

However, the only language Masefield has for this inward exploration is physical, and his reliance on terms like 'cells' and 'atoms' only secures him in that from which he is trying to escape.

John Drinkwater's 'The Fires of God' (*GP I*, 1911–12) also addresses the problem of how to represent the self in all its felt immediacy. Once again the task of trying to represent it while avoiding the language of representation proves too much and the whole project collapses, the poet escaping the contradictions his task imposes on him by a recourse to religion. Nature becomes a sign of God, a guarantee of his order – a motif, incidentally, common to a number of poets of this period – and the poet surrenders himself to 'The glory of ... mysteries'; he escapes the crisis of subjectivity by merging it with something outside himself, as indeed does the subject in W.J. Turner's poem 'Ecstasy' (*GP III*, 1916–17) who becomes one with the frieze. This fusion of subject and object in a new whole does produce that sensuous immediacy, or 'ecstasy', for which there was no place in the new discourse associated with citizenship. However, where nature is subject rather than object this merging cannot take place.

Some aspects of the style of Georgian poetry can perhaps be related to this crisis of subjectivity. To begin with there is plentiful use of archaic diction: 'blessed', 'wherewith', 'amid', 'thee' and so on. This conscious use of outmoded words may be seen as an attempt to re-create a past where the individual subject was at home in the world. In attempting to reanimate a tradition, it acknowledges both the authority of that tradition and itself as the descendant of it, and thus conjures up the ghost of paternalism to bolster itself in a decreasingly paternalistic age. Apostrophe is another characteristic of Georgian verse – 'Are you cold too, poor Pleiads? ...' (Robert Graves,' Star Talk' (*GP III*, 1916–17) – and this is simply personifying nature by addressing it as a subject so that it can stand in for the lost intersubjectivity of the social.

Ross has described how some early commentators on Georgian poetry were unhappy about the obtrusion of certain brutal and nasty details such as those describing the torture of a merchant in Lascelle Abercrombie's 'The Sale of St Thomas' (*GP I*, 1911–12).[20] But such details did more than point to the supposedly new realism of Georgian verse; their intensity was a form of a displaced subjectivity which could find no place for itself as the category of the individual increasingly gave way to the categories of the citizen and the collective. In this connection it is worth mentioning that these details were mainly to do with death, which perhaps can be interpreted as the demise of a particular type of subjectivity, the individual.

Another feature of Georgian poetry is its quantity of adjectives:

> ... the glowing bodies,
> Drunken with light, untroubled clouds ...
>
> Peter Quenell, 'Perception' (*GP V*, 1920–22)

is a fairly typical example. The adjective should describe the noun but here, as elsewhere, the latter is in danger of being overwhelmed. These multiple adjectives help to produce a poetic discourse that is the very antithesis of the new administrative and scientific discourses of the collectivizing state. The adjectives infuse the world with subjective impressions but at the cost of losing it as an entity in its own right. Indeed, this opens up another way of seeing the deployment of multiple adjectives in Georgian poetry: they are an attempt to capture what seems to be on the point of disappearing. In either case, this characteristic of Georgian poetry imparts to it a quality of excess that not only recalls that thickening of the signifier associated with symbolism but also suggests, once more, the redundancy of the category of the individual: the world can no longer support this particular subject's view of it; it collapses, leaving the subject alone without being able to understand its aloneness. The use of multiple adjectives is part and parcel of that strained grammar, yet another aspect of Georgian style. The grammar seems to break down under the strain of trying to make sense of a world which requires different sense-making operations, thus drawing attention to itself as language and, by doing so, calling into question that traditional judgement of Georgian poetry as approximating to the 'natural utterance'. What modernism does consciously Georgian poetry does by default.

One final feature of Georgian poetry is its tendency to 'doubling'; that is to say, an apparently straightforward narrative or lyric seems to be twice told. For example Wilfrid Gibson's 'The Hare' (*GP I*, 1911–12) reproduces the dream of killing the hare in different ways and in different contexts to the point where it disrupts the very distinctions on which the narrative is based, with the result that the poem mimics itself rather than, as it appears to do, tells a story. Here, language starts to escape from the poet as if it, not he, were autonomous and self-determining. The poet is ceasing to matter and this looks forward, albeit obliquely, to such modernist doctrines as Eliot's objective correlative. But perhaps there's more at issue than poetic language escaping the writer's efforts to fix it in a stable framework of meaning, for the moment of poetic doubling may parallel the general operations of discourses in the social field, where the subject is doubled as both private person and public citizen, with the emphasis on the latter, neither coinciding, as they did previously, in the category of the individual.

If part of the popular appeal of Georgian poetry lay in the tensions it generated in trying to establish a place for private personal experience in traditional forms when both were being historically sidelined, another part was almost certainly due to it being vigorously marketed by Eddie Marsh and Harold Munro, a process which was in sharp contrast to the pastoralism of the verse itself. Ironically it was the very forces of centralization which gave Georgian poetry such a high profile. Poetic activity in and around London was rationalized by Harold Munro's Poetry Bookshop which opened officially in 1913. From then he was in a position to establish an ever expanding network of contacts with poets, reviewers and publishers turning poetry into a profitable business. This economic centralization was part of the general trend to a more corporate style of economy.[21] The greatest irony, however, has to lie in the fact that it was Eddie Marsh, a top civil servant and Churchill's private secretary, who organized and presided over Georgian poetry, since he stood for the very discourse his poets opposed. This unlikely juxtaposition revealed poetry as economically central but politically marginal. Marsh being a full-time civil servant, his association with Georgian poetry signalled it as a leisure activity; thus it was referred to the private person and so banished from the public sphere in which it nevertheless appeared. Poetry was established in the market-place and, simultaneously, was socially marginalized. In the process, the reading subject was pushed to the periphery to make room for the subject as consumer and it is as consumer that subjectivity will from now on be constructed.[22]

FIRST WORLD WAR POETRY: DIFFERENCE AND CONFORMITY

Perhaps the abiding contradiction of this poetry is that, even though it is more obviously rooted in history than Georgian verse, it is discussed as if it somehow transcended it. Criticism of First World War poetry constructs it as a message – war is bad – to be understood against a scale of universal human values. But, by emptying this 'message' of its specific history, criticism disables First World War poetry from ever playing an effective part in anti-war arguments – witness the Falklands campaign and the Gulf conflict. Its generality disqualifies it from any specific occasion where war is an issue, yet, paradoxically, the universal values to which it supposedly attaches are invariably the ones which are invoked for going to war in the first place. First World War poetry is only allowed its own history on condition that it transcends it. But to allow it its own history proves yet another way of marginalizing it, for then it can be confined to its period and thus is seen as saying something only about its own time, not any other. Where it is permitted to aspire beyond its own conditions of production it is on the understanding that it does so in terms of a universal language, all very well in an ideal world but hardly relevant to whatever matter is in hand. So, whether criticism produces First World War poetry as contingent to or transcendent of its history, the effect is the same: to prevent it from having an effective voice in anti-war arguments. Of course, this only applies to that poetry which depicts the horror of war. Poems like Rupert Brooke's 'The Soldier' are reproduced to simultaneously transcend and enter history precisely because they connote an idea of Englishness which is held to be true of all periods and, for that reason, is appealed to in specific crises.

First World War poetry is contemporaneous with Georgian verse; indeed some of Sassoon's war poetry appeared in *GP III*, 1916–17, as did Asquith's 'The Volunteer' which, with its romantic view of the clerk going 'to join the men of Agincourt', presents that sentimental view of war which so repelled Sassoon. That the two could be juxtaposed in one volume shows how considerations of poetic worth overrode anything poetry could actually say. Generally, Georgian poetry disdained contact with the world but the poets at the Front had no choice but to write about what was going on around them. The achievement of Owen and others was to engage poetry with experience but it was not a lasting one in terms of the tradition out of which they grew for, after the war, there was a reversion to the styles of verse so popular before it. This may be explained in part by a desire to forget the war and get on with the peace but it was also something to do with the fact that the First World War poetry represented a unique moment in which to make verse pertinent and relevant just after it had been marginalized; it went, in other words, against the ideological current. More particularly, it threatened to revive the category of the individual, in so far as it showed the poet involved yet apart from the events he or she described. This suggested that the individual could transcend the social when through collectivization the individual was being merged in it. Again, what is found in First World War poetry is that sense of shared experience which is absent from Georgian verse, where the poet relates to nature, not others. This recent awareness of community represents a radical potential that could feed in to political discourse, but this too disappears with the end of the war, not because it suggests a common humanity but because it suggests a particular type of humanity, a flesh and blood collection of individuals rather than citizens with abstract rights, duties and entitlements.[23]

There can be no doubting the immediacy of First World War poetry that is absent from Georgian verse. Sassoon mentions 'The rant, stench of bodies'. In Isaac Rosenberg's 'Dead Man's Dump',

> A man's brains splattered on
> A stretcher bearer's face
> ...

Such details are typical of much of the poetry, concentrating as it does on the violence and suffering of combat. There is a desire to both report and shock, a desire to tell the truth, to counter the propaganda and disinformation disseminated by the authorities.

However, although these and similar descriptions reflect a direct engagement with the war, there is another sense in which it is almost avoided. Edward Thomas's 'Fifty Faggots' mentions the war in an almost casual way –

> ... they must
> Light several Winter's fires. Before they are done
> The war will have ended ...

– while Rosenberg can approach it through Old Testament legend ('Moses', 'The Unicorn'). This use of nature and legend represents a continuity with

Georgian poetry and serves to lessen the specific impact of a unique war by making sense of it in terms of natural processes or ancient traditions. The poets lack the necessary framework which would help them make historical sense of the details they record, and so their only other option is to *repress* what they're experiencing (Siegfried Sassoon, 'Repression of War Experience'). The unique character of the war meant that there was no tradition to which it could be assimilated and so there was a resort to nature and legend which only succeed in naturalizing it, 'the wild beast of battle' (Siegfried Sassoon, 'The Troops'), and thus war is brought within the bounds of familiar experiences the poets were trying to escape. Shock is followed by recuperation and incorporation.[24]

Under this kind of pressure the verse can start to disintegrate, a disintegration made all the more acute by some aspects of grammar remaining intact while others crumble.

> Sickens the light, and poisoned, withered, wan,
> The least defiled turns desperate to me.
> ...

> Edmund Blunden, 'Preparations for Victory'

There is a general sense of corruption here, but it is not organized in a subject–object relationship; that has broken down just as it did in Georgian poetry, and, it might be argued, the elimination of the subject in modernist verse is the culmination of this process. The crumbling grammar and the consequent undermining of the subject–object relationship heralds the collapse of other organizing features of language so that disconnected phrases follow one another as in Ivor Gurney's 'It is near Toussaints' without being built into a whole. Once more this recalls aspects of Georgian style and looks forward to modernism.

The fracture of the subject–object relationship means subjectivity now inheres in the scattered details it records. This is chiefly seen in the work of Ivor Gurney but it is also there in Edmund Blunden and David Jones. Other signs of disintegrating subjectivity include those dream or hallucinatory poems such as Owen's 'Strange Meeting' or Ford Madox Ford's 'That Exploit of Yours', and those poems of self-alienation where mind and body are at odds as in Herbert Read's 'Dialogue between the Body and the Soul of the Murdered Girl', or Edgell Rickword's 'The Soldier Addresses His Body'. Stability is only achieved by resorting to the language of religion, which takes the individual out of the world (Read, 'Meditation of the Waking English Officer'), or nature, where he or she is contained within its larger scheme and so assured continuity.

Another stylistic feature of First World War poetry is the predominance of verbs. In Georgian poetry the stress was on the adjectives which ultimately implied a static world, whereas the prominent and graphic verbs of First World War verse convey movement and violence. This violence obviously reflects the destructive nature of war but it also represents an energy, something that's paradoxically life affirming, as in Blunden's 'Midnight Skaters' where death is depicted beneath the ice.

> Then on, blood shouts, on, on,
> Twirl, whirl and whip about him,.
> ... Court him, elude him, reel and pass
> And let him hate you through the glass.

This troubling ambiguity is found in a different form in the verse of Wilfred Owen who in setting out to report the horrors of war only succeeds, in certain poems, in aestheticizing them. What the reader notices in 'Anthem for Doomed Youth' is the perfectly worked sonnet form, the consistency and ingenuity of the imagery, and the effective alliteration; not the pain, suffering and waste. By being aestheticized war is made manageable and even, to some extent, justified; it becomes attractive by being transformed into art.

First World War poetry then both describes and doesn't describe war, and is the place and yet is not the place where the individual voice asserts itself. Its verse is where the contradictions of the social process are most apparent because they are most concentrated. The experience of war both includes the individual within the collective and causes him or her to protest against it. First World War poetry is used in the construction of bourgeois subjectivity as a site for the production of universal human values which are somehow ineffective whenever armed conflict is imminent. This is chiefly because they are articulated in a context where individuals are perceived as being powerless to confront their fate. Hence values such as pity and compassion are reactive rather than active and, as such, they help produce a passive bourgeois subject.

Although criticism uses First World War poetry to produce this kind of subject it is important not to forget that subjectivity in the poems themselves is manifested in different ways but, for the purposes of the development of modern verse, the most important is the fragmentary, discontinuous one.

IMAGISM

Imagism was part of a number of prewar movements which included, among others, vorticism and futurism. In contrast to the more conservative Georgians, these ideas formed part of a climate of opinion which encouraged experimentalism in art, which was anti-representational and anti-humanistic and which glorified newness for its own sake. Futurism lauded violence, self-assertion and primitivism. It idealized the machine, speed, danger, noise and the unrestrained ego. Futurist poetry was almost unreadable since words and symbols were used interchangeably and with almost total freedom, there was no syntax and verbs appeared in their infinitive form. It had little effect in English poetry. Vorticism, which was imagism's brief successor, was launched in 1914 and its principles were expounded in the magazine *Blast* edited by Wyndham Lewis. Unlike futurism, which stemmed from Italy, vorticism was a homegrown phenomenon. Building on futurist ideas, particularly the celebration of the machine and the reality of the present, it too challenged realism, sentimentalism, aestheticism and the moral, didactic quality of previous poetic traditions. Vorticism, like futurism and imagism, passed with the war.

John Press has argued that imagism was 'the only poetic movement of the century that has profoundly altered the course of English verse'.[25] And this view is partly echoed by Stead, who argues that modernism was a product of the divergent qualities of both symbolism and imagism, creating open-ended works that imposed new, creative responsibilities on the reader.[26] Imagism contained three distinct phases. The first was the 1909 group led by T.E. Hulme who, for a year or so, in their weekly meetings in a Soho restaurant, called The Eiffel Tower, discussed the possibility of a new poetic. Then there was Pound's belligerent school of 1912 and, finally, there were the post-Poundian imagists led by Amy Lowell and dubbed by Pound as 'Amygists'. As a movement, imagism could be said to have begun in 1909 and to have died in 1917 when the last imagist anthology was published in Boston.

Although imagism is related to symbolism in its emphasis on form, it differs from it in as much as it seeks to remove the poet from the poem, giving it as objective a character as possible. There was an insistence by poets like Hulme, Flint and Pound that the new poetry should contain no verbiage and should aim for absolutely accurate presentation. In addition, Edward Storer, along with other poets, declared war on the iambic pentameter. 'There is no absolute virtue in iambic pentameters as such ... however well done they may be. There is no immediate virtue in rhythm even ... judged by themselves, they are monstrosities of childish virtuosity and needless iteration.'[27] The Imagists' concern for accuracy and economy and the adoption of *vers libre* was a reaction to the sloppy, prolish, meandering and imprecise verse which they felt characterized the state of English poetry.[28] Their aim was to revitalize language, to get away from vagueness by means of precise definition.

This aim was reflected in a number of highly prescriptive programmes such as Pound's 'A Few Don'ts by an Imagiste' and Flint's checklist in 'Imagism'.[29] This emphasis on selection, on what counted as good or bad verse, chimed with the ethos of Social Darwinism, which was the philosophy behind much state intervention. But it was not only on the matter of selection that imagism reflected the move from an individualist to a collectivist ideology, for the scientific tone of its various manifestos and the discussions concerning which techniques produced the best results mirrored the new scientific approach to social problems.

Richard Aldington's 'Evening' is a typical example of imagist work.[30]

> The chimneys, rank on rank,
> Cut the clear sky;
> The moon,
> With a rig of gauze about her loins
> Poses among them, an awkward Venus –
> And here am I looking wantonly at her
> Over the kitchen sink.

This is short, there is no moralizing tone, there is no fixed metre or rhyme and no vagueness. The reference to the chimneys is a sign that the city is now a suitable subject for poetry, even though the chimneys are pointing away from it. The urban environment is seen as highly structured 'rank on rank' to which the moon offers a pleasing contrast. This is slightly puzzling in terms of imagist aesthetics which valorize order and precision, as indeed is the use of the first person pronoun which introduces a subjective element into the poem, given imagism's anti-subjective bias.

Pound saw the image as 'that which presents an intellectual and emotional complex in an instant of time'.[31] It was something which unified and thus perhaps combated the fragmentation characteristic of urban life. More significantly Pound's formulation, especially the reference to time, manages to anticipate the way in which information comes to be transmitted in the modern world, instantly and dramatically: instantly, because there's so *much* information to be conveyed and dramatically for the same reason. This is particularly evident in advertising which, of course, constantly structures the subject as consumer. And this leads to the key question regarding Aldington's poem; namely, what sort of response does it require? The strange thing about imagism is that it seems to require no response, not just because it is non-discursive, but because it has a kind of absolute quality which defies comment.

> Golden peacocks
> Under blossoming cherry-trees,
> But on all the wide sea
> There is no boat.
>
> Amy Lowell, 'Yoshiwara Lament'

Imagism arrests the reader in a quasi-specular fashion which uncannily catches the way in which consumer society presents itself as self-contained spectacle. Nowhere is this spectacle more in evidence than with the commodity which is ubiquitous and inescapable. The manner in which the commodity is packaged and presented means that its origins and mode of being, that is its place in the production process and the circulation of capital, are hidden. Imagism too is self-contained by the primacy and purity of the image which, in requiring no real critical response, helps to prepare the subject for its specular and therefore passive relation to society.

Although imagism is quintessentially modern in some ways, in others it seems like an edited or improved Georgianism in that the bulk of it is concerned with the country rather than the city. It is allusive like Georgian verse, but in a more élitist way, and there is a liberal use of the apostrophizing mode:

> You are clear,
> O rose, cut in rock,
> hard as the descent of hail.

> H.D., 'The Garden'

It is different in being concerned to establish a relation between things rather than people.

> Whirl up, sea
> Whirl your pointed pines,
> Splash your great pines
> On our rocks,
> Hurl your green over us,
> Cover us with your pools of fir.

> H.D., 'Oread'

It also shares with Georgian poetry an exoticism that consoles the subject with luscious sensuousness—... 'thy lips Are night-born poppies' (Skipwith Cannell, 'Nocturnes') – as it splits between the categories of individual and citizen. Imagism also looks back to Decadence with its emphasis on bodily experience.

> As a young beech-tree on the edge of a forest
> Stands still in the evening,
> Then shudders through all its leaves in the light air
> And seems to fear the stars –
> So are you still and so tremble.

> Richard Aldington, 'Images'

Imagism looks forward and back. In the detailed observation which characterizes the best of it, it is a mark of the resilience of the subject – object relationship which was under attack by the new Zeitgeist. The active, perceiving subject asserts itself in the verse at the same moment that the verse seeks to deny that subject's existence. Furthermore, since the poet is making the connections, the claim of the Imagists to objectivity is undermined. Indeed, this is just one of many contradictions regarding imagism. Another is its pretension to scientific criteria while being resolutely non-analytic and non-discursive. As with other poetry, it is possible to exploit the contradictions to make it mean other than what it has been made to mean. The only problem in this case is that imagism has been marginalized as a prelude to full-blown modernism and so made to mean very little. The type of criticism which the poetry invites is simple aesthetic appreciation, once more constructing the subject as passive when a closer examination reveals the potential in imagism for an active subject. One such subject was Ezra Pound, an American, and his involvement with imagism draws attention to one of the important characteristics of modernism, its internationalism. Art, like capitalism, was becoming transcultural.

MODERNISM

Internationalism is just one of the characteristics of modernism; others include a self-conscious experimentation in art, a belief in the work of art as autonomous and a view of the artist as isolated by the intensity of his or her vision.

As far as poetry was concerned, the dominant form was the lyric and it occupied this position because the poet had been set apart from the public sphere. Part of the reason for this again lies in the shift from the ideology of the individual to that of the collective with its associated discourses aimed at representing the citizen, making him or her visible at all levels of society. With an increasingly public dimension, language lacked the resources to cater for and communicate private experience. The result was a disjunction between literary and social discourse, with the former's complexity being proportionate to the latter's simplicity.

Traditionalists objected to modern verse on the basis that 'The poet writes no longer for the reader, to communicate an emotion, to reveal the beauty and meaning of the world, to enlarge experience and to sharpen sensitiveness'.[32] Whilst traditionalists in their turn were attacked by Middleton Murry who, with the Georgians as his specific target, wrote 'They were only individuals by courtesy whose flavour is almost wholly corporate'.[33] The interesting thing about this is that it shows that even those on the side of modernism still clung nostalgically to the idea of the individual as the most important index of art, while the traditionalists, who were opposed to mass corporatism, could, at least in Murry's eyes, be accused of upholding such views. The distinction between traditional personality and modernist impersonality is therefore not as clear cut as it seems. The Georgians for example sought to lose the self in nature, while symbolism, which was responsible for, among other things, modernism's acute consciousness of language and its juxtaposing of images and ideas leaving readers to make the connection themselves, was a doctrine that by an intricate and complex association of ideas and metaphors attempted to communicate unique personal feelings. Such contradictions show that, though traditionalism and modernism may have been opposed, both were nevertheless plagued with internal contradictions concerning connotations surrounding the categories of individual and citizen.

Modernism then seems to be as concerned with personality as impersonality for, as Gillian Rose, following Adorno, has pointed out, 'any aesthetic which seeks completely to deny the illusory power of the subject will tend indirectly to reinstate that illusion'.[34] The subjectivity found in Eliot's 'The Love Song of J. Alfred Prufrock' and 'Portrait of a Lady' is able to observe in a reflective, cultured manner the world it is fastidious of entering. Even the discontinuities of modern life which threaten to violate such a subjectivity are used to uphold it. As Eliot wrote at the end of *The Waste Land*, 'These fragments I have shored against my ruins' ('What the Thunder Said').[35] And for all Pound's vaunted impersonality there is an egotism as well as truth to his poetic programme evidenced in much of 'Salvationists'.[36]

The problem faced by writers like Pound and Eliot was not just finding the right poetry for the times but also coping with the consequences of the diminuation of the category of the individual. The severance of literary from social discourse ipso facto precludes the writing subject from representing itself in, or being represented by, the latter; but the modernist subject could not simply employ the existing categories of literary discourse because writers like Eliot, Pound, Amy Lowell and H.D. were all American and therefore not only had little sympathy with native tradition but were uniquely placed to see that those traditions could not answer the needs of the modern world. So the modernist subject, caught between two cultures and two discourses, had to use what he or she could of both and the effect is a kind of collage. This is particularly true of Eliot who mixes literary quotation, philosophy and mythology with the idiom of common speech and the images of the contemporary world.

The poet is an assembler of fragments which are pieced together, but the significance of the relationships they form is something the reader must work out because there is no unifying authority or controlling narrative voice and, perhaps in reaction to the new scientific discourses, the connections here are not logical but associative. Perhaps, too, Eliot's possible élitism and his reluctance to explain his poems can be understood as a desire to prevent them from being known and therefore appropriated by those discourses devoted to certain types of humanistic knowledge. In an age where the accent is increasingly on knowing, the poet presents his or her discourse by allusion, obfuscation and ellipsis. As such it cannot be absorbed into the forces of collectivization and corporation but remains outside itself, a fragment, and therefore of that order of the world which it deplores. The poet may lament the fragmentary condition of modern life but, as fragment, the poem shows its opposition to the totalizing operations of culture which is thus revealed not as broken images but as homogeneous and monolithic.

A consequence of the rift between the ideological categories of individual and citizen means the subject is called upon to play different roles in society and this leads to a potential schizophrenia. As G.M. Hyde has argued,

> the debate with an imagined but for that reason only too real interlocutor has become the very mode of existence of many Modernist works of art ... often it is as much a dialogue with self as a dialogue with another, and seems to relate to the characteristic disease of modern civilisations, schizophrenia.[37]

The problem is how to centre the subject, or how to situate it in relation to its various guises. For the Eliot of *The Waste Land*, the answer is a symbol borrowed from the myth of the Holy Grail, for Pound it is in the Chinese ideogram and for Yeats it is in Irish legend, then in occultism. Each symbol in its own way acts as a unifying force and, also functions as a critique of the spiritual impoverishment of the modern world. The drawback with this manoeuvre is that by identifying itself with other cultures and older traditions the subject further distances itself from the world at the moment that it is trying to come to terms with the consequence of that distance; thus, it is in danger of infinite regression.

Modernism, then, is in part the story of the subject collapsed in its own space. It struggles to make sense of its new condition, using myths, symbols or idioms from different cultures, but only succeeds in further dispensing itself in different symbolic systems. To this extent it almost does history's work for it, carrying on the process of eroding the ideological category of the individual. Given this context, the doctrine of impersonality seems like a rationalization of what had to be the case, rather than a desired end, and modernist poetry, far from being anti-representational, reflected what was happening only too well. However, it is important not to forget that the vanishing subject is only one function of modernist verse for it is also possible to view verse as an assertion of the subject, as can be seen in the case of the active perceiving subjection in imagism. This and other contradictions are held together by the lyric form, which is not only highly flexible in itself but, because its form predates this particular crisis of subjectivity, it is to some extent immune to it.

The modernist lyric took the form of free verse, and there were at least two reasons for its adoption. The first was a desire to replace a stylized lyric 'self' with one more intimate and authentic and the second was to get away from the tyranny of the iambic which imposed its pattern in the object rather than let the object's natural rhythm emerge. In both cases free verse contradicts the generally anti-representational aesthetic of modernism. Pound defined verse as being based on cadence; it must have a perfect balance of flow and rhythm and, Pound continued, it should be 'as rounded and recurring as the circular swing of a balanced pendulum'.[38] But free verse was not just a matter of aesthetics, it was also a reaction to the rhythms of technology and communication which, had a rhythm of their own, one to which poets were forced to respond. To the extent that technology works for human beings it is humanized, but because it has its own rhythm it always conveys something more than just what humans put into it. Free verse seems to have represented a break from the ordered, regular rhythms of late romanticism nevertheless it kept some affinity with the rhythms of traditional verse. Its very discontinuities could be said to mimic the jolting jazz rhythms which are also part of the urban experience.

Modernist verse turns out to be just as contradictory as the other verse that we have examined and its relation to the world just as complex. It seems by its allusiveness and symbolism to aestheticize experience and thus confer unity on the split subject of the modern age. The subject is drawn up into the world of culture from which he or she can view the desolation of the Waste Land, but only at the expense of not being able to participate in it. Thus, modernist poetry, so convincingly evoking the modern world, removes the reader from it. Criticism of modernism is concerned with teasing out the underlying unity, and its negotiation of paradox and contradiction encourages bourgeois subjectivity, through an encounter with the poetry. Should this strategy fail, criticism can always flatter the readers that, like Hugh Selwyn Mauberley, they may not be integrated into the great scheme of things, and that this somehow confirms them as unique and individual. Finally, by presenting such a daunting body of knowledge about modernism, criticism sets it apart and so creates a hierarchy of readers corresponding to the possible hierarchies of class society. That modernism should test criticism in this way is a sign that the contradictions it brought into being have still to be resolved.

NOTES

1. C.K. Stead, *The New Poetic*, revised edition (Philadelphia, 1987).
2. For an excellent account of this period see M. Langan and B. Schwarz (eds), *Crises in the British State 1880–1930* (London, 1985), esp. S. Hall and B. Schwarz, 'State and Society 1880–1930', pp. 7–33.

3. Clive Scott, 'Symbolism, Decadence and Impression', in Malcolm Bradbury and James McFarlane, *Modernism: A Guide to European Literature 1890–1930* (Harmondsworth, 1991), p. 215.
4. Ernest Dowsen, the first line from the entitled poem, in Christopher Ricks, *The New Oxford Book of Victorian Verse)* (Oxford, 1987), p. 582.
5. Lionel Johnson, 'The Dark Angel', in Ricks, p. 559.
6. Scott, in Bradbury and McFarlane, p. 218.
7. See Peter Ackroyd, *T.S. Eliot* (London, 1984), p. 34.
8. It should, however, be noted that a number of poets who appeared in these anthologies objected to being called Georgian, among them Graves, Sassoon and Blunden. Some poets who may now be regarded as Georgian, such as Edward Thomas, did not appear in the anthologies at all. The issue of who was and who was not a Georgian is vigorously taken up by James Reeves in his introduction to *Georgian Poetry* (Harmondsworth, 1962) and by T. Rogers in *Georgian Poetry 1911–12, The Critical Heritage* (London, 1977).
9. R.H. Ross, *The Georgian Revolt: Rise and Fall of a Poetic Ideal* (London, 1965), p. 146
10. Stead, p. 82.
11. Reeves, p. xx.
12. Ibid., p. xv.
13. David Daiches sums up the consensus on Georgian poetry when he writes that 'Georgian ... poets had nothing very new to say; neither their subject matter nor their technique was in any degree original. They took traditional motives, romantic accounts of the East, "nature subjects", meditative description of English scenery or accounts in a subdued lyrical strain of personal experiences in listening to birds or watching sunsets and produced what was, on the whole, a quiet, unambitious verse, restrained in mood, low in temperature'.
14. Quoted in Ross, p. 125.
15. The battle between the modernists and the Georgians was fought out in the magazines and newspapers. They can be roughly divided into three camps which though they were Left, Centre or Right aesthetically were not necessarily so politically. Indeed, one of the baffling contradictions of modernism is that between progressivism in art and reaction in politics. Among the Left magazines one can include *The Egoist* (1914–17), *Rhythm* (1911–13), *Blue Review* (1913) and *Wheels* (1916–22), at the Centre *Poetry Review* (1911) and *The Athenaeum* (1828–1920) and, on the Right, *The Times Literary Supplement* and the notorious *London Mercury* (1919–34). Battle lines were drawn so fiercely that the centre ground was extremely difficult to hold. For an overview of this aspect of the period see Ross, and Bradbury and McFarlane, 'Movements, Magazines and Manifestoes: The Succession from Naturalism', in Bradbury and McFarlane, pp. 192–206.
16. Reeves, p. xx.
17. For a wide-ranging introduction to the many dimensions of ideology see Terry Eagleton, *Ideology: an Introduction* (London and New York, 1991).
18. The whole question of how criticism makes sense of a text needs to be explored in all its complexity. Two points can be noted here. First, criticism *in general* attempts to situate a text in a literary tradition rather than in its historical context. Second, this procedure means that criticism is constrained to think of a text which comes after as a kind of fall or lapse from some original standard. This view is never explicit but it informs a good deal of thinking about literature, as has been

demonstrated by Harold Bloom. It is not germane to criticism but is related to an apocalyptic type of thinking which, in aiming to establish a concordance between beginnings, middles and ends, offers a way of making sense of existence which might otherwise seem no more than a succession of unrelated moments. On this view, Georgian poetry had to be seen as marking the end of an era partly because of the dates, 1912 to 1922, and partly because it seemed to gesture backwards to romanticism; it was the decadent moment prior to the renewal of poetry through modernism. Mythic structures of thinking, in other words, may use history for their own ends and may be more deeply rooted in our cultural consciousness than we realize. Frank Kermode explored this whole question in *The Sense of An Ending* (New York, 1967).

19. The exotic has been defined as a way of 'salvag[ing] values and a way of life that had vanished, without hope of restoration from post-Revolutionary society but that might, beyond the confines of modernity, still be figured as really possible'. See C. Bangie, 'Exotic Nostalgia: Conrad and the New Imperialism', in J. Arac and H. Ritvo, *Macropolitics of Nineteenth Century Literature: Nationalism, Exoticism, Imperialism* (Pennsylvania, 1991), p. 270. This is quite close to the imperialist belief, echoed in the exotic allusions of 'What the Thunder Said' (Shackleton in South Georgia, and Doughty's Arabia Deserta), that the frontier renews values that have fallen into decay. The exotic in Georgian poetry and the exotic in Eliot obviously have different inflexions but they both share this broad assumption.

   Part of the Georgian exotic is made up by frequent references to the moon and the sea. Both have overlapping significations, beauty, nature, romanticism and the like. However, perhaps their true importance may be located in relation to the problem of subjectivity. The sea as its shapeless mass, the moon as a sign of its sought for transcendence, able to accommodate change.

20. See Ross, p. 149.

21. See B. Schwarz, 'The Corporate Economy, 1890–1929', in M. Langan and B. Schwarz, pp. 80–103.

22. One reason for the success of Georgian poetry was the fact that it was published in anthology form, for a reasonable price. The public could sample the work of a number of poets and have an overall view of what was happening in the field. However, the anthology system also works to submerge individuals into a group and thus it is part of that general trend to collectivization already mentioned.

23. Although there is an undoubted democratic potential in First World War poetry, it is as well to remember that most of it was written by the officer class, hence making criticism's task of using the verse to procure bourgeois subjectivity in the reader that much easier.

24. Siegfried Sassoon, 'The rank stench of those bodies haunts me still', in John Silkin, *The Penguin Book of First World War Poetry* (Harmondsworth, 1981), p. 124. All quotations are taken from this edition.

25. J. Press, *A Map of Modern English Verse* (London, 1969), p. 30.

26. For a detailed account of this view see S.K. Stead, *Pound, Yeats, Eliot and The Modernist Movement* (London, 1986).

27. Edward Storer, cited in P. Jones, *Imagist Poetry* (Harmondsworth, 1976), p. 16.

   For an interesting history of the iambic pentameter and its role in the construction of bourgeois subjectivity see Antony Easthope, *Poetry as Discourse* (London and New York, 1983). In this context imagism's – indeed modernism's – abandonment of the iambic can be seen as the end of one type of subjectivity and the beginning of another. Much work needs to be done here but a starting place may be the self-contained structure of the iambic. Each line is complete in itself yet leads on to the next. This suggests progress and development, primary characteristics of the bourgeois subject. It is these which are lost in modernism.

28. For a good introduction to *vers libre* see Clive Scott, 'The Prose Poem and Free Verse', in Bradbury and McFarlane, pp. 349–68.
29. For the full texts see P. James, pp. 129–34.
30. All quotations from imagist poems are taken from Jones.
31. Quoted in James p. 39.
32. M. Wollman (ed.), *Modern Poetry 1922–1934* (London, 1939).
33. M. Murry, cited in Ross, p. 231
34. Gillian Rose, 'The Dispute Over Modernism', in Francis Barker *et al.*, *The Politics of Modernism* (Colchester, 1979), pp. 27–36, p. 33.
35. For a stimulating if flawed account of the subject in Eliot see S. Smith, 'Scars and Emblems 1936' and 'The Crisis of the Subject', in Francis Barker *et al.*, *Practices of Literature and Politics* (Colchester, 1979), pp. 344–79. His view is that the self in Eliot 'is finally a container, unchanged by the social contents in it' (p. 364).
36. See *Ezra Pound, Collected Shorter Poems* (London, 1990).
37. G.M. Hyde, 'The Poetry of the City', in Bradbury and McFarlane, pp. 337–49, pp. 338–9.
38. Pound, 'Preface to Some Imagist Poets' (1916), reprinted in Jones, pp. 136–40, p. 138.

CHAPTER TWO
The Novel as Art Form

Jim Reilly

THE VERY SOUL OF THE WORLD IS ECONOMIC

British fiction from 1900 to 1929 poses an intriguing test case for the claims of a sociology of literature. The novel is the literary form traditionally chosen to articulate socio-economic realities, to contain the contemporary banal, the quotidian, the contingent, and to uncover their significance – in a sense the selfsame ambition of sociology. As D.H. Lawrence (1885–1930) puts it, in poetry the Word is allowed to fly a bit too free but 'in a novel there's always a tom-cat, a black tom-cat that pounces on the white dove of the Word'.[1] And, he adds, a novel always has a water-closet – that emblem of quotidian physical necessity – on the premises. This is, of course, the period of modernism's ascendancy and at first sight modernist fiction looks like a much-needed reaffirmation of such earthy contingency after nineteenth-century reticences, or even the very first occasion of their entry into fiction. There may always have been water-closets in novels but Joyce's *Ulysses* (1922) and Proust's *A la recherche du temps perdu* (1913–27) are surely the first fictions to have set-piece scenes showing characters – Bloom and Marcel – using them. This rather absurd example at least helps us consider one of the myriad paradoxes of modernism. On the one hand it can appear to have a resolutely sublunary aesthetic and register a quite un-Victorian taste for the sensuous, fleshy and visceral – 'Mr Leopold Bloom ate with relish the inner organs of beasts and fowls ... Most of all he liked grilled mutton kidneys which gave to his palate a fine tang of faintly scented urine'.[2] On the other, it is perhaps unprecedentedly unworldly, aesthetically self-conscious and unconstrained by fiction's wonted duty to transcribe social reality.

There is a single story to tell about the novel in this period: how the assumptions about literature's engagement with such reality prevailing at its beginning were in tatters at its end. To consider in succession Bennett,

55

Galsworthy, Wells, Forster, Ford, Conrad, Lawrence, Woolf, Joyce is to encounter such leaps in methodology as to constitute a revolution in representation, one so decisive as almost to call into question whether these works can be contained within the same ontological category. A key component of this revolution is what one might see as an exponential growth in the complexity of the relations between literature and the socio-economic 'base'. Modernism was a profound interrogation of literature's representational function. The contract between fiction and the social reality it felt bound to transcribe, as underwritten by Bennett, Galsworthy and Wells, was torn up by Lawrence, Woolf and Joyce. In these latter authors the realist intentions which persist to varying degrees are now in dialectic with, or often subservient to, quite un- or anti-representational ambitions. Social reality has been crucially displaced as self-evidently both origin and goal of representation. A sociology of Joyce seems a much more problematic proposition than one of, say, Bennett. History itself is anathema to modernism. Modernism's twin opposing temporal categories are the moment and eternity, permutated in strange combinations throughout its texts. These quite fill the narrative space which, in the nineteenth-century realist novel in particular, was the site of dramatization of that now apparently excluded middle term, historical time. Of course, one could argue that this disappearance of a certain kind of meticulous socio-historical register from high literary fiction is itself a socio-historical phenomenon – but these are big questions and this is to anticipate.

Surveying a period of such rich and varied achievement one can be forgiven for brevities, or for viewing its pre- or anti-modernist authors purely in the light of modernism's critique of them. For Virginia Woolf (1882–1941), for example, there was something fatally unachieved, a crucial lack of artistry, in those pre-eminent popular and critical successes of the first decade, Bennett, Galsworthy and Wells.

> … I think that after the creative activity of the Victorian age it was quite
> necessary, not only for literature but for life, that someone should write the
> books that Mr Wells, Mr Bennett, and Mr Galsworthy have written. Yet what
> odd books they are! Sometimes I wonder if we are right to call them books at
> all. For they leave one with so strange a sense of incompleteness and
> dissatisfaction. In order to complete them it seems necessary to do something –
> to join a society, or, more desperately, to write a cheque.[3]

Overt sociological content provokes Woolf's ridicule. That the work of fiction should be completed only by ameliorative activity in the social realm – an attractively radical notion – is to her unthinkable. In the same essay she invents a psychodrama around the figure of a distressed woman she has seen in a railway carriage and dubs Mrs Brown. How, in contrast, would Galsworthy represent her?

Can we doubt that the walls of Doulton's factory would take his fancy? There are women in that factory who make twenty-five dozen earthenware pots every day. There are mothers in the Mile End road who depend upon the farthings which those women earn. But there are employers in Surrey who are even now smoking rich cigars while the nightingale sings. Burning with indignation, stuffed with information, arraigning civilization, Mr Galsworthy would only see in Mrs Brown a pot broken on the wheel and thrown into the corner.[4]

Woolf's hauteur and facetiousness here about a politically conscientious fiction may say more about her complete psychic containment within her own class position – snobbishness would be a blunter term – than about Galsworthy's supposed failure of artistry. For Lawrence too, Galsworthy exemplifies the decisive limitations of Edwardian fiction. His characterization particularly is fatally flawed, his Forsythes provoke 'repulsion' and 'an emotional refusal to have them identified with our common humanity'. Like Woolf, Lawrence finds Galsworthy exhaustively sociological. His characters have 'lost caste as human beings' and 'sunk to the level of the social being'. With them money 'goes right through the centre and is the controlling principle' – Lawrence probably has the aptly titled *The Man of Property* (1906) in mind – whereas the artist should struggle to depict 'the alive human being' in whose 'last naked skin [money] does not enter'.[5] The issue is a complex one: to do as Woolf and Lawrence urge and refuse to depict characters entirely in terms of their social and economic determination can be either a radical and utopian gesture or a naively individualistic and hence reactionary one. One could raise questions about the motivation for this apparent occlusion of economics given that literary modernists (Lawrence we will exempt) were typically rather well-heeled. Alasdair Gray objects to a swathe of modernist fiction as 'a literature almost completely class-bound, and bound to the propertied classes ... Forster, Virginia Woolf, Wyndham Lewis, Aldous Huxley, Elizabeth Bowen are dissimilar writers, yet all describe people so detached from their source of wealth in land, trade or industry that they can ignore it, because it is handled by their bankers'.[6] Woolf was left five hundred pounds a year 'for ever' by an aunt who died falling from a horse in Bombay. She perfectly exemplifies Gray's point about a puzzled incognizance of the source of one's own wealth.

> There was another ten-shilling note in my purse; I noticed it, because it is a fact that still takes my breath away – the power of my purse to breed ten-shilling notes automatically. I open it and there they are.[7]

Woolf is like E.M. Forster's (1879–1971) liberal Miss Schlegels in *Howards End* (1910) who also puzzle over their own unearned wealth (they each have six hundred pounds a year) though, since they are in a Forster novel, they feel guilty about it. They favour the sort of worthy activities about which Woolf registers such irony, including attending discussion groups on 'How ought I to dispose of my money?'. Margaret Schlegel has a perceptive image for their financial security and the 'independence' it brings.

> You and I and the Wilcoxes stand upon money as upon islands. It is so firm beneath our feet that we forget its very existence. It's only when we see someone near us tottering that we realize all that an independent income means. Last night, when we were talking up here round the fire, I began to think that the very soul of the world is economic, and that the lowest abyss is not the absence of love, but the absence of coin.[8]

The rigidity of this social hierarchy and the immensity of difference between the various strata of classes is the premise informing – directly or obliquely – all Edwardian fiction, be it reactionary, utopian, aesthetically opaque or scrupulously realist. Forster perfectly exemplifies the dilemma of a fictional discourse intending to survey the whole spectrum of contemporary social reality – this had always seemed the honourable ambition of the great realist novels – when that reality is carved so decisively into mutually hostile class registers. The novel of his which famously attempts to survey the social spectrum and makes the liberal plea 'Only connect ...' itself also admits – with exactly what degree of irony? – 'We are not concerned with the very poor. They are unthinkable, and only to be approached by the statistician'. Not all registrations of the dilemma are as stark as Forster's. Consider, for instance, how it informs with a marvellous obliqueness a passage by Joseph Conrad (1857–1924) from the very beginning of our period in *Lord Jim* (1900). He describes the night journey of a ship crowded with Muslim pilgrims.

> ... above the mass of sleepers a faint and patient sigh at times floated, the exhalation of a troubled dream; and short metallic clangs bursting out suddenly in the depths of the ship, the harsh scrape of a shovel, the violent slam of a furnace-door, exploded brutally, as if the men handling the mysterious things below had their breasts full of fierce anger: while the slim high hull of the steamer went on evenly ahead, without a sway of her bare masts, cleaving continuously the great calm of the waters under the inaccessible serenity of the sky.[9]

Here perhaps a sophisticated sociology of literature comes into its own, pointing out how a passage making apparently no reference to social hierarchies seems itself utterly structured by the registration of differing layers of ontology: social, discursive, aesthetic. Here are three distinct levels. There is the threatening and mysterious 'base' of a currently subservient but loud and restless labour, one from which human agency has been largely abstracted, the scrape of a shovel, the slam of a door; above this a layer of dreamy incognizance, a troubled dream, however, perturbed at an unconscious level by the labour below; and, surrounding and over-arching all – and this is utterly Edwardian – a 'great calm' and 'inaccessible serenity', a highly aestheticized register of a conjectured transcendence. This last motif reminds one of Ruskin eulogizing sky-scapes in *Modern Painters* (1846) and how poor soon-to-be-unemployed Leonard Bast in *Howards End* has a weakness for Ruskin and sky-scapes and that whole Edwardian transcendent register. His increasing poverty and humiliations, which the well-meaning intervention of the Schlegel sisters has unwittingly provoked, force him to learn that this is a mode of privilege to which the socially lowly cannot aspire. The Ruskin-register palls, 'For it was the voice of one who had never been dirty or hungry, and had not guessed successfully what dirt and hunger are'.[10]

ARTFUL DODGES AND SIMPLE TALES

An expatriate Pole of aristocratic background and conservative sympathies, Joseph Conrad strained to be more Edwardian than the Edwardians and yet achieved in the process a towering proto-modernism. Politically, Conrad's novels, and the sea-tales most obviously, are never far from the anti-egalitarian emphases of the favourite amongst his boyhood reading, Captain Marryat's *Mr Midshipman Easy*, in which the work-shy and Paine-spouting landlubber is transformed into the exemplary officer by the rigours, and rigorous hierarchies, of the maritime service. They celebrate the service's traditions of duty and discipline and what one harassed captain contemplates reassuringly as 'the blessed simplicity of its traditional point of view on life'. They bear the imprint of Conrad's own desire for the simplicity of traditional tale-telling in their subtitles: *Lord Jim: A Tale* (1900), *Nostromo: A Tale of the Seaboard* (1904), *The Secret Agent: A Simple Tale* (1907). The emphasis on yarn-like intimacy and moral directness is reinforced by frequently couching the narrative as an oral reminiscence of much-travelled, loquacious sailor Marlow, 'a most discreet, understanding man'. But Walter Benjamin in *Illuminations* (1955)★ famously diagnosed the crisis of literary modernism of this period's inability to exchange stories or to believe in the proverbial wisdom orality was intended to convey. Thus Conrad's disingenuously dubbed 'yarns' are transformed by all the relativizing, problematizing devices which are his decisive contribution to emergent modernism; hesitant and fractured telling, writing which writhes within the agonized intuition of its own lack of reference, evocation of the moral opacity of a world congealed into secret and deceptive forms, a radical indeterminacy of meaning. This disturbance of the moral and representational assumptions of storytelling, in some sense the very inversion of them, is suggested in the famously enigmatic formulation from 'Heart of Darkness' (1902):

★Benjamin's famous collection of essays was published long after his death.

> The yarns of seamen have a direct simplicity, the whole meaning of which lies within the shell of a cracked nut. But Marlow was not typical (if his propensity to spin yarns be excepted), and to him the meaning of an episode was not inside like a kernel but outside, enveloping the tale which brought it out only as a glow brings out a haze, in the likeness of one of these misty halos that sometimes are made visible by the spectral illumination of moonshine.[11]

One such Marlow narrative is *Lord Jim* in which the characteristic Conrad complexes are set in play. Jim is an idealistic young officer and apparent exemplar of maritime virtue who is put on trial for an inexplicable and disastrous dereliction of duty. His plight fascinates the refined Jamesian analyst in Marlow who contemplates the moral enigma of the defendant, in an arresting Conradian paradox, as if 'I was being made to comprehend the Inconceivable ... I was made to look at the convention that lurks in all truth and on the essential sincerity of falsehood'.

Through the image of the fort-da game in *Beyond the Pleasure Principle* (1920), in which the child alternately rejects and retrieves the cotton reel that represents the supreme desired object of the mother, Freud was to speculate on the playful strategies the mind devises to stage and hence control a potentially tormenting absence/presence of meaning. He thus anticipates the post-structuralist conception whereby language itself conducts an endless game of signification and deferral. Conrad's novels are another staging and analysing of such teasing strategies, the 'artful dodges' with which dangerous truths are both obscured and disclosed, presented and deferred: 'no man ever understands quite his own artful dodges to escape from the shadow of self-knowledge', 'The truth is hidden, luckily, luckily'. The second half of the novel shifts, perhaps degenerates, into a boisterous romance mode as Jim redeems himself as the heroic overlord of a remote Malayan trading post whose islanders confer on him the honorific of the novel's title. Marlow is fascinated by the moral 'plague spot' which has been uncovered in Jim and we might say that Conrad's own debilitating 'plague-spot' is a recourse to the vigorous assurances of the adventure mode when the issues he has uncovered prove too fearfully intractable. His last novels, *The Arrow of Gold* (1919), *The Rescue* (1920), *The Rover* (1923) and *Suspense* (1925), as their titles suggest, revisit the adventure mode but without the buoyancy and conviction the genre needs they degenerate into, as Virginia Woolf put it, 'stiff melodrama'. Here the romance mode and its motifs are not, as they are in the consequently more rewarding *Under Western Eyes* (1911), *Chance* (1913) and *Victory* (1915), subject to ironic scrutiny and reversals.

A more sinister and farcical representation of the ambiguity of loyalties, drawing on Edwardian fears of terrorism and social unrest, is *The Secret Agent*. The parlour behind a backstreet pornography emporium – all seedy enticement with no actual goods – houses a moribund Marxist/anarchist cell which itself unwittingly harbours the supine and ineffectual double agent, Mr Verloc. This brilliant recession of duplicities is a suitable metonym for the ubiquity and deceptions that make up the alienated and unlovely social formation of Edwardian London and which both repel and fascinate an author whose titles habitually hint at the inscrutable: 'The Secret Sharer' (1912), *The Secret Agent*, *The Shadow-Line* (1917), 'Heart of Darkness'. Verloc is guardian of the demented innocent Stevie who, feeling social injustice as a personal anguish, immerses himself in the furious depiction of 'circles, circles, innumerable circles', a 'mad art' which, in an echo of Marlow's response to Lord Jim, attempts 'the inconceivable'. He becomes the hapless victim of Verloc's reluctant and spectacularly futile attempt to blow up the Greenwich Meridian. Largely a cynical survey of a paranoic and stultified political scene, the novel does, in its conclusion, wring a tawdry tragedy from the plight of Stevie's long-suffering mother Winnie who reaches her own breaking-point. In 'Heart of Darkness' Marlow, travelling through the Congo jungle, is fascinated to find a little manual on the breaking-strains of ships' cables. Conrad's novels are also studies of breaking-strains – mental, ethical and emotional – and the crises that can bring one, to quote one if his titles, to 'The End of the Tether'. Alongside another circumscribed and tragically self-repressing wife, Mrs Gould in *Nostromo*, Winnie is a powerfully sympathetic characterization from an author whose female characters tend, like Kurtz's Intended in 'Heart of Darkness', to archetype and abstraction.

Conrad's greatest novel and 'largest canvas' *Nostromo* (1904) is perhaps also the finest paradigm of a key feature of modernist narrative: it is hushed and quelled by history. This panoramic parable of capitalism's pitiless advance to world hegemony enshrines a profound political pessimism within an artfully repetitive and ponderous narrative. Western 'material interests' achieve a gradual stranglehold upon the politics and economy of a Central American republic and everywhere distort the various integrities and idealisms of those drawn into its machinations. A viscous narrative curls sluggishly around the congealed masses of stately and descriptive set pieces, themselves characteristically mesmerized by lowering images of stasis; a mountain, an equestrian statue, a monumental urn, the statically suspended corpse of a hanged man, the preternaturally dark and still gulf metonymically named 'Placido'. This last is the setting for a famous scene where Conrad's artistry reaches its bleak acme in evoking the obliterating alienation of the fugitive Decoud, soon to commit suicide, amidst 'the silence like a still cord stretched to breaking-point, with his life, his vain life, suspended from it like a weight'. With reference to this scene Terry Eagleton has suggested that we should trace Conrad's 'radical pessimism' to its social and historical root:

> The pessimism of Conrad's world view is ... a unique transformation into art of an ideological pessimism rife in his period – a sense of history as futile and cyclical, of individuals as impenetrable and solitary, of human values as relativistic and irrational, which marks a drastic crisis in the ideology of the Western bourgeois class to which Conrad allied himself.[12]

Plagued with illness and self-doubt, particularly during the agonizing periods of composition, Conrad would complain of being 'complètement embourbé' – completely stuck. Such deadlock is dramatized, if that is quite the right word, in the ordeal of the young master with his first command in *The Shadow-Line*. With illness raging on board, the ship languishes in a slough so absolute that the sails hang 'like granite'. The novel is dedicated to Conrad's son Boris and the whole contemporary generation of youth who were then languishing in the slough of the First World War, literally 'embourbé' in the sodden trenches. This chillingly Medusan novel thus depicts a tripartite crisis of reification and debility affecting simultaneously the author's sense of artistic deadlock, the characters' own agonizing ordeal of stasis and the historical context of a dead-end, deadlocked world. Despite, or perhaps because of, its modernistic obliqueness of reference, this sea novel set in the nineteenth century is perhaps fiction's greatest evocation of the despair and debility of those later war years. Its layered inertia is a fitting testimony to the stalemate which characterized this first real 'war of attrition', a conflict which Walter Benjamin describes as being the first in human history from which even the victors – one thinks of Woolf's shell-shocked combatant Septimus Smith whose suicide is the dark centre of *Mrs Dalloway* (1925) – brought back no narrative, no wisdom and no insight.

A CHASM IN A SMOOTH ROAD

It is worth pausing here to consider how immense were the ramifications for discourse of the Great War. The fatuous carnage of the trenches utterly despoiled the monumental historical optimism that had persisted as a keynote of thought since the nineteenth century. As Henry James puts it,

> The plunge of civilisation into this abyss of blood and darkness ... is a thing that so gives away the whole long age during which we have supposed the world to be, with whatever abatement, gradually bettering, that to have to take it all now for what the treacherous years were all the while really making for and *meaning* is too tragic for any words.[13]

James voices the grim realizations with which modernism contends. The war exploded the progressive, positivistic myth that had prevailed in culture for at least a century: 'like a chasm in a smooth road, the war came' (Woolf), 'The cataclysm has happened ... there is now no smooth road into the future' (Lawrence). The war was like modernism itself: a tremendous shattering of wonted meanings and perhaps, and perhaps irrecoverably, even of meaning *tout court.* Furthermore it provoked a sense that twentieth-century history had broken the former alliance between history and discourse. Such experience is 'too tragic' – James is left reaching for the old, discredited grand terms – 'for any words'.

We would expect James to be primarily concerned with 'meaning', but it was the opposite in this case. The war changed meaning. Thought, speech and representation were altered for ever. Perhaps no single historical event before or since has so changed its culture's discourse, so transformed the totality of its expression. In *The Great War and Modern Memory* (1975) Paul Fussell has demonstrated how profoundly aestheticized a culture was prewar Britain; and how decisively de-aestheticizing was the war. He contrasts narratives of serving soldiers – letters, diaries, memoirs, literary works – in the First and Second World Wars. The former, and strikingly this applies across the ranks, were uniformly mannered, literary, ever reaching for an elevating allusion to myth, poetry or the visual arts; sunsets were habitually Turneresque, birdsong Keatsian. There is nothing comparable in writings from the latter conflict where style is vehemently vernacular, baldly un-decorative, terse, cynical and free of mythic or literary precedent. Fussell traces the decline of this Georgian high tone as the conflict drags on through four years of gruesome attrition. The most famous poem of the war turns angrily on 'the old lie' of 'Dulce et decorum est ...' and one senses that it is as much the dignified, old-world register evoked by an elevating tag from Horace as that poet's sentimental militarism that Wilfred Owen, and the war, negates.

The war's impact on fiction was at first sight slight, at second, profound. Martin Amis has said that there is no classic of representation of the nuclear age, Adorno that there is no adequate drama of fascism and we might push the argument back in time to add that, in fiction at least, the Great War also never found adequate expression. All these instances illuminate the assertion of Adorno's on twentieth-century conditions that 'the coming extinction of art is prefigured in its inability to represent historical events'.[14] In English fiction the war is characteristically circled rather than represented. D.H. Lawrence called *Women in Love* (1921) his 'great war novel', though the event is never mentioned. It is in *Kangaroo* (1923) and in fact rather hijacks the novel's ostensible theme of an Australian proto-fascist movement as Lawrence gives a querulous, embittered account of his hounding by the authorities on suspicion of spying and repeated degrading medical examinations assessing his fitness for service. Lawrence just avoided conscription rather as his fiction just avoids depiction of the war, the structuring absence of all his later work. The peculiarly truculent and unseductive quality of the novel's address of its reader – 'If you don't like the novel, don't read it!' – its suspension of story for long periods of invective and a chapter called 'Bits' as if metonymic of a modernist denial of coherence and sequence, all suggest Benjamin's conclusion that this was the World War that stubbed out storytelling. Even Ford Madox Ford's (1873–1939) stylistically more sober *Parade's End* (appearing between 1924 and 1928) registers something of this malaise in its lugubrious, directionless narrative – a tetralogy no less – and fragmented characters bereft of values. For Virginia Woolf the war is present, or rather absent, as metaphor. In *Jacob's Room* (1922) we infer Jacob's death in action from lingering depictions of his unoccupied room and undisturbed possessions, imagery revised as the desolation and decay of an uninhabited house in the central section of *To the Lighthouse* (1927). On the very last page of the former novel Jacob's mother hears – like the unsettling rumbling from the engine-room in *Lord Jim* – inexplicable muted thunderings, 'Was that someone moving downstairs?' But she lives on the South Coast, from where the booming guns in France and Belgium were distinctly heard. For Woolf the war is an inexplicable disturbance at the margin of consciousness, it is implied in its evidences of ruin and absence, another of which is Septimus himself.

CLASS, CLIQUES AND CONSCIOUSNESS

Though the war is not a direct presence in the work of Woolf or Lawrence, what both authors do forcefully express, though in their very different registers, is the vibrancy of change which was the immediate postwar experience transmuting everything from politics and its discourse to manners and the construction of the feminine. It seemed as if one world had been replaced by another.

> Those five years – 1918 to 1923 – had been, he suspected, somehow very important. People looked different. Newspapers seemed different. Now, for instance, there was a man writing quite openly in one of the respectable weeklies about water-closets ... And then this taking out of a stick of rouge, or a powder-puff, and making up in public.[15]

> It was in 1915 the old world ended. In the winter of 1915–1916 the spirit of the old London collapsed; the city, in some way, perished, perished from being a heart of the world, and became a vortex of broken passions, lusts, hopes, fears and horrors. The integrity of London collapsed, and the genuine debasement began, the unspeakable baseness of the press and the public voice, the reign of that bloated ignominy, *John Bull.*[16]

The interleaved concerns – class, democracy and mass culture, a deeply alienated and doomed social formation and the emergence of new fraught forms of identity and consciousness – everywhere animate the work of Lawrence. Characteristically he articulates them with another urgent issue which, ever since Simone de Beauvoir in *The Second Sex* (1949) castigated his supposedly phallocentric rendering of it, has become nearly the sole topic of Lawrence studies, sexual politics. The collier's son from Eastwood, Nottinghamshire looked to Hardy as a literary mentor and found in him the last notable instance of an artist concerned to present working people who were yet 'aristocrats of the spirit'. Alasdair Gray reads the whole of Lawrence's career as novelist, traveller and social critic as an attempt to come to terms with his voluntary deracination from the working community of his Midlands youth.

> In the mining town where he grew up he had known a community: people who accepted each other for what they had in common as workmates, neighbours, chapel-goers. His mother wanted her children *not* to be common, but professional and monied. By his talents he became these things, and found that the professional, talented, wealthy folk he now mixed with, though good friends who recognised his uniqueness, had no community beyond cliques based on love-affairs and on conversations about art and ideas. So he went searching through Australia, New Mexico and Italy for a working community like the Eastwood of his childhood, but not based on wage-slavery, and with room for a free spirit like his own.[17]

Such an analysis is underlined by the much-needed moment of comedy in *Kangaroo* (1923) when the characters based on Lawrence and Frieda rent a bungalow in Melbourne called *Torestin*. He takes the name to be aboriginal until she points out it means to-rest-in. They quickly move on – one of the chapters of *Women in Love* is called 'Flitting' – in an illustration of how Lawrence never found the home in which to rest. But some aspects are unacknowledged by Gray: Lawrence's revulsion at the 'uncreate' ugliness of the mining country and its denizens – 'Everything is a ghoulish replica of the real world, a replica, a ghoul, all soiled, everything sordid'[18] – and the fact that his bête-noire is the emasculating 'merging' of democracy – 'the hateful, unmanly insolence of these lords of toil, now they have their various "unions" behind them and their "rights" as working men, send my blood black'.[19] Lawrence is as contemptuous of workers' solidarity as high-born Conrad ever was. However these outbursts of Lawrence's can perhaps be accommodated to Gray's reading as denunciations from a man who, having discarded community, can only vilify it and the politics which might restore or revitalize it. Perhaps after all Lawrence has the true ambition of the modern artist as Paul Klee describes it in *On Modern Art* (first delivered as a lecture, 1924): 'But we seek a people'.

Birkin, the opinionated disputant and moody champion of 'passional consciousness' of *Women in Love* – every Lawrence novel has one – is readily identified with his author. But this identification obscures, and perhaps Lawrence desired it thus obscured, an alternative identification between the author and Birkin's lover, Ursula, a character who had first appeared in *The Rainbow* (1915). This magnificent novel has a form and intent comparable to Thomas Mann's *Buddenbrooks* (1901). Each is a family saga stretching through the nineteenth century and, in Lawrence's case, into the twentieth which is a brilliant recapitulation, but crucially also a purging or laying to rest, of the great nineteenth-century realist narratives on which it is modelled. In these novels Lawrence and Mann both trace and enact the emergence of the new human identities and narrative forms characteristic of the twentieth century and of its new articulation, modernism. *The Rainbow* is focused on three generations of the Brangwen family of Midlands farmers from which, in the last phase, Ursula emerges as a spirited protagonist and voice of a truculant, commonsensical feminism. She is decidedly in the tradition of Hardy's predominantly female spiritual aristocrats. In the shift from *The Rainbow* to *Women in Love* Ursula moves from the Northern working community famously celebrated in the former's lush opening paragraphs to the cosmopolitan, bohemian 'cliques' described by Gray. In the process she forges a resolute creed of self-protective individualism – 'striving for more consciousness' – which proves both blessing and curse. 'The Bitterness of Ecstasy' is the ambivalent title of the chapter in which, contemplating a living cell through a microscope, she has her epiphanic intuition of the splendour of isolated selfhood – 'To be oneself was a supreme, gleaming triumph of infinity'. Lawrence's poignant 'Autobiographical Sketch' testifies to the emotional deracination which has exchanged a deeply social 'blood affinity' for cliques and consciousness.

> I cannot make the transfer from my own class into the middle class. I cannot, not for anything in the world, forfeit my passional consciousness and my old blood-affinity with my fellow men and the animals and the land, for that other thin, spurious mental conceit which is all that is left of the mental consciousness once it has made itself exclusive.[20]

Lawrence gave yet another version of his own quest in the great autobiographical Bildungsroman *Sons and Lovers* (1913). A young painter and writer strives in his work and relationships for the sublime ascendancy of the soaring Gothic as opposed to the dour, ground-hugging Normanness of his Northern working mileu of which his collier father is the exemplar. He struggles with a possessive mother and contrasting lovers: Miriam, who embodies the old, rooted, rural *Rainbow* world, and Clara, who is a precurser of the morally adventurous, modern bohemianism of *Women in Love*. Critics have been quick to dub the novel Freudian and Oedipal – it is Terry Eagleton's prime instance of the novel open to a 'psychoanalytic' reading in *Literary Theory* (1983) – which seems rash given Lawrence's provocative denunciation of Freud as the prurient purveyor of the 'dirty little secret' and of 'sex-in-the-head' of *Psychoanalysis and the Unconscious* (1921) and *Fantasia of the Unconscious* (1922). As this anomaly suggests, it is impossible in so brief a survey to do justice to the ironies and complexities of Lawrence's representation of his abiding concerns around gender, sexual expression, sexual politics and pornography and to the turbulent history of their critical discussion. Lawrence has lived many lives: as a sensualist and pornographer (*The Rainbow* and, most famously, *Lady Chatterley's Lover* (1928) were banned on these grounds); as a priest of love and champion of free sexual expression (a mentor adapted to the experimental sixties with some help from F.R. Leavis, Ken Russell and the *Lady Chatterley* trial); as the Ur-patriarch preaching an eternal reification of oppressive sexual hierarchies (Simone de Beauvoir, Kate Millet and many others) and as a great antagonist for the capitalist/Freudian confining, domesticating and neuroticizing of sexual identities with which we remain burdened (Deleuze and Guattari). Thus successively liberal humanism, feminism and post-structuralism have made their own reconstructions of Lawrence as a crucial figure. Suffice it to say here that while Conrad, Joyce and Woolf may be more unreservedly admired and secure in their canonical status than the embattled and mercurial Lawrence, he is the writer who generates the most provocative debate, a debate which has a habit of flaring just when it seems staunched.

One of Lawrence's claims which has become a touchstone of modernist innovation was that one must not look in his works for 'the old stable ego of the character'. The assertion seems riven with paradox given Lawrence's obsessive championing of an isolated, integral selfhood which looks suspiciously like a spruced-up version of the tired old bourgeois ego. However, it is true that his work is filled with a sense of that particularly postwar phenomenon of the emergence, as with Ursula or the war-devastated lives of the *Three Novellas* (1923), of new tentative and exploratory identities uncontained by the old forms. Meanwhile 'the old stable ego of the character' is apparently well enough to be enjoying something of a convalescence in the novels of Lawrence's contemporary E.M. Forster (1879–1970). His characters' anxieties are more conscious and worldly than the passional urgencies that animate Lawrence's and, confronted with a world which challenges and perturbs rather than negates them, they are all rather like the figure in *Howards End* who had 'no muscles, only nerves'. Though he was only six years older than Lawrence and actually outlived him by forty years, Forster had nearly completed his fictional career before Lawrence began his with just post-Edwardian *The White Peacock* (1911). Four of his six novels were written between 1905 and 1910 and his works seem distinguished from Lawrence's by an Edwardianism which is as much a matter of temperament as it is of dates.

We have already seen Forster cited by Gray as one of those broadly modernist writers who write from a position of social and financial privilege and are consequently incognizant and incurious about the structure of the society that facilitates their leisure. Forster could be partly exempted since perhaps the prevailing theme of his work is an embarrassed recognition of the injustice of precisely this position. His creed – never untroubled in his novels – is a near sacramental conception of the value of personal relations. Forster perfectly illustrates the ambitions and failings of liberal discourse. A meticulous and critical anatomist of how things are, Forster never makes the true modernist gesture of utter rejection. As Lawrence put it,

> Am reading *Passage to India*. It's good, but makes one wish a bomb would fall and end everything. Life is more interesting in its undercurrents than in its obvious: and E.M. does see people, people and nothing but people: *ad nauseam*.[21]

Where Angels Fear to Tread (1905) and *A Room with a View* (1908) are particularly marked by socio-economic naivety stemming from precisely the disabling emphasis Lawrence diagnoses on people relating to people as if free of external determinants. These works, and somewhat less so *Howards End*, are weakened by a glibly professed innocence of politics and espousal of the flimsy creed of 'personal relations'. Britain is seen as the class-dichotomized environment where

> Life, so far as she troubled to conceive it, was a circle of rich pleasant people, with identical interests and identical foes. In this circle one thought, married and died. Outside it were poverty and vulgarity, for ever trying to enter, just as the London fog tries to enter the pine-woods … [22]

And in reaction Italy is celebrated as the country where one can enjoy that thoroughly absurd and bourgeois conception – 'that true socialism which is based not on equality of income or character, but on the equality of manners'.[23] As is said of the well-intentioned and ineffectual Miss Schegels,

> In their own fashion they cared deeply about politics, though not as politicians would have us care; they desired the public life should mirror whatever is good in the life within.[24]

An impressive sign of growth in Forster is that *A Passage to India* (1924) reappraises this early insipid humanism – also enshrined in the regrettably whimsical *Aspects of the Novel* (1927) – with circumspection. This maturation of Forster's into a sense of the immanence of political reality is registered in the reflections of the protagonist Fielding:

> The complexion of his mind turned from the human to political. He thought no longer, 'Can I get on with people?' but 'are they stronger than I?'[25]

One feels the effect of this leap of understanding everywhere in *A Passage to*

India, a story of British administration in India centring on the trial of an Indian doctor accused of assaulting a white woman and handled with a Conradian density of emotional and moral ambiguity. The primordial caves where the incident may or may not have occurred are full of resonances for the characters as well as for feminist and postmodern critics alive to the implications of textual penetrations, hollows and absences.

Another meditation on obscured sexualities, *Maurice* (completed 1914, published posthumously 1971), finally confronts the issue of homosexuality over which this gay author's writing had been hesitating since the first fiction in 1905. For Edwardian discourse gay men are like the poor – unthinkable. Until *Maurice*, in Forster's fiction and elsewhere, not only does this love not dare speak its name but it seems to have no name nor any other signifier that could render it present in fiction. Forster's entire oeuvre can be read as the search for this signifier. The timid *The Longest Journey* (1907) opts for contortionate circumlocutions; an effete protagonist is burdened with an evidently symbolic and psychosexual gammy leg which he suspects he inherited from a father whose unmanliness is parenthesized by a flair for flower arranging. *Angels* and *A Passage to India* both feature strangely forceful yet undeveloped emotional relationships between men as Forster brings his fiction to the threshold of the issue. The threshold is firmly crossed in *Maurice* which cannot be the first representation of gay male desire in fiction but is certainly the first to place this sympathetically at the centre of representation and actually to allow its gay couple a happy ending. The story whereby the otherwise unimaginative Maurice first becomes infatuated with his Cambridge contemporary Clive and then finds true love with the gamekeeper Alec has the simple earnestness and wish fulfilment of a project never intended for publication but undertaken as the poignant and therapeutic gesture 'to grant one's creations a happiness actual life does not supply'.

As a footnote to a more contemporary sociology it is interesting to note that Lawrence and Forster have each been granted substantial but contrasting posthumous revivals. F.R. Leavis, Ken Russell and the trial and subsequent unbanning of *Lady Chatterley's Lover* all contributed to making the 1960s Lawrence's decade. Seen as sexual radical and prophet of free expression he was a suitable champion for an era socially and sexually iconoclastic, experimental and libertarian. The 1980s, however, thanks to lush film adaptations of five of the six novels, culminating with that definitive instance of reverent and ultra-tasteful literary adaptation, Merchant and Ivory's *Howards End* (1992), were Forster's own. Film stroked Forster's texts with the appreciative caress of a heritage consultant appraising some charming and precious *objet de virtu*. Novels that carefully teased and tested the limits of naturalism, narrative and humanist optimism are reprocessed into films that lushly reassert them, as Lawrence would put it, *ad nauseam*. While Lawrence's status faltered, Forster, reprocessed as elegantly nostalgic entertainment, suited a period of political and aesthetic retrenchment. Forster would have been repelled by the strident philistinism and conservatism that characterized the decade that rediscovered him and which lived out its own crassly consumerist version of his own creed of purely private values.

THE SMASHING AND THE CRASHING

James Joyce's (1882–1941) *Ulysses* (Paris, 1922) is the modernist novel par excellence, a work which he imagines entering a tradition of Irish art seen as 'the cracked lookingglass of a servant', an intriguing intimation that national dispossession and servitude are the premises of his own shattered mimesis. The reverberations of a tremendous shattering of representation are felt everywhere in modernism. Woolf describes the discursive mode she senses as prevalent after 1910.

> And so the smashing and the crashing began. Thus it is that we hear all around us, in poems and novels and biographies, even in newspaper articles and essays, the sound of breaking and falling, crashing and destruction. It is the prevailing sound of the Georgian age ... [26]

Woolf's image suggests the ambivalence of a climate of destruction that could be read as tragic ruination or an exhilarating iconoclasm. Lawrence chooses to lament the age as a shattered apocalypse: 'Ours is essentially a tragic age ... The cataclysm has happened, we are among the ruins ... We've got to live, no matter how many skies have fallen.'[27] For the émigré protagonist of Kafka's *America* (1924) the falling skies of modernity are an exhilarating spectacle. The glassy scintillation of light upon his arrival in New York expresses all the thrilling destructiveness of a brash modernity 'as if a glass roof stretched over the street were being violently smashed into fragments'.[28] Joyce's Stephen Dedalus surveys the shattered scene without apparent regret – 'I hear the ruin of all space, shattered glass and toppling masonry, and time one livid final flame. What's left us then?'[29] Modernism is art's ambiguous Krystallnacht.

Joyce was born in Dublin, the city where all his fiction is set, but which in each successive appearance is more transmuted and transfigured, further detached from realism, increasingly shot through with epiphany and enfolded within corruscating linguistic invention. It is the stifling site of small lives in the spare and naturalistic *Dubliners* (1914); the myth-saturated life of *Ulysses* and the hometown of the publican who is the human centre of the dazzling semantic web of *Finnegans Wake* (1939). In the movement from the first to the last of these works Joyce seems to enact within one career the entire momentous shift in discourse we are attempting here to survey. His career is a vast evolving experiment in language and intellection and, like Lawrence's, a restless peregrination through styles and geographies. He moved between Paris, Trieste, Zurich, Paris again and then, when disturbed for a second time by world war, back to Zurich where he died. Malcolm Bradbury and James McFarlane exactly express his work's profound but apparently oblique engagement with the turbulent Europe of these years. 'The European disorder of the century does not figure directly in Joyce's work, but it is an émigré art of linguistic pluralism, a modern semiology which both releases the word and rigorously defines its modern potential; hence Joyce's persistent appeal to Post-Modernist writers.'[30]

The paraphraser of *Ulysses* is stumped except perhaps to suggest that here all modernism's strategies are set in a great symphonic conversation: Lawrence's humanist fidelity to the textures of life, sex and 'selfhood'; Woolf's fraying of the distinction between mind and world and registration of an all-swamping interiority; Proust's exhuberant superabundance of observation; Eliot's erudition and palimpsestic overlaying of discursive archaeologies; Kafka's intuition of history as rooted in persecution and 'nightmare'. It is, amongst other things, a rhapsodic elaboration of the relations between fathers and sons allied to an immense meditation on begetting, authority and authorship; a compendium of the public topics of 1904; an encyclopaedia of discourses – literary and (hitherto) extra-literary – from epic narratives to the language of advertising, journalism, and music-hall and an aesthetic structure dedicated to the simultaneous evocation of conflicting registers and representations – recondite and banal, mythic and quotidian, impressionistic and meticulously structured. The introduction to this volume has raised the question whether *Ulysses* is modernist or postmodernist. Another possibility is that its ambitions are essentially realist, if we take that to mean dedicated to the healing of severances and the revelation of continuities, the re-establishment of relations between words and world, parents and children. At the level of plot the novel accepts as its premises cruel severings of relations, primarily familial but also of all kinds of reference, representation and relatedness. Stephen Dedalus has refused to pray at his mother's deathbed. His relations with his father are cold. Leopold Bloom's father committed suicide, his son died in infancy. Sexual relations have ceased between Bloom and his wife Molly. Home does indeed seem to be in the site of lack evoked in the jingle which keeps running through Bloom's head, 'What is a home without Plumtree's Potted Meat? Incomplete'. Indeed the world itself for Stephen is predicated upon such absence and incompletion, 'founded ... upon the void. Upon incertitude, upon unlikelihood'.

Ulysses is complexly patriarchical and structured around innumerable evocations of the model of 'The son striving to be atoned with the Father': the Holy Trinity, Homer's Ulysses and Telemachus, Stephen's theory that Hamlet is the ghost of his own father. Fathers are severed from sons, words from reference, Ireland from power, art from representation. But at the level of discourse Joyce is assiduously repairing reference and knitting up new, metaphorical relations to repair the loss of the traditional and literal, positing new paradoxical forms of relation, the prime example being the intriguing elective affinity between the disaffected Catholic intellectual Stephen and Bloom, advertiser's runner, cuckolded husband and butt of anti-semitic jibes and slights. Modernism finds its sparse consolations in such surprising and unresolved intuitions of affinity as in the startling moment in Woolf's *Mrs Dalloway* when the wealthy and self-absorbed heroine is checked in the preparations for her society party by thoughts about the suicide that day of war-devastated Septimus Smith.

> Somehow it was her disaster – her disgrace. It was her punishment to see sink and disappear here a man, there a woman, in this profound darkness, and she forced to stand here in her evening dress.[31]

Here we have a Joycean moment in the sense that it simultaneously registers the rigid demarcations of social status and sensibility – and Woolf adds gender – we have sensed everywhere in discourse in this period, as well as the vital flash of recognition which, in fiction at least, can be thrown across such boundaries.

If *Ulysses* is, for all its radical linguistic intent, in some sense a paean to patriarchy, Woolf's best fiction represents an alternative, female and feminist, strand in modernism. Her most achieved and distinctive novels, *Mrs Dalloway* (1925), *To the Lighthouse* (1927) and *The Waves* (1931) are intensely aestheticized and anti-materialistic, mood poems saturated with consciousness and exactly registering the passage of labile and haphazard impressions. Transmuting the explicit feminism voiced in the nonfiction *A Room of One's Own* (1929) and *Three Guineas* (1936), these novels characteristically pit a critical and in some perhaps unrecognized sense creative female sensibility – self-dissatisfied artist Lily Briscoe, unintellectual and motherly philosopher's wife Mrs Ramsey, epiphanically inclined society hostess Mrs Dalloway – against rational and conservative male norms. Woolf's is a thoroughly female modernism and it is an indication of her own influence that one checks a sloppy use of 'feminine' for 'female', rightly questioning, as Woolf does, their supposed synonymity. She was, as she called another great woman modernist, Katherine Mansfield, 'a terribly sensitive mind', where we need to see the word 'terribly' as uncoloured by irony and denoting a real fear and fragility. Woolf suffered repeated breakdowns and committed suicide in 1941.

Orlando (1928) is a jeu-d'esprit that toys absurdly with historical and sexual identities as it follows the mutations through centuries of its eponymous hero/ine with not an old stable ego, or gender, in sight. One splendid and strikingly dark passage from the last pages of the novel brings us right up to the date of composition and consequently almost to the very end of the period we are examining. It also exactly exemplifies some key modes and motifs of modernism. Orlando is driving through London.

> The Old Kent Road was very crowded on Thursday, the eleventh of October 1928. People split off from the pavement. There were women with shopping bags. Children ran out. There were sales at drapers' shops. Streets widened and narrowed. Long vistas steadily shrunk together. Here was a market. Here a funeral. Here a procession with banners upon which was written 'Ra-Un', but what else? Meat was very red. Butchers stood at the door. Women almost had their heels sliced off. Amor Vin – that was over a porch. A woman looked out of a bedroom window, profoundly contemplative, and very still. Applejohn and Applebed, Undert—. Nothing could be seen whole or read from start to finish. What was seen begun – like two friends starting to meet each other across the street – was never seen ended. After twenty minutes the body and mind were like scraps of torn paper tumbling from a sack and, indeed, the process of motoring fast out of London so much resembles the chopping up small of identity which precedes unconsciousness and perhaps death itself that it is an open question in what sense Orlando can be said to have existed at the present moment. Indeed we should have given her over for a person entirely disassembled ... [32]

Here the city-scape is rendered, rather as in a cubist canvas, as abstraction, discontinuity and shock. Compare Joyce's 'Cityful passing away, other cityful coming, passing away too: other coming on, passing on'.[33] We readily recognize the keynotes of high modernist prose: abrupt encounters; suspended recognitions; abortive narratives; reality and identity seen as semi-legible, 'disassembled', even nonexistent. One recalls the features of modernism as described by Bradbury and McFarlane, 'the shock, the violation of expected continuities, the element of de-creation and crisis'.[34] World, self and prose share a common fragmentation. The restless eye is continually distracted by a scattering of unassimilable detail; identity is bitty, scattered and refracted; the prose itself staccato, paratactic, 'schizophrenic' in the specific sense of being only able to perceive detail, difference, disconnection. As Forster puts it , 'It is impossible to see modern life steadily and see it whole'.[35] Things are frustratingly illegible; both world and script withhold their meaning like the evanescent sky-writing which puzzles Londoners in *Mrs Dalloway*. As the narrator of *To the Lighthouse* puts it, it is as if 'divine goodness' teases us maliciously, never showing things whole but so breaks them, so confuses them that it seems impossible that their calm should ever return or that we should ever compose from their fragments a perfect whole or read in the littered pieces the clear words of truth.[36]

Death, shock and violence is threaded through all. The mad, tearing progress of technology provides the impetus of the whole.

Here is a severity we would not usually associate with Woolf. As the passage continues, however, the landscape ruralizes and the prose pastoralizes. 'Green screens' appear on either side and Orlando's mind regains 'the illusion of holding things within itself' on seeing 'a cottage, a farmyard and four cows, all precisely life-size'. This fragrant whiff of Georgian pastoral illustrates the very English inflection of Woolf's modernism but surely articulates something more urgent than nostalgia. Woolf, who has given wholly convincing depictions of mental illness in *The Voyage Out* (1915) and *Mrs Dalloway*, registers the mental strife which is one function of a modern world of lost sanities and freakish disproportions. This passage precisely reverses the movement from Nature to Culture the fantastic acceleration of which was the primary fact of the modern period. It thus serves to illustrate Fredric Jameson's view of modernism as an essentially anti-representational protest refusing to reproduce an alienating and alienated social formation, 'a symbolic act which involves a whole Utopian compensation for increasing dehumanisation on the level of daily life'.[37]

NOTES

1. 'Reflections on the Death of a Porcupine', *A Selection from Phoenix*, ed. A.A.H. Inglis (Harmondsworth, 1979), p. 163.
2. *Ulysses, The Corrected Text*, ed. Hans Walter Gabler with Wolfhard Steppe and Claus Melchior (Harmondsworth, 1986), p. 45.
3. 'Mr Bennett and Mrs Brown', *Collected Essays*, vol. 1, ed. Leonard Woolf (London, 1966), p. 326.
4. 'Mr Bennett and Mrs Brown', *Collected Essays*, p. 328.
5. *A Selection from Phoenix*, 'John Galsworthy', p. 286.
6. Postscript to Agnes Owens, *Gentlemen of the West* (Harmondsworth, 1986), p. 133.
7. *A Room of One's Own* (London, 1973), p. 42.
8. *Howards End* (Harmondsworth, 1989), p. 72.
9. *Lord Jim* (Harmondsworth, 1981), p. 20.
10. *Howards End*, p. 62.
11. 'Heart of Darkness' (Harmondsworth, 1981), p. 8.
12. *Marxism and Literary Criticism* (London, 1976), p. 7.

13. *The Letters of Henry James*, ed. Percy Lubbock, 2 vols (New York, 1920), 2, p. 384.
14. *Minima Moralia: Reflections from a Damaged Life*, trans. E.F.N. Jephcott (London, 1974), p. 143.
15. *Mrs Dalloway* (London, 1988), p. 65.
16. *Kangaroo* (Harmondsworth, 1988), p. 240.
17. Postscript to *Gentlemen of the West*, p. 132.
18. *Women in Love* (Harmondsworth, 1982), p. 12.
19. *Sea and Sardinia* (London, 1989), p. 39.
20. 'Autobiographical Sketch', *A Selection from Phoenix*, p. 18.
21. Letter to Martin Secker, 23 July 1924, *Selected Literary Criticism*, ed. Anthony Beal, (London, 1969), p. 139.
22. *A Room with a View* (Harmondsworth, 1990), pp. 129–30.
23. *Where Angels Fear to Tread* (Harmondsworth, 1975), p. 53.
24. *Howards End*, p. 41.
25. *A Passage to India* (Harmondsworth, 1976), p. 59.
26. *Collected Essays* 'Mr Bennett and Mrs Brown', p. 334.
27. *Lady Chatterley's Lover* (Harmondsworth, 1988), p. 5.
28. *The Collected Novels of Franz Kafka* (Harmondsworth, 1988), p. 465.
29. *Ulysses*, p. 20.
30. *Modernism: 1890–1930*, 'Pelican Guides to European Literature' (Harmondsworth, 1981), p. 625.
31. *Mrs Dalloway*, p. 164.
32. *Orlando: A Biography* (Oxford, 1992), p. 164.
33. *Ulysses*, p. 135.
34. *Modernism: 1890 to 1930*, p. 24.
35. *Howards End*, p. 164.
36. *To the Lighthouse* (London, 1987), p. 119.
37. *The Political Unconscious: Narrative as a Socially Symbolic Act* (London, 1983) p. 42.

CHAPTER THREE

Popular Fiction and Middle-Brow Taste

Michael Hayes

THE PROBLEM OF DEFINITION

Nearing the end of the twentieth century, in a 'postmodernist world' that increasingly seeks 'The breakdown of the distinction between high culture (art) and popular culture'[1] it would be all too easy to judge popular fiction as being synonymous with bestsellers. Bestsellers – those publishers' and authors' dreams of massive and immediate sales that, like Mario Puzo's *The Godfather* which sold over fifteen million copies, get turned into blockbuster films and then a mere eighteen months later can be bought at market bookstalls or parish jumble sales for thirty pence; desirable books that in spite of the scorn of academics and the neglect of literary reviewers generate prodigious pounds for their publishers and authors alike.

Were this the case a discussion of popular fiction in Britain for any period of the twentieth century could be conducted quite simply by focusing on those books that notched up record sales at the time. Unfortunately such a simple and basic identification of popular fiction with bestsellers is fraught with far too many difficulties. For one thing, clear statistics are not available. It was not until the 1970s in England that any attempt was made, and then not by publishers but by journalists and booksellers, to present the public with a bestsellers' list. Furthermore, there is the problem of those books that sell in very large numbers on the basis of their author's name but any one of whose titles never make the hall of bestseller fame. Then too there are the types of fiction that sell so well they have sections to themselves in the bookshops but whose individual titles are not as significant as their genre labels. Even more problematic are those 'penny dreadfuls' that twenty, thirty or a hundred years later re-emerge, this time on the literary curricula of institutes of higher education and on the examination syllabuses of schools.

The key problem is that no definition of popular fiction can ever be finally arrived at by a simple enumeration of properties, even for example such apparent commonplaces as, all action narrative, preponderance of dialogue, a resolution that conforms to the moral convictions of the readers and good sales. As John Ellis cogently argues, most categories of objects, whether 'weeds' or 'literature', cannot be defined solely by reference to their common features because implicit in the use of the name is a notion of value.[2] Terms like 'weeds', 'literature' and 'popular fiction' are used to describe those objects that society agrees to call weeds, literature and popular fiction.

I have deliberately borrowed the argument about the impossibility of giving a constitutive definition of popular fiction from the field of literary study. It is in respect of literature rather than popular fiction that the discussions about definition have been most thoroughly rehearsed. Antony Easthope in *Literary into Cultural Studies* spends the first third of his book giving excellent and clear coverage of the often intricate arguments as to what constitutes the nature of literature.[3] But he obviously feels no such necessity in relation to books that he might wish to include under the term 'popular'. Rather, he contents himself with a couple of pages giving Raymond Williams's account of the three uses of the word, namely: referring to something many people like; popular as opposed to high culture; and representing a culture that arises spontaneously out of a social group. To these he adds the version of popular as 'mass media imposed on people by commercial interests.'[4]

These uses are all plausible although located in very different contexts and ideologies. What they have in common is that they are all grounded in a notion of social expression, one either of consensus judgement or of group determination of preference or of an imposition by a powerful group on a less powerful one. It is in this inclusion of a social dimension that definitions of popular culture differ from most attempted definitions of high culture, including literature, which concern the nature of the contents rather than the use. It is just this reification of judgement in definitions of literature that Ellis attempts to reverse, redefining it as that which people chose to use as literature.

No definition then of popular fiction is to be elicited by a close investigation of a specific range of books or scrutiny of a fixed catalogue of bibliographic items. Since questions of value and use are involved it is necessary to consider the whole range of factors that might contribute to a fiction being classed as popular. Popular fiction is less a fixed category than a historically contingent relationship between producers, the literary critical establishment and book readers, mediated through fictional narratives. In other words, popular fiction is a cultural nexus for a historically determined and evolving relationship whose understanding requires us to reflect on the period, the people and the state of book production as well as the books themselves. A corollary of course is that a text having popular use at one time does not therefore necessarily preclude the possibility of it having other uses or values at other times. Yesterday's popular fiction can be today's literature. The purpose of this essay is to shed light on the nature of the cultural relationship that goes under the name popular fiction during the period 1900 to 1929.

THE READING PUBLIC

Knowing that a thousand or even a hundred thousand copies of a particular novel were sold does not tell us who bought them, what effect it had on them, or even if they read it. We can point to strategies employed by the writer and the bookseller and reveal ideological positions maintained in the book, but without a good deal more information we know neither the reading repertoires employed nor how readers might have been positioned in their approach to the text. The early years of this century are particularly problematic since 'From the point of view of social history the early twentieth century still lies in an academic limbo'.[5]

Nevertheless there are important sources of knowledge about the nature of the reading public that can be examined. For one thing, history is a continuum and any period owes something to processes already unfolding at earlier times. We know, for example, a very great deal about popular fiction during the Victorian period due to the researches of scholars such as Cruse, Dalziel, James and Neuburg. We also know of the economic and social circumstances which were the context for the people's lives and helped create the presuppositions which governed their world view. We also have a mass of diaries, autobiographies and collections of oral material which reveal the social history and consciousness of the people, harvested by enthusiastic local historians over the last twenty years. But it is only now that this wealth of material is being scrutinized with a view to making the appropriate classifications which can underpin and validate generalizations.

R.C. Terry sees in the period 1860–80 the inception of that transformation of reading consciousness that dominates the early years of this century; at this point 'the problematic of the individual and mass society begins, and the paths diverge between literary culture and popular fiction'.[6]

The beginnings may be in the earlier period but it is not, according to the *Oxford Dictionary*, until 1904 that we see the distinction between literature and 'popular' literature confirmed in nomenclature.

During most of the nineteenth century there was a tendency to see the reading of fictions as one single activity, 'readers ... still able to share spontaneously in the common pursuit ... untroubled by the aestheticism of a later generation'.[7] During the early years of the twentieth century a cultural divide between high- and low-brow readers becomes apparent, a divide which by the twenties is confirmed in terms of a mass market as against a market for literature.

To be read books have to be obtained, and at the beginning of the century that generally meant buying or library subscription, both of which meant disposable income. A guide to the economic state of the population can be found in the figures for men's occupations. While it is true that in some areas, such as Lancashire, there was comparatively well paid employment for women, making them independent, like W.S. Houghton's heroine in *Hindle Wakes*, it was predominantly the position of men that determined the status and prosperity of the household. Seventy-eight per cent of men were in working-class occupations ranging from skilled to unskilled with semi-skilled the largest group. Twenty-two per cent were in middle-class, mainly profes-sional, occupations, leaving a fraction of one per cent in the upper class. It took the war to reveal officially the depths of privation experienced by many of the working class. Among the recruits medically examined for fitness for the trenches four out of five, for example, had such bad teeth that they could not eat properly.

This shortage of money meant that for many working-class families it was not books that provided the main reading but newspapers. Cheap newspapers and the new family magazines set target figures for sales that the new mass readership was capable of delivering. In 1897 *Pearson's Weekly* sold a million and a quarter copies. In 1910 the circulation of the Sunday paper *News of the World* had reached one and a half million. It is significant that it was the Sundays that had highest circulation figures since that was the only day on which many poorer households bought a paper.

During the twenties in spite of depression and the national strike there were significant economic improvements. By the end of the decade a *New Survey of London Life*, using the same yardstick as Charles Booth had used in the Victorian era, found only 8.7 per cent as opposed to 30.7 per cent below the poverty line. Accompanying this enhanced prosperity was the advent of mass entertainment. What newspapers had done in the latter years of the nineteenth century was followed by cheap books, radio and cinema in the twentieth.

But a people's consciousness is not simply formed by their economic situation. Culture is a mysterious amalgam of socio-political context, educa-tion and the influence of aesthetic and moral imperatives. Sometimes an event or a behavioural change becomes the basis of a myth which can go some way to sum up the consciousness and anxieties of an age. The sinking of the White

Star liner *Titanic* is not merely a metaphor for civilization heading for the First World War, the augmentation of its narrative offers us a portrait of the age.

Built as the exuberant expression of technological progress and manufacturing excellence, it sailed on its maiden voyage with a cross-section of society on board. A few days later it sank with the loss of 1,635 lives, but it was not merely the extent of the loss that was remarked but the disproportions between the classes. *The Daily Herald* of 22 April 1912 observed:

	per cent
Proportion of 1st class saved	61
Proportion of 2nd class saved	36
Proportion of 3rd class saved	23
Proportion of crew saved	22
Proportion of whole Ship's Company	29

Not only were doubts about the benefits of science and industry thrown into relief but the inequalities of the social structure highlighted. Furthermore, myth had it that this secular triumph bore the legend 'Neither God nor man can sink this ship' as it rolled down the slipway. Reputedly it sunk to the strains of passengers and crew singing hymns. Resonating clearly through the story are major anxieties particular to prewar society: concern at the pace, nature and extent of industrialization, unease about the inequalities of the established social order and the continuing crisis in religious belief. However, it must also not be forgotten that 732 lives were saved by ships summoned to the disaster area by that new invention, the wireless.

These apprehensions of consciousness were matched by the uncertain state of literacy. Compulsory child education had been introduced in 1870 with the express purpose of expanding numeracy and literacy among the population so that it might adequately serve the expanding new economic and industrial developments. In spite of the best efforts of Matthew Arnold and like-minded school inspectors, education among many in the working class remained largely irrelevant, or at best narrowly utilitarian. Almost in vain does one search through John Burnett's collection[8] of twenty-seven working-class autobiographies for any sense of the acquisition of literacy as a gateway to a fuller imaginative or cultural life, or even as an escape from poverty and effort. The school attendance figures for children aged 5 to 11 years between 1901 and 1931 range from 89.3 per cent to 91.7 per cent. But these figures tell us neither how many working-class children were literate nor, if they did learn to read and write, what scope they had to exercise their abilities. Melvyn Bragg's Wigton informant probably speaks for all too many when she says

> But you see we left school at fourteen, just when you were beginning to take an interest in things, and it was all lost that. You didn't get any further because you had to go right out to service and you never saw a paper or anything.[9]

One sign though of the increasing confidence of the young in the prewar years was the spread of comics. In 1906 *The Magnet* was founded, the comic that introduced Billy Bunter to the world. Another production, the pink paper *Chips*, was also circulated even in quite poor homes by means of the practice of 'swopping'. It was this younger generation who, increasingly confident in their literacy, became the popular-fiction readers of the postwar period.

The implications of this historical context for people as readers must be fairly self-evident. Easthope writes that popular culture 'in some degree expresses the values of the working class'.[10] At the turn of the century popular fiction as written text had very little to do with the majority of the working class. Most of them could not afford even the cheapest books and, even among the skilled and semi-skilled, reading appears to have been limited to newspapers, particularly Sunday papers, with the occasional school or Sunday-school book prize.[11] The titles of these prize books were carefully restricted to those deemed suitable by the middle class who controlled the purse strings. The public library system, instituted in 1850 as an alternative means of access to books, was as yet undeveloped and under-used. At the turn of the century less than two books per head of the population per year were borrowed. Magazines, particularly aimed at women, appeared in great numbers and variety but the rapid turnover in titles meant that none achieved market dominance.

The war killed one in ten of all Edwardian males under the age of 45, but after it society was never quite the same again. In the twenties society began to move in more egalitarian ways in spite of economic difficulties, to retrieve a sense of purpose. In 1926 some half of all the Cambridge undergraduates, 2,600 of them, registered for emergency duty, to help break the general strike. But by the end of the decade a mood of active concern had turned many of the privileged young into active socialists if not communists. The radical political society, the Labour Club, which had normally had some 150 members, began to grow. 'By 1931 it claimed to have over 1000 members.'[12] Women, who had done so much in the war, and many of whose marriage prospects had been destroyed by it, would never again be content to be shut up in their dolls' houses. Young working-class men, like their middle-class counterparts, were becoming confident in their literacy, they read and enjoyed books which they could now afford, including much fiction.

As John A. Lester suggests, 'the years from 1880 to 1914 severely jarred and shifted the bearings of man's imaginative life and left him at times bewildered as to how to recover his lost meaning and purpose'.[13] After the war, popular fiction was to play its part in shaping and reflecting the mind of the age, but the imaginative parameters within which this process took shape owed more to the rapidly growing and developing cinema than to the wholesome and improving literature of their erstwhile betters.

PUBLISHERS AND FORMATS

Publishers are entrepreneurs bringing together the craft of authors and the skills of printers in order to market the results as profitably as possible. In our late-twentieth-century world of hype, advertising and mass marketing it is all too easy to think of buyers as merely the dupes of media manipulators. Adorno, in his mid-seventies article 'Culture Industry Reconsidered', argues that

> the culture industry undeniably speculates on the conscious and unconscious state of the millions towards which it is directed, the masses are not primary but secondary, they are the objects of calculation: an appendage of the machinery. The customer is not King, as the culture industry would like to have us believe, not its subject but its object.[14]

In other words, the reader is inscribed in the text whose meanings then produce, rather than simply reflect, ways of looking at the world, which in turn determine patterns of consumption.

In some sense this has become more true as the century has progressed. If you are going to speculate millions, your prospective buyers are certainly going to be the object of calculation. But what the argument misses is that the relation between sellers and buyers is not just one transaction but a process of transactions. The word 'speculates' has two meanings, speculate in the sense of investing money, but also speculate in the sense of hypothesize. The investing comes after the hypothesis which leads to the decision making. The actual selling is only the end of the process and its success or failure feeds back into the thinking which determines the new investment and the making of the next object for sale. The customer might not be king but he or she is certainly an *active* participant in the continuously evolving relationship. The producers/publishers of the early years were of two kinds, those who inherited the paternalistic mantle of the Victorian tradition and the new breed who responded to the market as sellers rather than as the self-conscious guardians of moral values. Although the ideology of the former has persisted even to the end of the century, it is to the latter that we look in the twenties and the creation of a genuinely plural market.

In their time the great Victorian entrepreneurial publishers had shown invention and imagination in exploiting urbanization to establish new and vastly increased markets. Print runs went from tens of thousands to hundreds of thousands and they availed themselves of the greatly enhanced networks of communication to sell more books. The Brontës in Haworth receiving their box of books from the circulating library courtesy of the railway, or passengers purchasing cheap railway editions sold by W.H. Smith from their railway station outlets inaugurated on Euston Station, 1 November 1858, were just two of a range of nineteenth-century innovations. Here were initiatives that reduced the prices of books from guineas to shillings, making them no longer the privilege of the rich and middle classes but also the right of the upper-working class. Charles Knight was a typical Victorian publisher. He gave his support to the book club movement whereby groups formed themselves into a society; each member then paid a small weekly subscription, often only a penny or tuppence, for the purchase of cheap editions. These books were then available to each member on a lending library basis, finally they formed the basis of a permanent library or were sold off to subscribers at the end of a specified period. But even as he promoted the benefits of such a scheme he also made quite clear what sort of books he thought suitable. They should be 'such books as were unexceptionable in their morality, interesting as well as instructive, and containing an abundant provision of truly national literature'.[15] His ideals, like those of many of his fellow publishers , might be summed up as pious, preachy and patriotic!

The publishers of the late Victorian age had, as entrepreneurs, an investment in the stability and continuity of society. They believed in making money from stories of adventure and romance, provided the stories were patriotic and wholesome. Above all they believed in the work ethic, that everyone had the capacity to improve their station in life by their own efforts. The part they saw books as playing in this was to transmit practical information of all kinds and to promote moral values. When Harmsworth added 'Pluck Library' and *Boys' Home Journal* to his 'juveniles' list

> the editorial policy was the same in each instance: the cultivation of physical fitness in the young, the encouragement of adventure abroad and enterprise at home. In all of them the bugle-call of patriotism was loudly sounded, pride in Great Britain and the Empire. 'No more penny dreadfuls!' was long the ruling theme and in at least one of the Harmsworth boys' journals it was stated in those words.[16]

Needless to say the market for such action stories was assumed to be exclusively male.

Publishers like Chambers and Cassell produced part works on all manner of information from science to British History. On the fiction side, series of classic and literary works were published in a popular format at cheap prices. In 1875 'Cassell's Library of English Literature' was commenced in sevenpenny monthly parts and continued for nearly six years. Routledge produced a weekly series of editions of the classics at threepence and sixpence entitled 'World Library'. Another enterprise of the late Victorian era was to offer book coupons with tea: after drinking gallons of tea the coupons could be exchanged for books. At the turn of the century the publication of literature was given a boost as many leading Victorian authors came out of copyright. The books could be published cheaply without the added burden of having to pay royalties, and the titles and authors were an advertisement in themselves.

But new works supposedly of quality were by no means ignored in the cost-cutting exercise. In 1894 circulating libraries refused to take any more expensive 'three deckers', the format that had dominated novel publishing for over a hundred years. In competition with cheap reprints, pushed by demand for the latest titles and rivalled by free libraries their pressure on publishers resulted in the one-volume six-shilling novel. This price was to remain the norm until after the war when the price went up to seven shillings and sixpence.

But the real developments in mass publishing had their roots in the social and technical achievements of the last quarter of the nineteenth century that are associated with names like Harmsworth, Pearson and Newnes. Urbanization and an improved transport had delivered a national retail distribution network, universal education was creating a younger generation increasing in confidence and willingness to exercise their growing literacy, and technology had delivered cheap paper in large quantities and 'printing processes capable of turning out newspapers and periodicals by the million at high speed'.[17] The final link in the chain was the development of advertising which was capable of bearing as much as half the costs of producing newspapers and magazines.

The primary concern of newspaper and periodical publishing was news and miscellaneous information. Even so both forms of publishing had a place for fictions, short stories and serial publications. Harmsworth in his *Daily Mail* found room to serialize fictions that supported his own pet views. In 1906 he serialized Le Queux's fictional account of a German invasion of Britain, which he had been warning the nation about, entitled *The Invasion of 1910*. The original route of the invasion lay through East Anglia, but since the march was through areas of minimal *Daily Mail* sales Harmsworth changed the route 'to ensure that the Hun sacked those towns where chances of securing a boost to the *Daily Mail's* circulation were strongest'.[18] The book was eventually translated into twenty-seven languages and notched up sales of a million.

The magazines and penny novelettes directed at women, with a mixture of 'mother and home' features and romantic fiction, offered almost limitless scope for short stories. The house rules for these fictions were few and simple:

> They must be complete, have two or three characters and a mild love interest, a little bit of mystery, and deal with everyday or 'romantic' affairs in a way that most people can understand.[19]

One might add that the conclusions of the stories must necessarily coincide with and reinforce the moral convictions of their readers. This prescription is confirmed by interviews that J. Haslam recorded at the beginning of the century with Manchester and Salford newsagents and customers and published in his book *The Press and the People* (1906). One Manchester woman for example said,

What sells best with me is penny novels ... These yo' know is good stories; no silly kissin' and lovin' about 'em. Of course they is all good stories about love, but it's proper love – sensible like – an' all ends happy – an' that kind o' thing. [20]

The repetitive simplicity of these romances, ensured there were no shocks, no disruptive outbursts of sensuality, and the undemanding morality conformed to the acceptable social mores of an essentially subservient readership. In their anodyne character they released their female readers for half an hour or so from the very real anxieties of everyday life. A dominant vision of women identified by sex and bounded by role as mother and homemaker was reinforced and elucidated.

The arrival of *Vogue* from America in 1916 heralded a sea change. This was an altogether more adventurous publication offering articles over a whole range of topics cultural, worldly and contentious. It assumed that women wanted more than just the conventional role of mother and homemaker that pervaded the English magazines. It assumed that women wanted and were entitled to be people in their own right and that they wanted to achieve their goal through education. The recognition that women, after their war experiences, had money to spend and that the new working-class woman constituted a potential market was acknowledged by the inauguration in 1919 of *Peg's Paper*. It was aimed at working class women and it embodied a subtle but significant shift in its fictional practices. Instead of avoiding difficult issues entirely it sought to incorporate them, although disguised, into a fiction that identified with the concerns of its readers. Not that the stories were realistic, but the glamour, sensation, mystery and revenge were a means of subsuming the wider range of experiences that the earlier stories had sought to ignore. Interestingly, elements of their content and style owed as much to the rapidly growing popularity of the cinema as they did to the tradition of written stories. The success of this venture was such that the magazine lasted until the outbreak of the Second World War.

One thing both newspaper and periodical publishers had in common with book publishers was that they were frequently self-made men in the Victorian tradition. John Cassell's father was a Manchester publican who died when John was only 13. George Routledge served an apprenticeship with a Carlisle bookseller before making his own way. Harmsworth's father was a barrister at the Irish Bar whose health broke down when Alfred was only 15, leaving him with responsibilities for his six brothers and three sisters. Cyril Pearson actually won his job as a journalist with *Tit-Bits* when it was offered as a prize in one of *Tit-Bits* famous competitions. With such backgrounds they were often Liberal in politics while at the same time deeply orthodox in their views on what constituted a proper order in society. If there was a difference it was that the book publishers promoted work articulating the attitudes and social values of the active middle class, while the newspaper barons sounded the innate conservatism of a mass audience that was being increasingly drawn from all levels of society. A conservatism that in its own turn was elaborated and reinforced by the published fictional work.

The major undertakings of the book publishers were firstly to control the price of books and secondly to publish new work that they considered to be of literary quality. The demise of the three-volume novel and its replacement by the one-volume six-shilling novel has already been mentioned, but not the practice of issuing sevenpenny and shilling reprints in cloth covers. Popular series such as 'Everyman's' and 'World's Classics' specialized in cheap reprints of world literature at one shilling a volume, though during the war prices were forced up to two shillings.

One of the liveliest of the new book publishers was T. Fisher Unwin who inaugurated the 'Pseudonym Library' of paper-backed books, priced eighteen pence, in order to promote new authors. The series, which published Olive Schreiner and W.B. Yeats among others, was certainly a notable success, but a notable success is not a popular success. Heinemann with his 'International Library' published cheap editions of writers such as Turgenev, Tolstoy and Maupassant, but again the venture was worthy rather than broadly appealing. Book publishers generally took themselves, and their role of promoting what they considered 'good' literature, seriously. The fictions of prewar writers such as Marie Corelli, Conan Doyle and Rider Haggard were essentially Victorian in tone, argument and moralizing: the reader is patronized.

The postwar period brought about a change. Publishers had to recognize, albeit unwillingly and often only partially, the power of the greatly democratized market, the influence of the new opportunities for access to books which created a readership who no longer wanted to be patronized. They wanted fictional reading that would show life as vivid and intense, but also under its ramifications essentially simple and above all shaped. Readers of popular fiction moved from being patronized by their betters to a state of being positioned within what Clive Bloom has called in his introduction the 'controlled collective and mass produced experience'.[21]

AUTHORS AND GENRES

At the turn of the century authors, for the most part, came from cultured, literate, middle-class families and they wrote in the genres inherited from their Victorian predecessors. The adventure writers A.E.W. Mason, Anthony Hope and Conan Doyle, for example, were all educated at public schools, while

Marie Corelli and Agatha Christie were privately educated. Two writers with less orthodox backgrounds were H.G. Wells and Edgar Wallace, and it is significant that both of them contributed to changes in popular genres.

Leaving aside Wells and Wallace for the moment the implications of the strongly middle-class background of many popular authors became clearly manifest in their books. Brought up in an atmosphere that encouraged and valued literacy they had had some education in the classics as well as familiarity, as readers, with the major Victorian writers. In this way they shared a common culture of images, ideas and references remote from the working class. Authors, being part of the class that considered itself the backbone of society, felt entitled to resent and criticize both the abuses and extravagance of the rich and what they saw as the irresponsibility of the poor. There was a tradition of critical discussion among them inherited from Dickens, Ruskin and Matthew Arnold, but in fact going much further back to roots in their class's puritan conscience. The result of this is that even in their lightest works there is a vein of moralizing and self-justification.

Possibly the most characteristically Victorian of all genres was that of religious fiction. Not only did it present a safe theocentric world view but it also used religion to validate the morality of the ruling class. By the end of the century of Darwin few were so naive as to accept religion unproblematically but at a time of ideological crisis it had its comforts. Marie Corelli[22] published her first book, *The Romance of Two Worlds*, in 1886; however, it was several books later, with the publication of *Barabbas*, in 1893, that she achieved her popular métier. By the beginning of the twentieth century she was the outstanding popular author whose books went into reprint after reprint. Nevertheless some ten years later, well before the war, her star had waned. It is not irrelevant that Marie Corelli was among the first to have her novels published in the new one-volume format at price six shillings. This price meant that the middle classes had even greater access to books than before, but does not in itself explain her popularity. Her books were an entertaining way of encountering questions of religious, moral and social behaviour; they were often vivid and spectacular scenes from all strata of life which appealed to the innately human but also serious propensities of her readers. Unfortunately she began to take herself, rather than the problems, too seriously and her self-dramatization as prophetess alienated many of her readers. The middle class, who were the basis of her popularity were changing. The market was changing and the author who had so fully expressed their mass sentiment became no longer relevant. Marie Corelli began to apply the rather overblown sentimental style, which had once been anchored in the very real social and religious concerns of middle-class life, to the sentimental creations of her own imagination. The later novels are an evasion of or even a collapse of moral responsibility in the face of a changing world.

And with a deep vow of fidelity sworn to his secret soul he sat alone, watching the shadows of evening steal over the landscape – falling, falling slowly, like a gradually descending curtain upon all visible things … Then silently bidding farewell to all his former dreams of happiness, he set himself to face 'the burden and hurt of the day' – that long, long day of life so difficult to live, when deprived of love.[23]

Any substance the man's emotions might have had, and in narrative terms he is a distant relative to Farmer Boldwood in Hardy's *Far from the Madding Crowd*, is vitiated by the insistent clichés, the 'deep vow', the 'secret soul' and the 'farewell to all his former dreams of happiness'. The failure to root the inner emotion in language is not compensated for by the repetitions nor by the banality and generality of the landscape in which he is sitting. The sentimental is rendered trite. The book was published in 1914 just as trite sentimentality under the guise of patriotism was about to receive its awful punishment in the slaughter of the war.

The genre of the religious novel as part of the mainstream of popular fiction was past: the consistency of popular readership was changing, and the sustaining beliefs in religion as a concomitant of class position was going. The genre did live on among a more specialized middle-class Catholic audience. Isabel C. Clarke, for example, produced a wide range of novels and short stories published in the Catholic press on various topics. Her 1915 book, *Whose Name is Legion*, opposes Catholicism to Spiritualism, a topic in vogue at the time. But its unambiguous treatment of the contraries is neither sufficiently stylized nor sufficiently generalized to appeal to a nonsectarian audience. Robert Hugh Benson, another Catholic author, had rather wider appeal with this same theme and other topics but by the early 1940s the religious novel as a popular genre had virtually disappeared. There remained only individual writers like Morris West, and the occasional spectacular blockbusters such as *The Cardinal* and *The Robe* to suggest what had once been staple fare of the reading public.

One middle-class myth that not only managed to persist in the novel but underwent a variety of metamorphoses in order to survive cultural change was the myth of the perfect Christian gentleman. This heroic protagonist, descended from the days of chivalry via Sir Philip Sidney, was brave, sensible, not too intelligent, courteous, usually of independent means and always of independent views. Often, like his authors, he was adventurous and, when necessary, prepared to back his own views against those of his class. He was the agent of a continuing middle-class vitality and the backbone of the adventure and action novel. The author Rider Haggard held official positions in South Africa; Kipling lived and worked in India, A.E.W. Mason, whose best-known adventure book was *The Four Feathers*, travelled extensively to odd corners of the world; and P.C. Wren, who wrote *Beau Geste*, literally 'knocked about' the world until serving for ten years as an assistant education officer in India. As with the melodramas of the previous age, exotic locations and the history of the Empire provided ideal locations within which the heroes could undergo their baptism of fire. The excitement of the troubles in Egypt and the Sudan, evoking recent memories of Gordon and Kitchener, provided the narrative spur for Mason's *The Four Feathers* published in 1902. Probably because passions had so recently been aroused and there had been controversy about the handling of events by the British Government, the hero's redemption from cowardice included not just adventure but also some real analysis of character. More usually the hero was unselfconsciously heroic like Richard Hannay in *The Thirty-Nine Steps* published in 1915.

In narrative terms the movement of the adventures follows remarkably similar lines. The hero, sometimes from a flaw in his own character but more usually from a spirit of adventure or an accident of history, is pushed into a time of trial. All he has to rely on are the solid virtues of his middle-class upbringing: resourcefulness, common sense, good breeding, morality and bravery. Of course, as with Robinson Crusoe, these innate virtues are supplemented by certain material advantages: money gained by somebody else's thrift, a sound practical education provided by caring parents and a remarkable physical constitution that owes itself, in part, to the material comforts he has hitherto enjoyed. These latter are taken for granted where the former are seen as attributes earnt by right living. Armed with a heroic character (and a full money belt) the hero undertakes his quest only to be captured by an insidious enemy. He escapes, largely through his own bravery and resourcefulness, which is supplemented by the stupidity of his foreign or lower-class jailors. Sometimes escape is effected by some lower-class captor who recognizes the hero's innate qualities and attaches himself loyally to him, thereby hoping to gain enhancement by symbiosis (a noble death is not infrequently his only reward). The stage is set for the grand confrontation in which the hero triumphs finally to return to his loved one/fiancée/daughter of the empire who has so eagerly but passively awaited his return.

The basic narrative structure allows of variations and repetitions but it is remarkable how stories as varied as *The Prisoner of Zenda* (1894), *The Four Feathers* (1902) and *The Thirty-Nine Steps* (1915) can be seen to fit the pattern. These tales are intended as tributes to individualism and materialism, but at every stage they are marked by unspoken assumptions about the heroes. The character of the heroes revealed under pressure of narrative events asserts virtues and capacities which are typically supportive of and reflect the image the middle class have of themselves. The stories are escapist not so much in the improbable adventure they portray but in the unquestioning and unreflective stance they take in relation to the question, what does it mean to be a good and heroic human being? They are evasive in the unambiguous emotions they espouse. For Rider Haggard, love, loyalty and fidelity are absolutes. It is assumed that, like enmity or curiosity, they are essentially right, and whatever actions are taken in their furtherance are validated by the situation; there is no sense in which one's cause or motives need be questioned.

Just as in their narratives and characters the stories evaded present realities to affirm middle-class ideals, so too in their settings they avoided the problematic locations of urbanization and mass production. The plots usually unfolded in exotic, usually imperial, locations that provided, as the frontier did in America, a land of opportunity. A mythic territory free of contemporary neuroses, which held out an optimistic future for those adventurous and willing enough to seize the occasion.

Interestingly , even as the comforts of the religious novel were in decline there grew out of the adventure novel a new genre that was to be capable of expressing much of the unease of the century, the spy novel. In these stories the site of the action is not elsewhere but here and now. It is the covert battleground between industrial rivals, prior to the war usually Britain and Germany. The individual struggles against the shadowy espionage network of the enemy that threatens to suffocate his country. But his very condition of individual awareness of threat places him in an ambiguous position with regard to his own side, who collectively fail to recognize the threat. Le Queux, who with Erskine Childers virtually founded the genre, might have had a bestseller with *Spies of the Kaiser* (1909) which he claimed was based on fact, but neither government nor people took him seriously. The spy was set to be the individual in the shadows, neglected by his own side and pursued by the enemy, if not pursued by both sides.

If the adventure story was essentially masculine reading then the detective story could claim readers of both sexes. In detective fiction the prime mover is not the hero but the narrative event: a crime. This allows for a greater variety of protagonists and it even legitimizes the use of women and foreigners as well as eccentrics. Sherlock Holmes, Mason's Inspector Hanaud, Chesterton's Father Brown, Miss Marple and Hercule Poirot are all tributes to the diversity of characters who can be allowed to take centre stage. What these stories assumed is that there is consensus as to what is a crime and that the solution of the problem it poses lies between the twin poles of reason and intuition. Agatha Christie's detectives typify the extremes, Poirot with his 'little grey cells' and Miss Marple with her marvellously attuned intuition.

The rise of the modern detective story is attributed to Wilkie Collins, but the first great detective was Sherlock Holmes , who first appeared in the *Strand Magazine* in 1893. He died in 1894 in the famous struggle with Moriarty when both plunged to their deaths at the Reichenbach Falls, but he returned by popular demand in 1903. Holmes's great capacity lay in his intelligence and the advances in science which made deduction possible. Even between his demise and resuscitation progress had been made, when a satisfactory system of finger-printing was introduced in 1901. Thus the detective story satisfied the growing public confidence that problems could be solved and order could be restored even after the aberration of crime.

If the hero justified middle-class personal values, the detective story justified their sense that society could be restored to order even after such a serious disruption as crime. It is interesting that the crime in question is persistently murder. Murder was unequivocally the ultimate crime in that it represented the destruction of individualism. Sherlock Holmes, prior to the First World War, represents the pyrotechnic displays of an unusual and singular intelligence; Agatha Christie's books, starting with the *Mysterious Affair at Styles* in 1920, ushered in the classic period of detective fiction and represented the attempt of a beleaguered class to defend the order of their society.

Like Marie Corelli, Agatha Christie's original ambitions were in the direction of music. But her first book, in spite of having to be submitted to a number of publishers, was so successful that it set her on the path of authorship which was to be, by her death in 1976, so fruitful that her total sales could not be estimated. The crime sets both her detective and her reader a puzzle. The setting is upper-middle-class life, which provides a locale cut off from the real social life of the time. It is never-never land of privilege which is above question. There is very little description, very little character, only dialogue. The crime disturbs the even flow of life, and its solution restores order. The sense of isolation is heightened by events frequently taking place in a country house; a remove completed by the fact that the crime is not solved by the legitimate forces of law and order but by a private individual. Typically, the police force is peopled by lower-class incompetents, lacking both in manners and intelligence, the latter excusable, just, but the former demonstrating the deficiencies of society at large. The arrival at a solution is due to the ingenuity, persistence and peculiar talents of the protagonist. In the detection fiction of the twenties it is the cunning of nonprofessional sleuths which defeats the deviousness of the criminals. Crime breaks ranks, it is a deviation from the norm. Solution brings what has been concealed into the open to restore order to the group – in Agatha Christie's case a privileged and exclusive group.

In the success and popularity of her books we see the triumph of plot over character and sensation over reflection. The 'consumer generation' had either arrived or been created. The main types of fiction, such as the detective story, the domestic or intimate novel and the adventure, sensational and religious novel, had been established in the eighteenth or nineteenth century by middle-class writers. New genres were usually the creation of authors who fell outside the prevailing class. Spy fiction came from Erskine Childers, who was an Irish revolutionary, and William Tufnell Le Queux, who with his

French father, English mother and cosmopolitan background and all his popularity as a novelist was never really accepted by the establishment. Similarly both H.G. Wells and Edgar Wallace came from backgrounds each in their own way marginalized by society.

Wells was the son of a gardener who rose to the lower-middle classes by dint of professional cricket and shopkeeping. The shop failed and a broken leg destroyed his cricket, resulting in serious family poverty. His son Herbert George tried various careers but his real concern was writing. As a result of a fascination with science he wrote before 1900 a number of scientific romances that caught the public mood of interest in the nature of science. But his really popular books were the humorous accounts of lower-middle-class life *Kipps* (1905), *Tono-Bungay* (1909) and *The History of Mr Polly* (1910). Like Harms-worth and Wallace, Wells earned a good living from journalism, but like many self-taught men of poor background he overestimated the power of rational thought to change society. In the twenties his nonfiction books, such as an *Outline of History* (1920), achieved worldwide sales , but his reformist zeal prevented him from achieving all that he had hoped through his ideas. In a moment of self-realization he once said his epitaph would be 'He was clever but not clever enough' – an anonymous reviewer wrote of him, he could have been a comic writer to rival Dickens if he had stuck to fictions of lower-middle-class life.

But Wells as a popular author cannot be quite so easily dismissed. His scientific romances brought into being a series of images that have been reworked for mass audiences on radio, film and television, particularly *The Invisible Man* (1897), *The Time Machine* (1895) and *War of the Worlds* (1898). It is not really the books themselves that express what I have defined as the popular fiction relationship but *images from the books* that have struck popular chords. This ability to invoke powerful images was not restricted to his fiction, part of his *Outline of History* for example inspired William Golding in the writing of *The Inheritors*. Usually it is characters, for example Hamlet and Mr Pickwick, who transcend their sources, but in Wells it is the narrative movement itself. What he succeeded in doing was updating age-old story motifs, such as Gyges' ring, making the narrative concept live in the scientific age. It is the story process rather than the exploration of character under pressure that makes them inspirational for other tellers of tales.

Edgar Wallace had no pretensions about teaching society. An illegitimate child born in 1875 he was brought up in the family of a Billingsgate fish porter; at 11 he sold newspapers, at 18 enlisted and served in South Africa. He became a correspondent for both Reuter's and the *Daily Mail* and in 1905 published the *Four Just Men*. He wrote a great many novels but it was not until the twenties with *The Crimson Circle* (1922), *The Green Archer* (1923) and his play

The Ringer (1926) that sales moved from tens of thousands to hundreds of thousands.

Part of the reason for his phenomenal success in the twenties, as distinct from modest success before the war, lay in the accomplishment of those changes in the market previously only foreshadowed. As books became cheaper and more accessible, their ability to generate significant profits meant that the book trade progressively became part of the very centre of the capitalist economy. The mass market eschewed the moral and social concerns that middle-class entrepreneurial publishers still offered to their circle of patrons.[24] Instead sensational incident, graphic narrative and stereotypes rather than characters were offered to a mass readership. Those books that displayed these characteristics and could be reprinted cheaply began to dominate the market. At the Schoolboys' Exhibition of 1926 the favourites were found to be Ballantyne, Henty, Conan Doyle, Rider Haggard, Verne, Marryat, Kipling, Wallace and Wodehouse. Youngsters of all classes confident in their literacy were being turned into a new plural readership. Furthermore where books could be tied to other media products this increased their salability. In the 1920s Woolworths launched their 'Readers' Library' at sixpence a volume. As unlikely a book as *Metropolis* by Thea von Harbou had three reprints in 1927 alone amounting to a quarter of a million copies. The editor's note makes clear, 'She is responsible for the scenario of the film version of her novel, and actively assisted her talented husband, Fritz Lang, in its production.'[25] Books were no longer books but part of a product range.

The key to Wallace's success in turning books into products lay in the endless variety and originality of his narratives. Although the milieu is often middle-class his heroes appear classless: Richard Alford in *The Black Abbot* (1926) is the younger son with apparently no hope of the Chelford title, and only his own hard work and ability to rely on. In *The Squeaker* (1927), set among criminal classes, John Leslie Barrabal is frequently referred to as a 'gentleman' even though he is classless in origin and a chief inspector. However complex his narratives become and however many tricks of plot are exploited, there is an underlying simplicity of goal which readers are never allowed to forget. There is consistent sensation in the stories and although disguises and tricks frequently support the narrative line the pace never allows readers to feel they have been cheated. The characters may be stereotypes but they run a gamut of variations that are rooted in the realities of society, a trick learnt no doubt from journalism, so that attention never flags. Furthermore Wallace, like Wells, created in King Kong a modern version of Beauty and the Beast that lives beyond the confines of its representational form.

In the final section of this essay I am going to look more closely at two novels – one by Marie Corelli, *Holy Orders* (1908), and the other, *The Black Abbot* (1926) by Edgar Wallace – as examples of the change that took place

93

between the middle-class popular fiction of the early part of the century and the mass-market popular fiction of the twenties.

CASE STUDIES

In the writings of Marie Corelli and Edgar Wallace respectively we can see something of the changes in popular fiction that occurred during the early years of this century. At the beginning popular fiction was essentially a consumer-led product, its marketing demanding what social psychologists call 'high involvement' on the part of the purchasers. The change-over to mass marketing was a change to a producer-led product, entailing 'low involvement' on the part of buyers.

'The Methuen list had soon attracted to itself some of the best selling writers of the day ... and the outseller of them all, Marie Corelli'.[26] *Holy Orders* came at a time when her popularity was just beginning to wane; even so two editions were brought out in the first month of publication. There were several reasons for the book's success; among others, it was in the approved six-shilling format. But more important was her status as an author with an excellent record in giving her middle-class readers what they wanted. Her books were seen as relevant, the discussions provocative and having serious implications for readers, in other words a high involvement product. The novel, through the character of Richard Everton, newly appointed vicar of the Cotswold village Shadbrook, investigates the role and function of religion. For the middle class the doubts about God consequent on Darwin and scientific rationalism had created a void at the heart of one of their most cherished institutions, namely religion. This led to a need for reassessment of the divine calling in everyday life.

In private life Everton is married to the pretty but empty-headed Azalea; there is tension between his duty as a minister and his natural desire to please his wife. In the village, drink is the curse of his poor parishioners, represented by Dan Kiernan. Here the problem is knowing how far it is right for him to interfere in the lives of his flock, and the realization that even good actions can have bad effects. Then there is the question of ambition, his own ambition to be recognized as a good man of God – not merely to do good works, but to be seen and praised for good works. Finally there is sexuality, the spontaneous and natural sensuality of Jacynth, the prettiest girl in the village, who in the freedom and wildness of her upbringing represents the 'new woman'.

In these problems we have a microcosm of the anxieties that beset the middle class. Drunkenness, particularly among the numberless shadows of the poor, suggested sudden and violent forces that could disturb the increasingly fragile stability of their lives. Ambition was the threat of the individual to break ranks, to throw off the group loyalty that was the bulwark against a changing world. And finally sexuality, the 'dark angel' capable of destroying the patient accumulation of a lifetime. Against all this tide of disaster stands the figure of Parson Everton.

The narrative is melodrama. Everton by trying to dissuade Kiernan from drink invokes the hostility of both Kiernan and Minchin, the hypocritical brewer. The latter gives Kiernan a job with free drink and freedom to shoot rabbits on his land. Out hunting, Kiernan happens on Azalea and, in trying to frighten her, accidentally kills her. In an excellent scene, reminiscent of Bill Sykes's flight after killing Nancy, he escapes to London, only to be killed by Jacynth's car. For Jacynth village life had proved too restrictive so she had gone to London. After a brief career as a revue artiste she had married a millionaire Jewish press baron. His character gave Corelli the opportunity to display that blatant anti-semitism and hostility to the penny press[27] that were part of a deeply ingrained middle-class system of prejudices.

But what affords the reader a chance to engage these problems is the style of presentation. The story moves slowly, punctuated mainly by duologues. These, peopled by a limited number of characters, allow the reader to grasp easily the two sides presented. They even invite partisan readers to identify with one of the speakers, so exercising their interest in both religious and social controversies. Another stylistic feature is the lengthy extracts from Everton's sermons, which will have reminded readers of the collections of sermons and spiritual exhortations that played a significant part in their reading lives.

In proposing that Corelli's book was a high involvement experience for her readers I have suggested, first, that it dealt with problems of immediate significance and, secondly, that the style is an invitation to thought and argument. The final condition for high involvement is that the book should have implications for its readers, even affecting their self image. To some extent this is done in relation to various issues, so the role of wife is scrutinized in the person of Azalea, but the big question is 'where is God?'

Jacynth's death is a spectacular scene of great intensity which calls into question the religious convictions thought to underwrite the intentions of the book. Jacynth takes a trip in a hot air balloon with the drunken poet Claude Ferrers; when he dies, of a heart attack, she is left floating among the clouds. Her flight becomes a metaphor for her life and a study of her evolving relationship with God.

> 'There go the bells of Shadbrook Church!' she murmured – 'Make haste,
> Dan! I want you to see me there in my best frock. Don't be late. We must
> pretend to be good, you know. It's so easy to deceive Parson Everton! Come,
> come! It's Communion Sunday!'
>
> Here suddenly drawing herself up to her full height, she flashed her brilliant
> jewel eyes in the golden face of the sun.
> 'Yes, Parson Everton' – she said, in gentle accents – 'I know my lesson! I
> believe in God the Father Almighty, Maker of heaven and earth!'
> With that she folded her hands together, and resting them on the edge of the
> car looked placidly on at the growing splendour of the day.
> And when noon came both sun and sky were clear of anything more strange
> than the sea-birds flying across the roughening waves, and diving like winged
> sunbeams among the rising and falling crests of foam.[28]

Jacynth is a child of nature but from this extract we see she is also a child of
religion. Three alternatives emerge. Is she still the wild and natural creature
deceiving Everton? Has she, in the face of death, come to realize the truth of
religion? Is religion simply a poetic form whose true meaning lies in its
affirmation that God is life? The context makes it unlikely that she is simply
deceiving Everton, the gentleness of speech suggests real feeling, but feeling
for the person of the Church does not answer the question of its relationship
with God. The idea of a death-balloon affirmation of faith in God through
the Church would have been the sentimental choice of many of her readers.
But we are left with the third possibility, that having recited her creed, that
is performed her religious rituals, she returns to nature, identifying with 'the
growing splendour of the day'.

The translation of the implications into an answer is left with readers, who
will argue till bed-time, something nobody ever did with an Edgar Wallace,
though they may often have read him till morning. The first difference one
notices between a Marie Corelli and an Edgar Wallace is the books themselves.
Although book jackets were introduced in 1906 the first edition of *Holy Orders*
does not have one, it is on thick paper and is over five hundred pages long.
Edgar Wallace comes in smaller format comparable with today's paperbacks,
on cheap paper and less than half the length.

What Wallace does in his novels is set up a series of expectations and then
use the plot to delay their inevitable final resolution. In that way untidy
characterization and unlikely turns of events are rendered relatively insignificant because we have before us all the time the expectation of a solution. *The
Black Abbot* is set in the country seat of the Chelfords; Harry Alford is the
eighteenth Earl and Richard, his younger brother, runs the family estates. The
problems are, first, there is a ghostly figure called the Black Abbot haunting
the grounds and frightening the servants. Second, the Earl is searching
obsessively for the long lost Treasure of the Chelfords which reputedly consists
of gold and an elixir of life. Third, the Earl is engaged to Leslie Gine, the sister

of a solicitor who lives locally, and while the Earl himself appears thoroughly indifferent towards her, brother Richard obviously is not.

Readers, being too sensible to believe in ghosts, want to know who the Black Abbot is, they want the treasure found and they want Leslie to end up with Richard. And that, in spite of many vicissitudes of plot and the confusions of an extensive gallery of characters is just what they get. But what values underlie the book to make it so appealing to a vast audience?

Although the setting is ostensibly aristocratic there is no sense of any class-based superiority. Nearly all the characters are treated with a singular respect. For example, middle-class writers were persistently guilty of treating the official police as dunderheads – a combination of an inherited tendency to treat them as servants and resentment against them that was the result of the spread of the motor car! The spread of cars meant that for the first time the upper-middle classes were potentially criminalized in their everyday conduct (i.e. for speeding) in a way that they had never been before. To Wallace's credit a policeman, such as John Leslie Barrabal in *The Squeaker*, was as likely to be a hero as any other character. In *The Black Abbot*, detective-sergeant Puttler may look remarkably like a monkey but he is knowledgeable, cultured and behaves with remarkable sang froid whatever his situation.

Characters in Wallace seem to earn approval for the exercise of energy and ingenuity. Richard is approved of because he works to preserve the estate of his forbears without any hope of personal benefit. At the end of the book we learn that he is the Black Abbot, a role he played to keep his brother in the house during his progressively more frequent attacks of insanity. We learn also that the brother was bound to die in the near future anyway. It never occurs to the reader to apply a retrospective cynicism to his apparently selfless work for the estate that he was always certain to inherit.

Wallace's characters are defined by stereotypical patterns of virtue and vice. If 'energy' and 'ingenuity' are the virtues, then set against them 'cupidity or folly' are the vices. London and New York 'were filled with rich men who had founded their houses upon the cupidity or folly of men who were now almost penniless'.[29] It did not matter whether characters came from the aristocracy, the underworld or the Empire, their basic contribution lay in the colourfulness of their eccentricities and their simplicity of characterization. This lack of complexity means that readers have no difficulty in recognizing the moral function of any given character and that any identification with protagonists occurs purely at a naive wish-fulfilment level. It is a characteristic of low involvement that people 'appear to be affected by simple acceptance and rejection cues [in the story] and are less affected by argument quality'.[30]

In fact the characters have nothing to do with the manipulation of the plot, which is simply a mechanical working out of the puzzles set in motion. It just does not matter that much who the Black Abbot is so long as the revelation creates a sensation. In this way the real human concerns that characters might address are subservient to the needs of plot. It is as if real world events are no longer the genuine expression of people but the consequence of a massive reduction in individuality. The author exercises his skill in a play of nonsignificant meanings, characters are simply local colour, like the description of the abbey ruins or Fossaway Manor, and they neither inform nor interact with the movement of the story. There is no attempt to portray even stereotypes of serious concerns, rather there is sensation and the unravelling of puzzles, the happy conviction that the right man will get the right girl. As readers we are finally placed as the passive observers of a fascinating divertissement of nonsignificances. The end of *The Black Abbot* reads:

> 'There are a few minor trials and troubles for us, Leslie dear,' he said 'but when those are all over and everything is settled we will go abroad for a year and forget about these ghastly days and nights!' She took his hand between her two palms.[31]

. . . just as we might take in our hands another Edgar Wallace.

NOTES

1. Dominic Strirati, 'Postmodernism and Popular Culture', in *Sociology Review*, vol. 1 no. 4, April 1992, p. 2.
2. John M. Ellis, *The Theory of Literary Criticism: A Logical Analysis* (Berkeley, 1974).
3. Antony Easthope, *Literary into Cultural Studies* (London, 1991), pp. 3–61.
4. Ibid., p. 76.
5. Paul Thompson, *The Edwardians: The Remaking of British Society* (London: 1984), p. 1.
6. R. C. Terry, *Victorian Popular Fiction 1860–1880* (London, 1983), p. 7.
7. Ibid., p. 5.
8. John Burnett, *Useful Toil* (Harmondsworth, 1977).
9. Melvyn Bragg, *Speak for England* (London, 1976), p. 46.
10. Easthope, p. 75.
11. Thompson. Gives extracts from the oral evidence of a number of informants. For this point see Fred Mills, pp. 140–2.
12. Barrie Penrose and Simon Freeman, *Conspiracy of Silence* (London, 1987), p. 82.
13. John A. Lester, quoted in J. A. V. Chapple, *Documentary and Imaginative Literature 1880–1920* (London, 1970), p. 30.
14. Theodor W. Adorno, 'Culture Industry Reconsidered', in Bob Ashley, *The Study of Popular Fiction: A Source Book* (London, 1989), p. 53.
15. Victor E. Neuburg, *Popular Literature: A History and Guide* (Harmondsworth, 1977), p. 198.

16. Reginald Pound and Geoffrey Harmsworth, *Northcliffe* (London, 1959), p. 160.
17. Cynthia L. White, *Women's Magazines 1693–1968* (London, 1970), p. 60.
18. Phillip Knightley, *The Second Oldest Profession* (London, 1987), p. 16.
19. Quoted in White, p. 87.
20. J. Haslam, quoted in Neuburg, p. 213–14.
21. Clive Bloom, cf. Introduction, p. 9.
22. Marie Corelli, novelist, pen name of Mary Mackay, born London 1855, illegitimate daughter of Charles Mackay, poet and journalist who in 1861 married her mother.
23. Marie Corelli, *Innocent: Her Fancy and his Fact* (London, 1914), p. 238.
24. Of course established publishers continued in business with their traditional markets alongside the new mass market. They were supported by the strength of their lists and the occasional bestseller that came their way, for example Hodder and Stoughton with A.S.M. Hutchinson's *If Winter Comes* (1921), a novel of the war period that went to forty-three editions by 1923.
25. Editor's note to *Metropolis* by Thea von Harbou (London, 1927).
26. Maureen Duffy, *A Thousand Capricious Chances: A History of the Methuen List 1889–1989* (London, 1989), p. 7.
27. Thompson. Grace Fulford records that her father kept the book-case locked and never allowed his children even to look at a newspaper.
28. Marie Corelli, *Holy Orders* (London, 1908), p. 498.
29. Edgar Wallace, *The Black Abbot* (London, 1950), p. 200.
30. Richard Petty, John Cacioppo and David Schumann, 'Central and Peripheral Roots to Advertising Effectiveness: The Moderating Role of Involvement', *Journal of Consumer Research*, 10, 1983, p. 137.
31. Wallace, p. 254.

CHAPTER FOUR
Theatre: Roots of the New

Michael Woolf

> The modern is not like the reassuring landscape of the past, open and invadable everywhere. It is at once more immediate and more obscure: a blur of book titles, a mood of impatience with anachronism, a diffuse feeling of difference.[1]

Any study of culture and society between the years 1900 and 1929 is obliged to confront the presence of the First World War as the central fact of historical experience. An apocalyptic mode of thought became inevitable and the event shaped and distorted forms of perception as if all events led towards the cataclysm and all followed from it. In the theatre at this time, in contrast, the war seems to have passed across the stage making little impact outside a handful of plays. The history of theatre in this time is curiously untouched by the tragedy of war and its cosmic reverberations, strangely untroubled and persistently faithful to the patterns of the past and the imperatives of commerce.

In another and similar vein, this period appears to have a symmetry formed by the death of Queen Victoria in 1901 through the landmark of the war to end, as if with a natural momentum, in the Depression; as if history were crafted by some inexpert and melodramatic hand progressing inexorably from one death through many deaths to disaster. That view of history, for all its seductive attraction to the literary critic bred on the mechanics of fiction, distorts the reality of culture. The whole is further complicated by the romantic lens through which the 1920s is so frequently perceived: as a kind of gorgeous bubble framed by tragedy.

The object of this essay is to explore the shapes of theatrical experience and to assess their relationship with the culture in terms of their impact upon it and the degree to which they embody it. Theatre, like other forms of artistic endeavour, was engaged in a form of dialogue with new forces of social change. The first and probably most crucial factor in any discussion of this period is the reality of that change. This view must recognize the historical landmarks while simultaneously perceiving their essential untidiness and refusal to conform to some plot of history. The period is without neat beginnings or tidy ends and is characterized by a sense of nostalgia for the past and an uneasy relationship with the future. The emergence of a new kind of collectivism inevitably created both nervous dystopias and, simultaneously, impulse towards the reinvention of history in elegiac forms. Out of such tensions came, for example, the Edenic fiction of 'Edwardian England' as a kind of lost island of serenity. Inevitably, the notion of what constitutes the 'modern' was a key factor in the culture of the times and this involves both retrospective and futuristic perspectives.

It is necessary, however, to recognize the fact that theatre was the least innovative literary medium in these years. This was governed in part by the limitations of commerce and the conservatism of theatrical management. Of all art forms, the theatre is, of course, the most dependent on partnership between creativity and commerce. The control of the Lord Chamberlain as censor also acted as a restraining hand on the development of new forms and served, at times, to stifle impulses towards experimentation. The major impact of modernity in the British theatre does not really come until the 1950s. In the novel or in poetry (in Joyce and T.S. Eliot, for example) there exist major technical innovators self-consciously and determinedly creating the new by signalling separation from the forms of the past. In the theatre, there is no comparable figure. George Bernard Shaw's work marked a transition from Victorian to modern theatre, but it is expressed in terms of the material and the ideas contained within it, not in any formal innovation or radical departure from traditional techniques. The key figures in theatre in the period were, from a current perspective, largely minor figures with the exception of George Bernard Shaw.

None of this should suggest that the theatre was somehow a static form, however. In the first place, the status of theatre as an art form was being subtly changed by the relatively new process of publishing contemporary dramas. Prior to 1900 this had been quite a rare occurrence, but throughout the first three decades of this century the custom grew and influenced the development of dramatic theory and criticism. There existed a forum and a means for the critic to go beyond the newspaper or journal review and, more significantly, it enabled the writer to create a context for his plays outside of their performance. This had the most impact, quite clearly, on the work of Shaw. Perhaps the most startling example in this period is found in Shaw's *Androcles and the Lion: An Old Fable Renovated* (1914) where the Preface is about four times as long as the play itself. These extensive prefaces create, in a sense, an alternative existence for plays explicitly created to be experienced both inside and outside of the theatre.

It would also be misleading not to recognize the impact of European modernism in creating a climate for change. Ibsen, Strindberg and Chekhov were all known figures of increasing significance. In addition to that influence, while the great actor-managers were in decline, there were an emerging number of writer-directors gaining the kind of power that in later years would create the environment for the emergence of a Joan Littlewood. At an extreme end of this process was the enigmatic figure of Edward Gordon Craig whose career straddled the development of modern theatre. His mother was Ellen Terry and his lover Isadora Duncan. He lived until 1966 and saw the emergence of a theatre unrecognizable from that in which he grew. His strongest impact was, however, in the years between 1900 and 1920 when he aimed, under the influence of European culture, 'to bring a new kind of Impressionism into the theatre'.[2]

Another key figure in the growth of a modern theatre was Harley Granville-Barker. His major impact is less in his plays which will be discussed later than in his contribution to the development of the Royal Court Theatre. Popularly known as The Court, the theatre opened in 1904 and speedily became the focus for an emerging social realism as well as a location in which new drama might be performed. Under the manager J.E. Vedrenne, The Court became a crucial breeding ground for the new: a status it still retains.

The Court had several elements that came together to ensure its significance in the cultural history of modern theatre. In the first place, its location was central enough in London without being part of the West End theatre scene. It signalled a cultural as well as physical separation from mainstream commercial theatre. It also helped develop and restore a mode of playing that had been largely lost through the nineteenth century. It encouraged an ensemble approach to acting rather than relying upon the star system. All in all, with Granville-Barker's influence on the direction of the theatre, it created a place that became associated with producing plays by young playwrights and creating a platform for new material. Galsworthy's career was greatly assisted by the existence of the Court and Shaw's reputation was built there. In fact, in the first three seasons at The Court there were 988 performances. Seven hundred and one of those were of plays by Shaw.

The first decade of the century was indeed a time of great theatrical expansion. Between 1901 and 1906 a large number of new West End theatres opened including the Scala, the New Gaiety, the New Theatre, the Aldwych and the Apollo. The expansion of theatre building was in fact only halted by the war. As well as the growth of the West End, provincial theatres expanded significantly in the period. This created interesting dynamics. In the first place, the political significance of theatre began to be recognized in a growing number of People's Theatres directed to working-class groups. This was exemplified by the Yiddish People's Theatre in Shoreditch, east London.

The most important political dimension to theatrical development in this period was undoubtedly the growth of a nationalist theatre. The Glasgow

Repertory Theatre signalled the re-emergence of a Scottish nationalist theatre while in Dublin, the Abbey Theatre opened in the same year as the Court, 1904. The growth of regional culture and the nationalistic expression of that culture is characterized by the Abbey. Its impact upon the development of Irish nationalist feeling is well recorded but, in this context, it exemplifies and enforces the search for an alternative kind of theatre. The plays themselves may have, for the most part, maintained much of the conventional forms but the structure of theatre illustrates the pursuit of difference.

This search is further illustrated by pressure to establish a National Theatre led by Granville-Barker, William Archer and Arthur Jones. Jones made the case in a lecture in March 1904 to The Royal Institute. He argued the need for a National Theatre on several key grounds. He saw the need to separate drama from popular amusement, a process already begun by the publication of new plays. He wanted a theatre that would bring drama into line with the other arts as serious artistic endeavour. His other claims were for a theatre that would address real issues and actual moral problems. Most interestingly he also raised the issue of professionalization expressed by his desire to reward dramatists properly and to train the acting profession in a systematic fashion. All of this added up to a new sense of theatre as serious cultural production; and the need to recognize that seriousness of purpose in the formation of alternative locations and structures.

William Archer and Granville-Barker took this further in their publication of 1907, *A National Theatre: Scheme and Estimates*, in which they recognize the need for endowment or public support if there was to be a viable alternative to the conventional West End theatre. This campaign, in relation to the other campaign against the role of the Lord Chamberlain as censor, and in association with the growth of national and regional theatres, added up to a landscape of change which would in time create structures and institutions amenable to artistic development. James Woodfield summarizes this environment with particular clarity:

> The campaign to establish new modes of drama was not only against
> commercial interest, but also against the prejudices and taboos of a puritanical,
> middle-class society that was eminently satisfied with its own morality and mode
> of living, and suspicious of, or openly hostile to, innovations or new ideas,
> which it considered subversive.[3]

It is, then, possible to recognize a whole range of theatrical forms in the first three decades of the twentieth century some in decline and some emerging to form the basis of a developing modern theatre. In terminal decline was the theatre of the actor-manager exemplified by Herbert Beerbohm Tree at His Majesty's or by Charles Wyndham. This great age was over by 1914 and this reflected the emergence of new styles of acting and the growth of suburban and provincial theatres of which The Court and the Abbey are still the most significant. The strength of conventional theatre remained with the London West End and was enforced by the development of West End repertory companies such as Drury Lane. Provincial repertory theatres abounded and their work was enforced by the existence of any number of travelling companies.

Another theatrical form in some decline was music-hall. It is though too easy to prematurely write off the music-hall. In 1912, for example, the Royal Command Performance was composed substantially of music-hall performers. Harry Lauder, Vesta Tilley, George Robey and Little Tich appeared on the bill. The great performers of the music-hall are, however, in decline in the period. Marie Lloyd, for example, died in 1922 but the remaining influence of music-hall helped to create a form of theatrical experience that grew in popularity throughout the period: the musical revue. Several influences came together in this form, most notably that of European, particularly French, cabaret. The relationship to musical comedy was also clear. The combination of music-hall 'variety' with the sophistication of cabaret led to a form of entertainment that made major impact throughout the period. C.B. Cochran became an important figure with productions like *Odds and Ends* (1914) and *Wake Up and Dream* (1929).

Review reflects a number of trends. It is built on the relative prosperity of the 1920s, middle-class disposable income was available and could be spent on entertainment, and is nurtured upon the old tradition of variety; a theatrical performance that is built out of a combination of disparate elements. Audience pleasure is gained through shifting of focus from one self-contained part to another. It is an ephemeral form of theatre in contrast to the notion of theatre as published literary art. Above all, review contained many of the new attitudes toward sexuality and sexual relations that grew out of postwar society. Ivor Novello and, most significantly, Noël Coward built popular careers around this form.

The period is indeed marked by changing nature of attitudes towards sex and sexuality and this, inevitably, creates new (and shocking) subject matter for plays. In the social fabric of British society, there were profound challenges to the status quo in this area. The activities of the Rational Dress League combined with the battle for women's suffrage created an environment in which the so-called 'new woman' could emerge assisted, in no small part, by the pioneering work in the field of contraception of Marie Stopes. Towards the end of the 1920s, the transformation from Edwardian woman is dramatic and neatly symbolized by the Charleston:

> By 1927 a dance called the Charleston had come into vogue, the distinctive feature in which was a side-kick from the knees. Ladies' dresses were now worn short; the knees could be seen beneath an outdoor dress for the first time in civilized history. Hail emancipation! It was not unladylike to smoke, work for money, drink in public bars — cocktails were in fashion — or cast one's vote.[4]

This changing status of woman impacted on theatre in several ways. A succession of characters emerge with some or other of the characteristics of 'new women', most notably in the work of Coward and Maugham. As the following discussions illustrate, they exploit the comic and farcical potential of this transformation, for the most part, but also encapsulate the bewilderment or confusion of men when confronted with this domestic version of the modern. All in all, the shifting pattern of gender behaviour is a recurrent theatrical theme and the largely comic treatment masks a considerable unease in the perception of a transformed sexual reality.

There are, of course, other key events that signal the increasing momentum of change in the century. 1901 saw the opening of the first exhibition by Picasso and within two years the Wright brothers had begun a revolution in human mobility. In the same period a form of public entertainment was emerging that would have a huge impact on theatre. The history of movies from beginning to the first talkie more or less corresponds to the first three decades of the century: *The Jazz Singer* appeared in 1927. In his revisions of *Pygmalion*, Shaw recognized the potential of the movies and added scenes specifically with the possibility of a cinema production in mind.

These decades are then clearly marked by a sense of change and the creation of a landscape from which a changing culture will emerge. The roots of the new are settled even if, in the theatre, these roots have yet to grow many new branches.

GEORGE BERNARD SHAW: A CAREER FOR THESE TIMES

The figure of Shaw is inevitably central to this discussion and it is instructive to begin by considering the two plays that broadly cover the period: *Major Barbara* (1905) and *The Apple Cart* (1929). The key to *Major Barbara* is the notion that ethics are situational rather than absolute. The moral debates that run through Shaw's plays help define the period as one marked by shifting values and uncertainty. Undershaft is a typical Shaw figure in that he embodies the power of the individual and an approach to morality that is both individualistic and conscious of change:

> Well, you have made for yourself something that you call a morality or a religion or what not. It doesnt fit the facts. Well, scrap it. Scrap it and get one that does fit. That is what is wrong with the world at present. It scraps its obsolete steam engines and dynamos; but it wont scrap its old prejudices and its old moralities and its old religions and its old political constitutions!.[5]*

---

*Quotations from Shaw spelled as original

His view, in typical Shaw fashion, confronts Barbara's moral absolutism and in that lies whatever dramatic confrontation the play has. Barbara's moment of epiphany embodies the defeat of absolutism, the triumph of situational morality and the redundancy of middle-class morality:

> There is no wicked side: life is all one. And I never wanted to shirk my share in whatever evil must be endured, whether it be sin or suffering. I wish I could cure you of middle-class ideas ... [6]

There is certainly something of a Nietzsche-type view in these *Übermensch* figures in Shaw's plays who embody an alternative view of morality and exist outside of normal values as represented by the play's conventional figures. There is also though an implicit sense of moral and political uncertainty that defines the play's modernity.

The play offers, for example, a sceptical view of Salvation Army philanthropy and works with a most audacious duality. The arms manufacturer is set in confrontation with the Salvation Army, experience and cynicism confront innocence and faith and are found to be both stronger and more effective in terms of achieving desirable social objectives. The ironic triumph of Undershaft's view of the world reflects an environment in flux where the old ethics are becoming redundant without being replaced by any alternative form of moral structure. Undershaft's *realpolitik* is, in fact, a bleak projection of an amoral world governed by the needs of the arms trade rather than by any democratic will. If Lady Britomart represents the fading bastion of British aristocracy and Barbara represents the defeat of religious zeal, Undershaft embodies a conspiracy theory of international government. He is a representative of the military complex that is seen as governing the future of the world:

> The government of your country! *I* am the government of your country: I, and Lazarus. Do you suppose that you and half a dozen amateurs like you, sitting in a row in that foolish gabble shop, can govern Undershaft and Lazarus? No, my friend: you will do what pays us. You will make war when it suits us, and keep peace when it doesnt. [7]

In addition to some ideological weaknesses, the problem with the play, and with much of Shaw, is that it is essentially a debate rather than drama. It is in essence a closet drama designed to be read rather than a theatrical experience. The extensive prefaces to the plays almost suggest Shaw's recognition of that fact.

The Apple Cart (1929) sets up a confrontation in a political environment and Shaw uses the clash between King Magnus and Boanerges to examine the nature of democracy. The comedy projects a future of democratic decline, the break-up of national identity and America's political domination of Europe. The plot hinges on a scheme by the American Ambassador to cancel the Declaration of Independence and, thus, notionally to come back under British control. This is, of course, a device to extend US domination. It serves to reflect the notion of a world in flux where certainties have been removed and all values are open to negotiation and manipulation. Beneath its surface cleverness, it expresses a deep unease about the nature of political reality. The abuse of power is a recurrent concern in Shaw's work expressed in many forms from the abuse of political power to the personal control of another as in *Pygmalion* (1914).

The other major element in Shaw's work that reflects change in the social environment is shown in his representation of class. There are certainly some very traditional representations. Lady Britomart in *Major Barbara* is a purely conventional figure closely related to Oscar Wilde's Lady Bracknell from *The Importance of Being Earnest*. There is though a consciousness in Shaw's work which signals recognition of the fluidity of the class system and a sense that the old barriers are diminishing. In that respect, Shaw's plays bear some relation to the novels of Evelyn Waugh in their use of social comedy as a means of recording shifts in the nature of British society.

Many of these elements in Shaw's work can best be illustrated by reference to *Pygmalion*. The environment of the play reflects the conservative and nostalgic mood of much theatre of the time but there are also important undercurrents that encompass key social issues. At the centre of the play is an exploration of the relationship between language and class. Language is the means of defining social realities and of transforming self, but it is also an instrument for repression. The implications of social engineering underpin much of the emotional content of the play. Liza's angry exchange with Higgins exemplifies this theme:

> LIZA: Do my clothes belong to me or to Colonel Pickering?
> HIGGINS: What the devil use would they be to Pickering?
> LIZA: He might want them for the next girl you pick up to experiment on.[8]

Liza recognizes a distinction between scientific and emotional reality and her sense of herself as subject to experiment signals Shaw's jaundiced perception of emerging 'sciences' of personality. The preoccupation with new forms of social and linguistic classification and the related notion of social control are exposed in an implicit humanistic rejection of Higgins and his 'science'.

The play is also constructed with a notion of innovation inherent in Shaw's framework even if less apparent in the play itself. The use of the term 'Romance' in the subtitle is clearly ironic and indicates an attempt to break from traditional dramatic forms:

> The rest of the story need not be shewn in action, and indeed, would hardly need telling if our imaginations were not so enfeebled by their lazy dependence on the ready-mades and reach-me-downs of the ragshop in which Romance keeps its stock of 'happy endings' to misfit all stories. Now, the history of Eliza Doolittle, though called a romance because the transfiguration it records seems exceedingly improbable, is common enough.[9]

For all that declared intent, the work itself is less challenging than Shaw might like to suggest. It was a hugely popular success and the key reasons for that might well be that it exhibits a nostalgia for a Victorian and Edwardian past in the fabric of the society presented in the play, and it contains those elements of more disturbing modernity within a safe structure of comedy of manners. It sustains the tension described earlier between a culture uneasily perceiving the future while elegizing a quasi-Edenic version of the past.

It certainly shocked the contemporary audience, though, particularly by the use of the word 'bloody'. The play opened in April 1914 and was reviewed by the *Daily Sketch*:

> Mrs Patrick Campbell uttered the Unprintable Swearword at His Majesty's Theatre on Saturday night, and the play stopped for a whole minute till the audience had done laughing.
> The Censor did not intervene, and in *Pygmalion* Mr Bernard Shaw has been permitted once again to shock the British public.[10]

In this play and in the works of many contemporaries, there is a sense of pushing the boundaries further. Coward's *The Vortex* is an even more dramatic example, ten years further on, of the way in which the playwright's desire to move into new territory of expression exceeds the audience's willingness to go along with the process. In 1921, Somerset Maugham's *The Circle* was booed by the first night audience because of its content. The *Globe* considered *Pygmalion* to be 'a piece of vulgarity quite unpardonable ...'.[11] These outbursts of public moral outrage signify the degree to which public taste has undergone a major revolution since those times.

Pygmalion contains, as so often in Shaw, a moral outsider. For all the distinction of class and wealth, Doolittle is closely related to Undershaft in that his function is to expose the banalities of conventional morality:

> What am I, Governors both? I ask you, what am I? Im one of the undeserving poor: thats what I am. Think of what that means to a man. It means that hes up against middle class morality all the time.[12]

This reflects an essential characteristic of Shaw's work in these decades. Social convention is exposed through an exceptional individual who inverts expectations about virtue and vice, good and evil. The process of reviewing assumptions about reality in the new century finds full expression in this context. Shaw identifies a form of moral and political vacuum into which new ethical forms and conventions might be placed. There is also a sense, clearly, in which personality and identity too are subject to fictionalization and re-construction through 'art' or 'science'. That is, in essence, what Liza experiences: a new definition of self through a process of re-invention. It should further be recognized that Liza represents the young and that the rebelliousness of youth finds expression in Shaw's work in many guises. The perceptions of the young are frequently set in conflict with those of their elders, prefiguring the generational conflict that is to shape much Western culture by the middle of the century.

For all that *Pygmalion* contains these modern notions, it also signifies the continuation of earlier theatrical forms. There are elements of the 'new woman' in Liza and, in a comic sense, in Clara, yet they are still subject to the mores of 'Society': the set of social manners drawn from a very small group of rich London families. There is something still of the tyranny of that group and its values, a comic translation of tensions found in Oscar Wilde's *Lady Windermere's Fan* (1892) or *A Woman of No Importance* (1893):

> GERALD: I suppose society is wonderfully delightful!
> LORD ILLINGWORTH: To be in it is merely a bore. But to be out of it is simply a tragedy. Society is a necessary thing. No man has any real success in this world unless he has got women to back him, and women rule society.[13]

Some of this theatrical landscape remains in Shaw and his contemporaries and coexists somewhat uneasily with the demands of the new. The play may challenge conventional moralities but contains little sense, in the end, of a class structure that is subject to social change. The plot, in effect, depends upon a view of the class structure as static in two areas: 'Society' with its sets of rules and rituals, the penetration of which is the object of Liza's transformation; and the existence of an under class from which Liza is taken.

An intriguing aspect of Shaw's play, in its publishing evolution, is its explicit recognition of the potential impact of the cinema. *Pygmalion* was revised with a translation to the cinema in mind. As Shaw's technical instruction signified, he envisaged parts of the play as suitable primarily for production in the cinema:

> A complete representation of the play as printed for the first time in this edition is technically possible only on the cinema screen or on stages furnished with exceptionally elaborate machinery. For ordinary theatrical use the scenes separated by rows of asterisks are to be omitted.[14]

Shaw's career, long as it was, illustrates a transition from a Victorian world to a modern one, and the history of *Pygmalion* exactly illustrates the degree to which theatre in these decades contains both the remnants of what has been and the social and technological forces that will shape the future.

GRANVILLE-BARKER, MAUGHAM AND SOME CONTEMPORARIES

It is apparent that many of the key figures of the period who were Shaw's contemporaries and who dominated the British theatre have reputations now only as minor figures or, as in the case of Harley Granville-Barker, for their other contributions to drama. His contribution to the development of a National Theatre and The Court is already recorded but his most influential work is to be found in his *Prefaces to Shakespeare*. The play that best represents his own dramatic writing is probably *The Vosey Inheritance* (1905) and it retains some interest as much as anything for its analysis of the relationship between surface respectability and underlying corruption. The inheritance is precisely the legacy of the corrupted use of trust funds by the Vosey family. However, the Voseys are not, it transpires, guilty of exploiting the innocent. What is finally revealed is a system throughout characterized by different levels of corruption. The play offers an inclusive vision of a corrupted world in which the lines between moral and immoral become blurred: 'there's the danger of acting on principle ... one begins to think more of one's attitude than the use of what one is doing'.[15]

The ambiguity of the moral universe presented clearly serves to complicate the audience's expectations. What is an apparently moral solution may have consequences more disastrous than those that would result from the maintenance of what is ostensibly hypocritical and deceitful. Granville-Barker also attempted some theatrical experimentation in, for example, *The Marrying of Ann Leete* (1902) but his primary contribution lies elsewhere and *The Vosey Inheritance* is probably the only play that might make the transition from page to contemporary stage.*

Somerset Maugham's theatrical career is also, in retrospect, a minor matter but he did touch upon a number of the key themes of the period and he enjoyed a considerable theatrical success:

> In 1908 he had four plays running simultaneously in London; and he continued to captivate the theatrical public with some regularity thereafter, or at any rate until 1933, when he retired from the stage.[16]

His best plays are probably *Home and Beauty* (1919) and *The Circle* (1921). While his literary reputation is certainly best maintained in the novels and short stories, those plays signify some comic ability and a superficial but entertaining capacity to reflect the changing mores of society in the 1920s.

Home and Beauty is a farce that addresses the potentially tragic issue of a husband returning from the war to find that his wife has remarried his best friend having been told that her husband had been killed in action. The figure

---

*Staged in the West End of London in 1992.

of Mrs Shuttleworth is a familiar figure: a shallow female not unrelated to those invented by Evelyn Waugh in his novels of the 1920s. Collectively, these represent a jaundiced perception of the 'new woman' and an underlying unease about the potential revolution in the relationship between the sexes:

> You girls all talked as though the war would last for ever. Heroism is all very well, but at a party it's not nearly so useful as a faculty for small talk.[17]

The comedy is essentially based on wit though it circulates around a real social problem that is manifest elsewhere in plays of the period. Changes in patterns of sexual behaviour were not matched by any reform of divorce laws, and the absurd complications of those laws were both a subject for social comedy and a real cause of distress. *Home and Beauty* deals with the subject and further asserts the primacy of male friendship over marriage and sexual attraction. In the final outcome the two husbands combine to escape the stereotypical presentation of a wife as shallow and domineering.

Interest in Maugham's *The Circle* must similarly be seen as largely historical. It is also a comedy that exploits changing attitudes to sexual behaviour. The subject is adultery and the consequences of it. In essence, it translates the real social traumas of late Victorian England, expressed in Wilde's *A Woman of No Importance*, into comedy. The themes of the two plays are curiously close. Interestingly enough, the first-night audience at *The Circle* were outraged at Maugham's flippant representation of those issues, an indication that social attitudes had not changed quite as radically or completely as imagined. As in the Wilde play, Society is a tyrannical moral force: 'We're members of a herd. If we break the herd's law we suffer for it. And we suffer damnably.'[18]

The play contains little or no sense though of felt pain or suffering. Maugham's plays were a great commercial success precisely because they were able to express real issues in forms that made no emotional impact upon the audience. The dilemmas represented remained firmly at the level of language. Maugham partakes of the social and behavioural concerns of the 1920s without really offering perspectives upon them.

There are plays of considerable seriousness in the period, however. D.H. Lawrence's *The Widowing of Mrs Holroyd* might be seen as exemplifying didactic drama in the realist mode designed to reveal the suffering of particular classes. It was a play with an uneasy history. It was written in 1911 and rejected for production by Granville-Barker in the same year. Revised three years later, it was not finally seen in production until 1926. The play is set in a working-class mining district in Nottinghamshire. The life lived is seen as a form of imprisonment enforced by domestic strife, poverty and alcohol. Holroyd's death in a mining accident reflects both the harshness of the lives lived and the ending of hope. The play is in essence a slice of miserable life

having as its rationale the desire to reveal what was largely hidden from, or unseen by, the body of theatrical audiences:

> This vile hole! I'd never have come to live here, in all the thick of the
> pit-grime, and lonely, if it hadn't been for him, so that he shouldn't call in a
> public-house on his road home from work.[19]

Lawrence's play is at one end of a spectrum of theatrical possibility in the period with Maugham at the other. Maugham's sole strategy seems to be to contain and manage tension within a structure of light verbal exchange, whereas Lawrence creates an environment of such consistent gloom, despair and despondency that it is impossible to envisage change. Neither creates the condition for development out of which some kind of dramatic tension might emerge.

The contrast with J.M. Synge is marked. *Riders to the Sea* (1905) bears a superficial similarity to Lawrence's play in that it has a similar theme of poverty and suffering in an enclosed community. However, Synge's protagonists are ennobled not by the situation but by the power of their language. His treatment of a comedy of mistaken identity in *Playboy of the Western World* (1907) makes similar impact through the strength of language. Indeed, perhaps the greatest dramatic power in the period is in English outside of Britain in the work at the Abbey Theatre in the newly created Irish Free State. After 1922, the Abbey nurtured, among others, the major talent of Sean O'Casey. Irish nationalism, whatever else it produced, invigorated Irish theatre in a way that could not, for the most part, be found in Britain. J.M. Barrie, a Scot, and Shaw, an Irishman, made their names and their creative contribution largely to British theatre but in Ireland a breadth of theatrical vision existed that outshone nearly everything that was happening on the British stage. That, though, is the subject of another national history.

GALSWORTHY AND COWARD: CASE STUDIES FOR THREE DECADES

John Galsworthy was a playwright of high seriousness and stern moral purpose, as is fitting for a figure who reached maturity in Victoria's Britain and who gained the Nobel prize for literature, largely on the basis of his fiction, in 1932. A dramatic contrast is made by the figure of Noël Coward who in 1929 was only a few years older than the century. As a singer and actor he represented, perhaps more than any other figure, the popular mood of the 1920s. His role

was almost that of a British Scott Fitzgerald, embodying a new, sometimes amoral, world ostensibly committed only to gaiety and excess. That that 1920s is an 'invention' makes it no less a potent force in the culture. With these two figures, the contradictions and paradoxes of the first three decades of this century are embodied. Together, they represent a spectrum of possibility and no little theatrical talent. Ironically, it is Coward's influence that has lasted, illustrating perhaps that within his work there was a subtlety, literary ability and moral perspective that belied the mask of flippancy he wore with such skill.

Galsworthy's work falls within a tradition of worthy, didactic theatre. The plays, according to Benedict Nightingale, 'perpetuate an honourable liberal tradition'.[20] They are also limited in their theatrical force by a certain failure of vision: 'Galsworthy has no cosmic vision. Early twentieth-century English society is his interest, the practical ordering and humanizing of it his concern.'[21] That judgement, essentially a just one, should not obscure the strength of the best of Galsworthy's work, which is finely focused and frequently dramatically intense.

Strife: A Drama in Three Acts (1909) takes an almost documentary approach to the struggle between employers and employees. There is a rigorous refusal to judge and a retreat from any Dickensian sympathy with the plight of the labouring classes. There are no real villains except extremism. Roberts, the union demagogue, meets with Anthony, the unbending chairman of the board, in a clash that is unresolvable. In essence, Anthony's view of the division between Capital and Labour admits of no solution:

> 'It has been said that times have changed; if they have I have not changed with them. Neither will I. It has been said that masters and men are equal! Cant! There can only be one master in a house. Where two men meet the better man will rule. It has been said that Capital and Labour have the same interests. Cant! Their interests are as wide asunder as the poles'[22]

Galsworthy presents both conflicting figures in humanizing ways as well as in unbending conflict and the overall effect is to create a drama that is, while nonjudgemental, didactic in its presentation of the dangers of either form of extremism. Its other, and perhaps profounder intent, is to educate the audience in an understanding of the suffering of the poor. Inevitably, Galsworthy's confrontations sometimes approach the inflated level of melodrama but they always attempt to grapple with a social issue of genuine seriousness and widespread concern.

In *Justice: A Tragedy* (1910), for example, Galsworthy addresses the subject of penal policy and the play debates the nature of justice in a manner that approximates melodramatic simplicity but, nevertheless, most clearly focuses the issues both of the absurdities of the divorce laws and of the injustices inherent in a harsh penal system. Galsworthy's contribution to this latter issue

was not minor. In both this work and in his other activities he campaigned to raise public consciousness. The victim in *Justice* is a figure of goodwill with humane motives driven to suicide by an unforgiving system. The play caused a public outcry which contributed to a review of British policy in this area.

Galsworthy's contribution to the drama of the period was then a social one expressed in the themes he dramatically presented. As plays, they offer no technical innovation or formal experiment. In tone, they move, at times uneasily, between social documentary and melodrama. Noël Coward's subjects, in contrast, are not issues but *behaviour*. His major dramatic invention is indeed himself. He became, in fact, a performing self as actor, singer and cabaret performer. The figure he most resembles is Oscar Wilde and he brings some of Wilde's verbal elegance to the stage. Indeed some of his writing oddly combines the social structure of a Wilde drama with the behavioural patterns of the 1920s.

Coward essentially worked within given theatrical stereotypes but manipulated them into forms that illuminate issues of his time and that, quite clearly, addressed the concerns of audiences in the 1920s. In 1925, three Noël Coward plays were playing in London: *The Vortex, Fallen Angels* and *Hay Fever*. In 1926, *Easy Virtue* opened. This was the beginning of a career of astonishing popularity that, over forty years, transformed Coward from rebel to a sort of establishment eccentric. Unlike Wilde, Coward was able to obscure his homosexuality in a mask of eccentricity and become a public figure whose work was both his plays and himself. His major contribution is, arguably, in the twenties when he embodied and captured in his plays what Edmund Wilson characterized as 'The days when we embrace many and love none'.[23]

Hay Fever uses the conventional theatrical device of an upper-class weekend house party to bring together several players in a mêlée of sexual games across generations. The Bliss family operate a code based on theatricality that infuriates and profoundly confuses their various guests. As often in Coward's work the language is a form of game out of which protagonists are required to create meaning. The failure of the outsiders to do so is, in *Hay Fever*, the source of the comedy. Judith Bliss, appropriately a retired actress, is the creator of much of this linguistic comedy. Coward's dialogue is both profoundly mannered and a parody of traditional theatrical speech: 'You've answered the only call that really counts – the call of Love, and Romance, and Spring.'[24] While Judith's invented forms of reality are largely drawn from theatrical sources, her husband's sources are fictional. The counterpoint to Judith's role playing is David's novel, references to which run through the play. Like Judith's drama, it is a romantic fiction which is made ironic by the relation to the actions of the play itself.

One of the victims of this coded behaviour is driven to distraction and her anger focuses much of Coward's strategy in the play:

You're the most infuriating set of hypocrites I've ever seen. This house is a complete feather-bed of false emotions – you're posing, self-centred egotists, and I'm sick to death of you … I've been working up for this, only every time I opened my mouth I've been mowed down by theatrical effects. You haven't got one sincere or genuine feeling among the lot of you – you're artificial to the point of lunacy.[25]

As this outburst indicates, Coward's theme is essentially art itself. Like Wilde, he makes theatre from the perceived theatricality of behaviour and speech. The transaction between art and reality is continuous and bewildering. That bewilderment is the source of the considerable comedy. His other primary concern is the shifting nature of sexual behaviour. The moral codes that govern relationships between sexes and generations evaporate in the froth of interchange and intercourse.

The Vortex was altogether a darker drama, though in the mother, Florence, it contains a figure who is clearly related to Judith. She is both artificial and, in a far more extreme form, sexually promiscuous. Mothers in Coward's plays operate outside of the generational code that allocates to them a role as moral force and supporting parent. They exemplify the collapse of generational distinction in roles and the decline of family cohesion. The other subject of this frequently over-heated drama is drug addiction and Coward draws a direct line between the son's addiction and the mother's moral failure to be either a good mother or a loyal wife:

You're not to have any more lovers; you're not going to be beautiful and successful ever again – you're going to be my mother for once – it's about time I had one to help me, before I go over the edge altogether.[26]

What this reveals, of course, is Coward's moral conservatism that underlies his satirical view of social and sexual behaviour in the 1920s.

Fallen Angels returns to the less fevered tone of *Hay Fever* and explores much of the same landscape . The distinction between what is said and what is meant is again a source of comedy. The theme was, as with *The Vortex*, considered to be particularly shocking as it depended on the fact that the two female protagonists had a premarital affair with the same Frenchman. Coward uses the stereotype of the sexually attractive foreigner to contrast with the altogether less romantic British figures and the whole requires the recognition of women as sexually active. Although a relatively slight play, it is interesting in that it very specifically recognizes its own modernity, as in this exchange between one of the married couples involved:

FRED: I'm sure married life was much easier in the Victorian days.
JULIA: If you think women didn't discuss everything minutely in the Victorian days just as much as they do now you're very much mistaken.
FRED: But it was all so much simpler.
JULIA: For the men.

115

FRED: For the women too; they didn't know so much.

JULIA: They didn't give themselves away so much, poor dears, they were too frightened.[27]

Easy Virtue brings most of Coward's concerns together. It exists consciously at a point of social upheaval: 'Everything's changing nowadays, anyhow'.[28] It contains two contrasting women who are defined by theatrical stereotype. Larita, the older foreign women, is sophisticated, sexually 'dangerous' and exists outside English social convention. Her behaviour reveals the hypocrisy of respectable English society. In contrast, Sarah is the epitome of English virtue and decency. Larita's role is to expose the weakness of English social structures and to challenge the complacency and hypocrisy of its values. In a confrontation with her husband's sister, she makes a headlong assault on the conservative moral universe of the British upper classes:

> I'm completely outside the bounds of your understanding – in every way. And yet I know you, Marion, through and through – far better than you know yourself. You're a pitiful figure, and there are thousands like you – victims of convention and upbringing. All your life you've ground down perfectly natural sex impulses, until your mind has become a morass of inhibitions – your repression has run into the usual channel of religious hysteria. You've played physical purity too high and mental purity not high enough. And you'll be a miserable woman until the end of your days unless you readjust the balance.[29]

Larita represents an archetypal female outsider. She is sexually experienced, European, older than her husband, worldly and sophisticated: a 'dark lady' who, in her own consciousness, lives according to a diverse moral code, 'I don't live according to your social system'.[30] What she comes to realize, however, is the continued strength of the English moral code in this context. A newspaper cutting describing a scandal in Larita's past is accommodated in this way:

> LARITA: It was all very unpleasant. The Colonel stood by me, of course – John wasn't there – he doesn't know anything yet.
>
> SARAH: But Lari dear, don't give in like this and chuck up everything.
>
> LARITA: I must – you see, they're right; it's perfectly horrible for them. I'm entirely to blame.
>
> SARAH: But what does it matter? The past's finished with.
>
> LARITA: Never. Never, never, never. That's a hopeless fallacy.[31]

This exchange with Sarah is a reminder of the fact that social change is neither absolute nor complete. It recognizes the power of social convention in a fashion that recalls Mrs Arbuthnot's declaration in Wilde's *A Woman of No Importance*:

> You talk of atonement for a wrong done. What atonement can be made to me. There is no atonement possible. I am disgraced: he is not. That is all. It is the usual history of a man and a woman as it usually happens. And the ending is the ordinary ending. The woman suffers. The man goes free.[32]

The clash of past convention and modern manners was, then, a major subject for Coward and his work signalled the centrality of that theme in the theatre of the time. Galsworthy represented elements of Victorian high seriousness that persisted into the twentieth century and were expressed in a concern for serious issues of social reform. Coward, of a younger generation, represented a mood of scepticism and, at times, a conscious retreat from seriousness as his protagonists took refuge in wit. For all that, both Galsworthy and Coward, at opposite ends of an age, partook of the debate that character-ized the times. They knew what was disappearing but not the shape of what was to replace it. They formed in their respective plays patterns in which a modern life may be lived.

MAKING THE MODERN

Few men were able to welcome change whole-heartedly.[33]

Marcus Cunliffe.

To be modern is to find ourselves in an environment that promises us adventure, power, joy, growth, transformation of ourselves and the world – and, at the same time, that threatens to destroy everything we have, everything we know, everything we are.[34]

Marshall Berman

The plays and writers discussed here reflect the uncertainties of the opening decades of this century. Their subjects were the changes and dynamics apparent across the fields of politics, social behaviour, intellectual thought, philosophy, science and technology. A central fact of the age was the dynamics of transition from Victorian England to some version of modernity. These writers existed also in a broader age of ferment where, in an international context, the perception of the known world was undergoing revolution. That kind of upheaval is frequently unclear and never simple. It is accompanied by nostalgia for what has been lost and uneasiness about what lies ahead. It is also a process that is not over because it is in the nature of all cultures and civilizations to be unfinished, to be permanently moving from one condition to another.

In the theatre, this was not a heroic age. The British theatre had no practitioner of the status of those working in science, fiction or poetry who could, with justification, claim to be reforming the consciousness of a generation and remaking the nature of reality. The inexorable disappearance of the old certainties was both opportunity and anxiety: 'a swelling chorus of disaffection ... paralleled the age's sonorous hymns to progress'.[35]

For all the limitations of these works, they inevitably sustain the ambiguities and, in several ways, confront the key issues of what the modern world is and what it should be. The theatre, in conformity with the ethos of the age, took part in a search for the spirit of the new.

NOTES

1. Preface to Richard Ellmann and Charles Feidelson (eds), *The Modern Tradition: Backgrounds of Modern Literature* (New York, 1965), p. v.
2. Edward Craig, *Gordon Craig: The Story of his Life* (London, 1968), p. 155.
3. James Woodfield, *English Theatre in Transition: 1881–1914* (London and Sydney, 1984), p. 173.
4. Reginald Nettel, *Seven Centuries of Popular Song: A Social History of Urban Ditties* (London, 1956), p. 226.
5. George Bernard Shaw, *Major Barbara* (Harmondsworth, 1961), pp. 140–1. First produced 1905, first published 1907.
6. *Ibid.*, p. 151.
7. *Ibid.*, p. 144.
8. George Bernard Shaw, *Pygmalion: A Romance in Five Acts* (Harmondsworth, 1969). First produced, 1914, first published 1916.
9. *Ibid.*, 'Sequel', p. 140.
10. In Harold Hobson, *Verdict at Midnight: Sixty Years of Dramatic Criticism* (London, New York and Toronto, 1952), p. 98.
11. *Ibid.*, p. 99.
12. *Pygmalion*, p. 59.
13. Oscar Wilde, 'A Woman of No Importance', in *Plays* (Harmondsworth, 1984), p. 116.
14. *Pygmalion*, p. 11.
15. *The Collected Plays of Harley Granville-Barker*, Vol. 1 (London, 1967), p. 142.
16. Benedict Nightingale, *An Introduction to Fifty Modern British Plays* (London and Sydney, 1982), p. 139.
17. *The Collected Plays of W. Somerset Maugham* (London, Melbourne, Toronto, 1952), p. 236.
18. *Ibid.*, p. 87.
19. *The Complete Plays of D.H. Lawrence* (London, 1965), p. 15.
20. Nightingale, p. 10.
21. *Ibid.*, p. 107.
22. *The Plays of John Galsworthy* (London, 1929), pp. 150–1.
23. Edmund Wilson, *The Twenties* (New York, 1976), p. 376.
24. Noël Coward, 'Hay Fever', in *Plays: One* (London, 1989), p. 60. Written 1923, produced 1924.

25. *Ibid.*, p. 23.
26. *The Vortex*, in *Plays: One*, p. 174. Written 1923, produced 1924.
27. Fallen Angels, in *Plays: One*, p. 183. Written 1923, produced 1925.
28. *Easy Virtue*, in *Plays: One*, p. 256. Written 1924, produced 1926.
29. *Ibid.*, p. 330.
30. *Ibid.*, p. 344.
31. *Ihid.*, p. 355.
32. *A Woman of No Importance*, p. 133.
33. Marcus Cunliffe, *The Age of Expansion: 1848–1917* (Springfield, Mass., 1974), p. 15.
34. Marshall Berman, *All That Is Solid Melts Into Air: The Experience of Modernity* (London and New York, 1983), p. 15.
35. Cunliffe, p. 15.

CHAPTER FIVE

British Newspapers in the Early Twentieth Century

Nicholas Rance

ALFRED HARMSWORTH AND 'THE GREAT PUBLIC'

In 1899, W.T. Stead, former editor of *The Pall Mall Gazette*, praised journalism as a career: 'there is no calling that is so full of interest. In the theatre of life, the journalist occupies the front stalls, and instead of paying for his ticket, he is paid for attending the performance.'[1] Stead further remarked, 'for the great public, the journalist must print in great capitals, or his warning is unheard. Possibly it has always been so.'[2] Perhaps it had always been so, but the more common assumption was that specifically 'the 1867 Reform Act and the 1870 Education Act had produced a generation of young men and women who were sufficiently literate to read and vote but who did not have any solid educational grounding and were incapable of sustained thought'.[3]

This may have been too dramatic a view, implying a working class which was largely illiterate before 1870. In an essay of 1858, 'The Unknown Public', Wilkie Collins had characterized in similar terms readers of what he called 'penny-novel-journals', though the readers did not then have the vote. Of the serials in such journals, Collins remarked, 'the one thing which it is possible to advance in their favour is, that there is apparently no wickedness in them. There seems to be an intense in-dwelling respectability in their dullness.' He did not think that this indicated 'a rigid moral sense' permeating the unknown public, but rather that the public for 'penny-novel-journals' was unable to read anything more complex.

The 1870 Education Act made such a state of affairs an issue, helping to transform Collins's 'unknown public' into Stead's acknowledged 'great public'. Alfred Harmsworth, ennobled to Lord Northcliffe in 1905, proceeded to follow Stead's advice to 'print in great capitals'. He had begun his career in journalism by producing a magazine, *Answers to Correspondents*, which sated the curiosity of often imaginary correspondents by replying to such questions as 'Can Snakes Kill Pigs?' and 'Do Women Live Longer than Men?' Soon Harmsworth ran several such magazines. As Paul Ferris has remarked of the period,

> Basic costs of raw materials and manufacture fell steadily in late Victorian times. A magazine proprietor could exploit this twice, first by bringing down the cost of production, second by selling space to the advertisers of other cheap goods that were coming within the reach of millions. Here were fine pickings for the journalist and the salesman. Alfred was both. [4]

The turning point for Harmsworth, however, was founding the *Daily Mail* in 1896. Since Harmsworth was seeking profit from his newspapers, rather than being content to subsidize them like a traditional proprietor, he did not give his editors a free hand and was himself in effect editor-in-chief: to his staff he was known simply as 'the Chief'. *My Northcliffe Diary*, by Tom Clarke, who had edited the *Daily Mail*, records the proprietor's suggestions and interventions. 'Every day we must have a feature ... something different ... a surprise. As the Editor of the *Figaro* once said, "Every day you must throw your pebble into the pond".'[5] 'Don't forget the women, Tom. Always have one "woman's story" at the top of all the main news pages in your paper.'[6]

> Get more names in the paper: the more aristocratic the better, if there is a news story round them. You know the public is more interested in duchesses than servant-girls... the taxicab driver and the factory girl would rather read news about Society folk and West End doings than sordid stories about low life... Everyone likes reading about people in better circumstances than his or her own. Keep that in mind. Write, and seek news with at least the £1,000 a year man in mind.[7]

Such maxims duly governed the newspaper. 'Women are the greatest newspaper readers,' declared Northcliffe,[8] and they were advised on health and beauty – 'It is a delicate subject to touch, but I think that medical men ought, before now, to have warned women of the dangers to their beauty from too close association with dogs' – and provided with romantic serials.[9] These were often by Elizabeth York Miller (author of *Where Hearts Command*, *A Heart in Pawn*, etc.), whose photograph on the back page was sandwiched between Queen's Park Rangers in training and a West African landcrab. Titled folk reduced the newspaper to paroxysms of fawning when they married and of prurience when they divorced. As Paul Ferris aptly insists, however, the *Daily Mail* was 'a strange phenomenon, light-hearted but awake to serious matters, gossipy but literate, cheap but not nasty'.[10] A weekly column on 'Books and Their Writers' greeted Jane Austen's previously unpublished early work, *Love and Freindship*, as a 'delightful surprise' and 'a feast of delicious humour'.[11]

In 1903, Alfred Harmsworth founded the *Daily Mirror*, which was both 'the first daily newspaper for gentlewomen' and staffed exclusively by women. Within a few weeks, Harmsworth had sacked the women, which he compared to drowning kittens, and transformed the style of the newspaper. It then became the *Daily Illustrated Mirror*, with illustrations and smudgy photographs dominating fragments of text. The newspaper achieved the world's largest circulation, 1,200,000, by 1914, triumphing over the *Daily Mail* whose sales were still below a million, but did not retain the proprietor's interest, and Harmsworth, by then Lord Northcliffe, sold it cheaply to his brother, Harold, later Lord Rothermere. In 1907, Northcliffe bought *The Times*, whose circulation by 1910 was a modest 45,000, but stressed that 'the *Mail* is in my judgement a very much greater power than *The Times* will ever be, and we can make it an infinitely greater thing than it is ... '[12]

Robert Graves and Alan Hodge remark of *The Times, Daily Telegraph* (with a circulation of 230,000 in 1910) and *Morning Post* that 'it was a sign of gentility to take in at least one of these three select papers, all of which were Conservative: attempts to found a Liberal paper on the same solid lines had always failed'.[13] Among the penny papers, the *Daily News* was Liberal but often took an independent line, being owned by the Cadbury family, who were Quakers. The *Daily Mail* and *Daily News* were arch-rivals in promotion campaigns to lure new readers. The *Daily Mail* offered free insurance to those ordering the newspaper for seven weekdays and then till further notice. 'These Readers Signed the Form Below. Have You?', ran the publicity, and there followed a list of readers who had cashed in after breaking a leg at football, or being hurt in a motor-omnibus, or knocked down by a horse and cart. One of Northcliffe's bright ideas was to turn to advantage children's enthusiasm for playing in the sand. In 1922, the year of Northcliffe's death, Queenie Sizer won a prize for a design on the beach at Ventnor of Teddy Tail, protagonist of the children's cartoon in the newspaper, 'listening to His Master's Voice coming from the horn of a gramophone, announcing: " 'Daily Mail': World's Record Net Sale: Nearly 2,000,000" '.[14]

By 1922, however, Northcliffe was facing competition in the shape of Lord Beaverbrook's *Daily Express*. Beaverbrook had bought a majority shareholding in the newspaper in 1916. Northcliffe is reported as commenting in April 1922 that 'those who underrated Beaverbrook were fools. "He is a young man – far younger than I am. He is an ambitious man and a clever man ... " '[15] Beaverbrook was not himself an innovator in the design or content of his newspapers, though the *Daily Express* would be stylistically revamped from 1933 by its editor, Arthur Christiansen, who *was* a pioneer in newspaper design, but merely determined to beat Northcliffe at his own game. Under half a million in 1910, the circulation of the *Daily Express* rose to almost two and a half millions in 1939. It was not until 1934 that the *Daily Express* surpassed the circulation of the *Daily Mail*, but the newspaper of the early 1920s is already undoubtedly lively, aiming to appeal especially to women and youth. Canon Hicks, prebendary of Lincoln Cathedral, provided an opportunity to do both at once. In a sermon at Northampton, Canon Hicks imputed 'not mere frivolity, but downright immorality ... to the "flapper" ', and 'declared that the great danger to youths and young men nowadays is not so much the woman of the streets as the young girl with her hair down her back'.[16] The *Daily Express* rebutted the charge in a leader entitled 'Sexasperation'. 'Short skirts do not, and never did, make short morals, nor are cigarettes in the mouth of a woman a smoke barrage for vice'.[17]

DR CRIPPEN MEETS SHERLOCK HOLMES

Tom Clarke records of Northcliffe how one night at dinner,

> he asked if any of us had read *If Winter Comes*, and added, 'I cannot understand why people are reading it. It sends me to sleep. I am bored to death with the silly creature with the bicycle'. 'Why do you read it then, Chief?' I asked. 'Because', he replied, 'it is important for me to know why 500,000 people have bought or read that book. My business is to know what the public wants to read.'[18]

It will not be a surprise that a newspaper proprietor should be intent on purveying to the public 'what the public wants to read'. Notoriously, the *Daily Express* was to assure readers on 30 September 1938 that 'Britain will not be involved in a European war this year, or next year either', the last four words of the streamer headline being appended by Beaverbrook. His editor, Arthur Christiansen, recalls, 'I certainly did not seek to suppress the publication of the slogan. It seemed to me to suit the spirit of the time and the spirit of the people. It gave hope and reassurance that the worst need not befall. Was that so very wrong?'[19] Northcliffe's avowal, however, of seeking tips from popular fiction, whose popularity has standardly been credited to a capacity to inspire 'hope and reassurance that the worst need not befall', remains striking.

With particular reference to England in the early eighteenth century, Ian A. Bell has remarked on crime as constituting 'one of the pressure points of ideology', and suggested that, this being so, the press in propagating and diffusing conceptions of crime and legality 'can give us access to both the conservative and the more radical arguments at their most fully developed and articulate'.[20] In this section and the next, I discuss the treatment in the press of two of the more renowned crimes of the period precisely on the assumption that such cases may be seen as ideological pressure points, in the sense that 'common-sense' notions must be formulated or reformulated, made more dogmatic or perhaps extended to situate and contain the aberrant. It has been easier in the British press of the early twentieth century to discover the articulation of conservative than that of radical arguments. The Crippen murder case of 1910 was so constructed in the majority of newspapers as to yield 'hope and reassurance', evoking the consolations accredited to popular fiction; more specifically, the press echoes and sometimes invokes what were among the most popular of the popular fictions of the period, the Sherlock Holmes stories of Sir Arthur Conan Doyle. With an intermission following Holmes's supposed exodus at the Reichenbach Falls, the production of the stories spanned forty years, beginning with *A Study in Scarlet* in 1887.

Appropriately, at Crippen's trial, Sir Arthur was one of the 'few specially privileged ones' occupying 'the seats behind the Bar benches facing the jury'.[21] Expanding on the revelation that Crippen was almost certainly aboard the SS *Montrose* and sailing to Quebec, the *Daily Telegraph* flattered the captain of the ship with the headline, 'Captain Kendall as Sherlock Holmes'.[22] While aboard, Crippen himself had been reading less upright popular fiction, and the *Daily News* considered that his taste in books gave

> an insight into the morbid mind of the man. Nearly all of them dealt with the careers of more or less fictitious criminals who had spent their lives trying to escape the consequences of their crimes. *The Four Just Men*, which he was reading only a few hours before his capture, is Mr Edgar Wallace's well-known novel, the 'heroes' of which are obsessed with a sense of their own exceeding righteousness, and consequently imagine that their mission in life is to put an end to men 'guilty' of offences against what the four supermen conceive to be the law, even though the ordinary law looks upon the conduct as lawful. [23]

The trial of Crippen over, the *Daily Mail* published an article on 'The Psychology of Murder'.

> It is a common superstition, revived at every famous trial, that the murderer in aspect and character should conform accurately with a conventional form of savagery.... . Yet a little knowledge, a more vivid memory of the past, might convince the least imaginative that the murderer in his hours of ease is most often a kindly, amiable and sympathetic gentleman, *so long as his will, at once violent and infirm be not thwarted* [my italics].

Allowing that murderers are not outwardly distinguishable from the rest of us, the theory yet asserts an absolute distinction, even if not manifest. A perennial problem, however, of resorting to psychology is a tendency to seem to concur with the French tag, *tout comprendre c'est tout pardonner*. Such a pitfall is averted in the article only by a logical (or illogical) leap in the dark.

Maybe he has never measured the weakness of his will. Maybe he is constitutionally unable to understand the relation of cause and effect. The result is that his 'kindness' and his 'humanity' vanish in an instant, *and he proves by a pitiful lack of self-control that he is no longer fit for the society of men, that the gallows are his just and only goal.* (my italics).

The nod to Social Darwinism notwithstanding, there is a discrepancy between the 'pitiful lack of self-control' and the gallows being a 'just' goal, whatever that may mean in the context, let alone that one proves the other. The newspaper's leader on the Crippen case avoided such tangles by not meddling with psychology but resorting to a more fusty than trusty moral saw: 'The case teaches one lesson of surpassing moral importance, which, though it be an old one, cannot be too often emphasised. Murder will out, be the precautions of the murderer what they may.'[24] This is straightforward, but manifestly vulnerable to the evidence of crime statistics alike of 1910 and today. The summing-up in the *Daily News* was neither archaic nor convoluted, but nor was it consolatory, as the newspaper remarked of Crippen:

He was, in short, as reckless and imprudent in some respects as he was cool and ingenious in others, and his own mistakes undid him. Yet a man no less guilty but slightly cleverer might well have come through undetected; and that, amid all the not unmerited congratulations which have been heaped on Scotland Yard, will perhaps be the final comment in the minds of reflective people. [25]

The police had smoothed the way for Captain Kendall's elevation to the status of Sherlock Holmes of the mid–Atlantic by providing a contrast. Inspector Dew had searched the premises of the house in Hilldrop Crescent in the company of Crippen. Despite the suspicion thus evinced as to the fate of Mrs Crippen, anatomized in the cellar, the duly alarmed and alerted Crippen was allowed to flee the country. This lapse incurred questions in parliament and not only in parliament. 'The question everyone is asking is why, if they had sufficient suspicion to press him thus, sufficient suspicion to frighten him and induce him to decamp, they did not support their inquiries by watching him.' The Crippen case coincided with a moral panic about a spate of murders before which the police seemed impotent. 'Never in our recollection has a new week opened with such a forbidding list of murders and deeds of violence,' lamented the *Daily Mail*.[26] The *Daily Telegraph* felt justified in referring in a headline to a 'murder epidemic', comprehending a 'series of crimes in town and country', 'London actor shot dead', 'Cromer double tragedy'.[27] The actor's body had been discovered in a back garden in Battersea: the report of the incident was headlined, 'Impenetrable Mystery'. 'There is, indeed, this peculiarity about the crime, that no matter the number of theories that may be suggested to explain it – and the facts would permit of several – the chain of surrounding circumstances would seem to defy, or at least to evade, them all.'[28]

Thus was the scene set for a star to arise in the shape of Captain Kendall, 'a fine specimen of the shrewd, observant, genial, keen-witted seaman', according to the *Daily Mail*; this was a type which in its own right had been much celebrated in nineteenth-century fiction.[29] The Sherlock Holmes of the *Montrose* rescued the great detective from seeming too evidently a mere creature of fiction. The early phase of the Crippen affair had cast the amateur detective as a laughing-stock. As the *Daily News* reported,

> Scotland Yard's search for the perpetrator of the Hilldrop Crescent crime has not been without its amusing side. The huge building on the Embankment has probably not experienced such a rush of strange individuals offering suggestions and alleged clues in any big mystery previously. The Criminal Investigation Department has been simply invaded by amateur detectives since the police asked for the assistance of the public. It is really amazing on what small pretext, and with such little foundation, intelligent people have visited the Yard with 'correct' information as to the whereabouts of the wanted man.[30]

With regard to the myth of Sherlock Holmes, Captain Kendall was a resurrection-man.

Captain Kendall did show ingenuity more or less worthy of Holmes, which to an extent the press was merely faithfully reporting. Ethel Le Neve's masquerade as a young man had convinced nobody: Crippen's 'queer-looking, girlish companion was the topic of frivolous speculation from the first'. The police, however, had advertised Ethel Le Neve's height as being five foot five inches, and that of the girlish companion was five foot four inches. Together with his confidant, the chief engineer, Captain Kendall 'concluded that the police had got a wrong idea of the woman's height because they had not allowed for a woman's high heels and topknot on her head. Put Miss Le Neve into a man's shoes, cut her hair as short as she wears it to-day, and the difference of one inch disappears.' Kendall's masterstroke may have been in establishing whether the suspected Crippen tallied with the actual Crippen in the matter of false teeth. 'I told him funny stories by the yard. All the old chestnuts I ever heard were raked out for his benefit. You see, I wanted the man to laugh right out, and show his teeth, and he did laugh several times quite heartily, and then I knew that the teeth were false.'[31]

Nevertheless, the resuscitated myth of Sherlock Holmes was not simply handed to the press on a platter. The celebration of Kendall's feats of detection merges seamlessly with that of the new availability of wireless telegraphy as a means to relay the captain's suspicions. From the moment of Kendall's first wire until that of the arrest, enthused *The Times*, ' "Dr" Crippen and Miss Le Neve have been encased in waves of wireless telegraphy as securely as if they had been within the four walls of a prison'.[32] The *Daily Mail* commissioned an article from the deputy-manager of the Marconi Wireless Telegraphic Company.

The suspect fugitive flying to another continent no longer finds immunity in mid-ocean. The very air around him may be quivering with accusatory messages which have apparently come up out of the void. The mystery of 'wireless', the impossibility of escaping it, the certainty that it will come out to meet a fugitive as well as follow him in pursuit, will from henceforth weigh heavily on the person trying to escape from justice.[33]

Enthusiasm for the pursuit was exacerbated, perhaps, by two aspects which might have seemed in conflict. On the one hand, as the latest triumph of applied science, wireless telegraphy addressed and reinforced a 'scientific optimism' which had been in vogue since the 1870s, when *The Martyrdom of Man* was published, by W. Winwood Reade, a book receiving the compliment from Sherlock Holmes in *The Sign of Four* of being 'one of the most remarkable ever penned'. 'The interest which is now felt in politics will be transferred to science,' asserted Reade in 1872. The Sherlock Holmes stories, as tales of detection, were themselves informed by a scientific aura in accord with the spirit motivating contemporary investigative sociologists. 'Here the impulse came neither from politics nor from philanthropy, but from scientific curiosity; from the desire to apply the method of observation, reasoning and verification to the problem of poverty in the midst of riches,' recalled Beatrice Webb in *My Apprenticeship*. On the other hand, as the *Daily Telegraph* remarked, ' "wireless" is still a miracle to all but the learned in science, and when the clue, unfound on land, leaped suddenly out of the sea, it must have seemed to many little short of supernatural'.[34] There was thus scope for science to be seen as marching hand in hand with providence, a concept which since Darwin science might have seemed to undermine.

Newspaper readers were remarkably positioned in relation to the protagonists of the drama. *The Times* commented that 'there was something intensely thrilling, almost weird, in the thought of these two passengers travelling across the Atlantic in the belief that their identity and their whereabouts were unknown, while both were being flashed with certainty to all quarters of the civilized world'.[35] How, then, did Captain Kendall's contribution fit? It might have seemed to lend an air of fortuitousness to Crippen's arrest. The answer is not made explicit in the press and presumably could not afford to be, as looking somewhat tenuous in the flesh. As in the Sherlock Holmes stories, however, implicitly the triumph of the amateur detective gives promise of everyone being his or her own detective. A crucial difference is between seeing and observing. In 'A Scandal in Bohemia', Watson does not know how many steps lead up to the flat in Baker Street. 'Quite so! You have not observed. And yet you have seen. That is just my point. Now, I know that there are seventeen steps, because I have both seen and observed.' An exemplary figure, Captain Kendall could claim with his fictional forbear, Sherlock Holmes, that he both saw and observed.

Newspapers were suggested to enhance the scope for amateur detection to flourish. The press was not too diffident to bracket its own role in the affair with that of wireless telegraphy and with Captain Kendall as Sherlock Holmes. The *Daily Mail* remarked of the press generally that 'it circulated in all directions photographs and accompanying descriptions of the "wanted" couple. It made known every detail of their escape. It gave warning where they were to be looked for. Only after a study of the newspaper accounts and descriptions did Captain Kendall feel assured that he had the two in his grasp.' Obviously, modern newspapers were themselves entitled to bathe in the aura of 'science'. One of the features of the development of the press over the period was the increasing use of photography, and even the emergence of newspapers which were nearly all photographs, like the reincarnated *Daily Mirror*. By the early 1920s, the *Daily Mail* devoted its back page to photographs, a pictorial review of the news where murderers mixed with royalty and bathing belles. Apropos of the Crippen affair, the newspaper claimed that 'the photograph does not lie, and when reproduced by photographic engraving and the rotary press it affords in such instances as this an admirable means of effecting identification and of testing doubts'.[36]

In *The Strange Death of Liberal England*, first published in 1936, George Dangerfield presented the years leading up to the Great War in apocalyptic terms: the war itself, he argued, by diverting, at least, if not killing off the potential revolutionaries, preserved rather than undermined the social fabric. He invoked the rise of labour, the challenge to *laissez faire*, and the militancy of groups such as the suffragettes and the Ulster Unionists. Such a perspective on the period has been challenged by recent historians, and Clive Bloom's introduction to this volume stresses the extent to which suffragettes, for example, sought negotiation and accommodation rather than to build the world anew. Nevertheless, and while Dangerfield's own focus was on the immediately prewar years, 1910 to 1914, even the preceding years may be seen as putting traditional ideologies under peculiar strain. The enthusiasm for E.W. Hornung's Raffles fiction is perhaps indicative: collections of stories appeared in 1899, 1901 and 1905 describing the activities of the gentleman thief, and a novel, *Mr Justice Raffles*, in 1909. In a subversive parody of the Sherlock Holmes stories of his brother-in-law Sir Arthur Conan Doyle, E.W. Hornung made the hero a criminal, in itself implying the inadequacy of the black or white distinctions of the traditional moral ethic. The stories are dominated by images not only of monstrous women but of monstrous plutocrats, and a general anxiety about the anonymity of the processes of the new corporate capitalism, seeming to make redundant what is personified in one story as 'the Nonconformist Conscience in baggy breeches'.[37]

It was a dictum of Northcliffe's that 'crime exclusives are *noticed* by the public more than any other sort of news. They attract attention, which is the secret of newspaper success.'[38] As presented in the press, the Crippen case would attract attention by seeming to revalidate belief in the moralism of the self-help philosophy encapsulated in the work of Samuel Smiles, in which the capitalist exemplified virtue rewarded, with its contrast in the weak-willed and dissolute Crippen. The case allowed for the invocation of Sherlock Holmes, the unambiguously worthy hero and amateur, and Crippen himself might have seemed palpably an image of evil, combining wife-murder with having a mistress. Crippen was then duly arrested and executed, which might not in itself imply that good always overcomes evil, except that the contribution to the arrest of 'science' seemed to confirm that the hopeful old saw was the merest up-to-date wisdom. The treatment of the Crippen case combined criticism of bureaucratic ineptitude with a celebration of the heroic amateur, a fascination with technology and the science of psychology with a celebration of traditional values, fear of moral decline with a sense of justice upheld, reflecting the shifting accommodations between the old and the new.

MELODRAMA: THE CASE OF EDITH THOMPSON

With an aplomb that crime novelists might envy, the *Daily Express* reported in early October 1922:

> The flickering light of a match revealed to a doctor a dead man huddled against a wall in Belgrave-road, Ilford, at half-past twelve yesterday morning. It did not reveal the fourteen wounds in the man's back and throat or the trail of blood for nearly twenty yards along the pavement.[39]

These sentences not merely report a crime but impart an attitude to crime in harking back to the style of Victorian melodrama, which recurrently opposes good and bad, white and black, sheep and goats. Edith Thompson would be charged with living in melodrama, but the same might have been said of the newspapers reporting the case.

The *Daily Mail* whetted appetites by remarking that the Thompson–Bywaters murder case was 'one of extraordinary interest, and it is understood that evidence of a remarkable character will be given'.[40] What was the nature of the 'extraordinary interest' which the case aroused? A 'common-sense' response, which might invoke a mere delight in sensational and gruesome incident, allied with titillation, is inadequate, since any reader of the daily press will know that such cases are two-a-penny. More promisingly, the interest in the case may be linked with the undermining of definitions of sexual identity and sexual difference which was an effect of the war. In Virginia Woolf's novel, *Mrs Dalloway*, published in 1922, Septimus Smith, who commits suicide, is a victim of 'shell-shock' or neurasthenia. Symptoms of the hysteria which would declare itself a prerogative of women were exhibited by increasing numbers of men. Apart from the shock to assumptions about what constituted masculine identity, there was an awkwardness and embarrassment about parading allegedly masculine qualities in the wake of the slaughter of the war. Meanwhile, the war had enlarged the lot of women, so that it has been calculated that 'by 1921 the number of women in public administration and professional and commercial occupations doubled the 1911 figure, reaching over a million'.[41] Sexual and social restraints also relaxed: the obverse of the listlessness of the male neurasthenic was the vivacity of the flapper, the bane of Canon Hicks of Lincoln Cathedral in 1922. By the 1920s, it was not thought loose behaviour for young women to go out for an evening with boyfriend or girlfriends, and even to wear lipstick, which was considered disreputable before the war. This was the era preoccupied by the problem of the 'surplus woman', a potential threat to marriages by her availability and also to men's jobs, which she had performed during the war. The *Daily Mail*, fearing, too, that she would vote Labour, recommended the export of myriads of 'surplus women' to breed for empire.

In some respects, at least, Edith Thompson might have seemed the prototype of the modern young woman. She was an intelligent business woman in the city, earning more than her husband, a usurpation of the male prerogative repeated in her adultery with a lover eight years her junior. Where would it all end? With some strain, the answer might be construed as murder, which obviously was discomforting to an extent but also comforting, since Edith Thompson as an icon of social progress seemed to mark out that progress as disastrous and wrong, with a lurking implication that it might be or ought to be reversible.

The remarkable evidence in the case would be that of the 28-year-old Edith Thompson's letters to her lover, Frederick Bywaters. The 'dead man huddled against a wall' had been Edith Thompson's husband. A report in the *Daily Mail* during the inquest observed that 'Mrs Thompson, a slender, attractive-looking woman, with a strong personality, was more composed than she had been on the previous occasions'. Having bestowed 'a swift smile' on Bywaters, 'then, with feminine touches, she arranged the fur collar of her coat, folded her white-gloved hands in her lap, and gazed pensively out of the window'.[42] The newspapers cried up the mystery of the missing murder weapon. What was liable to be found more baffling was the admixture of 'a strong personality' and 'feminine touches'.

The case might then be interpreted as reinforcing a belief that women thus endowed are monstrous and should be cast out. There are echoes of Lady

Macbeth in the presentation of the relatively humble Edith Thompson: 'her gray eyes were lowered, and she walked uncertainly like a sleep-walker'.[43] The jury at the inquest was urged by the coroner to 'dismiss the question of morals. It was not a question of morals, but a question of law.'[44] Unfortunately for Edith Thompson, such a distinction was in abeyance at her trial. Similarly, this was a distinction too refined for several newspapers to appreciate. Unequivocally an adulteress on the testimony of her letters to Bywaters, Edith Thompson evidently should not have been found guilty of murder. As the *Daily News* commented temperately, 'it seems difficult for us to believe that she incited Bywaters to commit the particular murder which he did commit'.[45] More typically, newspapers suggested murder as a mere ramification of the status attributed to Edith Thompson, that of being, to cite the title of a novel by E.M. Delafield, published in 1924 and based on the Thompson-Bywaters case, 'A Messalina of the Suburbs'.

A trick of the press was to substitute for the actual complexities of the case a simple opposition between bad woman and good woman. The sole female juror became a star, her photograph appearing with those of other celebrities, including the defendants, on the back page of the *Daily Mail*. Whether female jurors should serve at trials where the evidence was liable to border on the salacious was a contemporary issue. The *Daily News* reported an action for slander in which a motor and carriage lamp repairer was suing a heavyweight boxer over 'an alleged statement by the defendant that the plaintiff had committed an act of indecency with the defendant's son'. The judge offered three women appointed to the jury the choice whether they would serve and, while one left, two remained. Mr Justice McCardie commented, with oblique phrasing but a liberal heart, 'there is a question as to how far it is wise to maintain the ideal of many men that women are purer and more dignified in the eyes of men if they are ignorant of the grim facts to which I have referred'.[46]

Messalina of the suburbs, then, was not opposed to any mere innocent, but to a woman presented as eagle-eyed in pursuit of reprobates among her sex: one 'who followed Mrs Thompson very closely'.[47] The verdict, one of guilty of murder, seemed also to punish and undo Edith Thompson's sexual allure: 'Edith Thompson, the pretty, pale-faced figure in black, is Edith Thompson, the convicted murderess of her husband, on whom sentence of death has been passed. A silent court watches her carried from the dock, now a collapsed, moaning, shapeless thing.' The woman once conceded to be pretty, or at least attractive (there was some debate: in the *Daily Mail*, Edith Thompson was 'a pretty woman' on 5 October, but 'attractive without attaining prettiness' on 7 October), was now shown exclusively in photographs depicting her as fleshy and disagreeable. While Messalina was being thus deflated, the woman juror came into her own. She 'remained composed throughout. Her head was held high as the jury returned with the verdict. There was a slight pallor as sentence of death was passed, but she looked at the prisoners as if determined to do her duty to the end, no matter how painful the consequences.'[48] The key phrase is 'a slight pallor': women as agents of justice and virtue need not be transformed into Furies, but may retain the marks of what they are defending, vestiges of which the *Daily Mail* had noted in Edith Thompson, 'feminine touches'.

Applauding the verdict, newspapers could not easily defend it. The *Star* was unusually frank in remarking that 'the verdict is a just one, and if society is not to dissolve into atoms the only one', which does not even pretend to focus on the evidence in the case as the criterion of what would be a 'just' verdict.[49] *The Times* was merely disgruntled in face of the public concern which the trial had provoked. Leaning on what was beyond dispute, that the defendants were guilty of adultery, the newspaper commented:

> a murder trial which, for no very clear reasons, has absorbed the public attention came to an end at the Central Criminal Court yesterday. A Mrs Thompson and her paramour, Frederick Bywaters, were both found *Guilty* of the murder of Mr Thompson, and were sentenced to death. There were no circumstances in the case to evoke the slightest sympathy.

The newspaper nodded cursorily to the issue of evidence or lack of evidence in relation to the charge of murder. 'Apparently no poison was given, but Mr Thompson was stabbed to death by Bywaters in a lonely road. The whole case was simple and sordid.'[50] The letters of Edith Thompson to Bywaters dallied with various exotic schemes for killing her husband. At the trial, Bywaters remarked of such schemes that 'she had been reading books' (such as *Bella Donna* and *The Fruitful Vine*, not to mention Lord Northcliffe's soporific *If Winter Comes*), and that Edith Thompson was 'a woman who lived in melodrama'.[51] The 'apparently' in the leader in *The Times* in relation to the question of the administration of poison was merely dishonest, since the full examination of the body after exhumation showed no trace either of poison or of powdered glass, which featured in another bookish fantasy. *The Times*, however, proceeded: 'as the Judge said, it was an ordinary charge of a wife and an adulterer murdering the husband. For that reason it is hard to understand why the entrance to the Court was besieged day by day by men and women.'[52] This, too, was beside the point. Doubtless, the charge was 'ordinary', but the question to be asked was whether the evidence supported the charge.

Reports of the trial in the *Daily Express* were symptomatically schizoid. There is a remarkable degree of identification with Edith Thompson: both this and the purple prose in which it is expressed are perhaps in accord with the tag which the newspaper ran in the top right-hand corner of its front page, 'The Paper that Women Prefer', though the editor of the *Daily Express*, Beverley Baxter, was passionately opposed to capital punishment and exerted himself for Thompson's reprieve. As the jury deliberates, 'the hands of the clock below the gallery look like the hands of fate. Nothing can hasten or retard their march round and round the dial. A sense of the irrevocable overcomes me.' Then the verdict is delivered: 'as she is borne out of our sight she bursts into a passion of weeping and wailing. The agony of it rends us.' Yet the author, James Douglas, nominally editor of the *Sunday Express*, but for whom more suitable employment had been found in writing sob-stories, was not inhibited from paying the only slightly back-handed compliment to the judge's adverse summing-up as 'a masterpiece of cold reason'.[53]

Following the trial, the *Daily Mail* published a verdict from a psychologist.

'Hers was a sex-disturbed mentality', a leading mind specialist, who is an expert on psychological medicine, told a *Daily Mail* reporter. 'Although neurotic literature has had its effect on a neurotic mind, I should say that inverted passion, which influences so many people, has influenced her so much that this action, which seems so terrible to normal people, seems such a small barrier in the way of her desires'.

As in the Crippen case, the pundit then had to cover his tracks. Categories such as 'inverted passion' might titillate the layman, but also might seem to imply that Edith Thompson was let off the hook of moral responsibility for the crime imputed to her. There is then a resort to bluster in order to avert the potential sense of contradiction. 'As a condition, it should not excuse her in any way from undergoing the full penalty. It is not the kind of mental case that the Home Secretary can worry himself with. He would soon be in tremendous difficulties if he began to excuse people on this account.'[54] That the Home Secretary should be spared difficulties was to be regarded as sufficient justification for hanging people conceded as mentally disturbed.

No less than other newspapers, the *Daily News* was morally appalled by Edith Thompson, but without seeing the issues of the trial through a blood-red moral haze. The leader following the trial conceded that the figure of Bywaters might seem 'quite engaging by contrast', 'but the legal case to be tried out was whether Bywaters murdered Thompson – which it is certain he did – and whether Mrs Thompson aided and abetted him in so doing. The jury's answer to this question is natural: we are not quite satisfied that it is correct'.[55] This was a significant advance on the position of the *Daily News*'s competitors. There was a further advance, however, the next day in the same newspaper, with the publication of Rebecca West's analysis of 'The Mind of Edith Thompson'. While stressing Edith Thompson's 'moral blood-guiltiness', the leader had also stressed that this was beside the point. Rebecca West enhanced the debate by approaching Edith Thompson as social product and symptom. It is an analysis anticipating to some extent, as in invoking the literature of the Renaissance if not in invoking God, the argument of Q.D. Leavis's *Fiction and the Reading Public*, published ten years later.

Here was Mrs Thompson, child ... of a favoured age; one of those well-fed, well-dressed young women that the suburbs have produced in the last twenty years; educated up to a point; given an opportunity to realise what a wonder she is ... by being allowed to hold a responsible post in commerce, and being paid a salary for it that would have made her grandmother swoon. She was now at the stage when she developed an imagination.

Then, when what she needed was God and William Shakespeare, she was given cheap sweets and Gloria de Vere.

The Thompson case is a symbol of what happens to a State which attains to a certain degree of material prosperity, but lacks a general passion for art and religion.[56]

Such is F. Tennyson Jesse's emphasis in her novel inspired by the Thompson-Bywaters case, *A Pin to See the Peepshow*, published in 1934. Tennyson Jesse is much in sympathy with her protagonist, Julia Almond, roughly a fictionalized version of Edith Thompson. Nevertheless, to regret the lack of a religious sense in the denizens of the suburbs suggests a wish that they might be prompted to toe the line.

A varied combination of a snobbish fear of the *nouveau riche* middle classes of the suburbs, unease at the rising tide of a consumer society with its sensationalist, sentimental popular fiction, and ambivalence to the newly emancipated women of the period, shifted the balance of press comment against Edith Thompson. Once again there was a dabbling in modern psychology soon overtaken by more traditional Victorian values and a melodramatization of events that reflected popular literary forms.

' "ARTY" PEOPLE AND A SLICED VENUS'

'Suffragettes, indeed! I'd suffragette them if I had anything to do with them,' exclaims Julia Almond's mother in *A Pin to See the Peepshow*. If Edith Thompson's adultery and conviction for the murder of her husband made her a portent of a world turned upside down, other women earlier in the century had been rebels more overtly and consciously. The suffragettes were devotees of symbolism. 'I have tried to destroy the picture of the most beautiful woman in mythological history as a protest against the Government for destroying Mrs Pankhurst, who is the most beautiful character in modern history,' explained Mary Richardson, who slashed the painting by Velasquez known as *The Rokeby Venus*, in the National Gallery in March 1914.[57] Press reports of the activities of the suffragettes were also run through with symbolism and allegory. The *Daily Mail* published a photograph demonstrating the 'Bad Aim of the Suffragettes'. The photograph was captioned 'result of Suffragette stone-throwing. Of the sixteen shots aimed at a window of Sir Edward Grey's house only one hit it. Fourteen hit the wall between the two windows, and one hit below the railings.'[58] Some propaganda was more enigmatic. 'Mrs Pankhurst's Friends Outwitted in a Tunnel', proclaimed the *Daily Mail*.[59] When Mary Richardson slashed *The Rokeby Venus*, there was a fascination with the suffragette's 'chopper'. It was reported that the police promptly deprived her of it. One might assume that they would, rather than let her continue to clutch it, but symbolically, at least, the detail is worth recording: 'meanwhile the perpetrator of this deplorable deed, still glorying in her success but deprived of her dangerous weapon, was removed under close escort in a cab to Vine-street.'[60]

The emotions aroused by the suffragettes in their opponents perhaps could be expressed only obliquely or in disguised form. In the wake of the slashing of *The Rokeby Venus*, when museums and art galleries were temporarily closed, the *Daily Mail* claimed to report the comments of a French tourist. One may be suspicious whether actually he existed, since his English resembles that of a French character in Dickens. The 'Frenchman's Idea' was as follows:

> Your Venus has been sliced, it appears, because she is beautiful of body and Mrs Pankhurst is beautiful of mind. Good! I am going to tell you. Take away the pictures and put there all the Suffragettes, all these beautiful of mind, in the frames, and open the museums, and let all your English women who are beautiful of face come – and – oh! come and chip these mind-masterpieces! Ah, my friend, what feast; I would not miss it![61]

Meanwhile, the press continued to cater for what was confidently assumed to remain a huge market of feminine rather than feminist women. Under the heading in the *Daily Mail*, 'What Women are Discussing', there was no mention of the vote, though this was not to imply that feminine women were empty-headed: 'every woman who can is repapering her rooms, and although there may be this or that actually new fashion in papers and decoration, the majority of my sisters are following out their own ideas, I think'.[62]

In 1914, the *Daily Herald* was a socialist newspaper with consequently a tiny readership, though a Trades Union Congress-backed and Labour-inclined *Daily Herald* from 1929 achieved a circulation of two million by 1939. It has been remarked of the newspaper in its earlier incarnation that 'any middle-class person subscribing to the *Daily Herald* was suspected and shunned by his neighbours; though the London clubs usually had a copy on their files for information – the *Daily Herald* printed a good deal of news that other papers would not touch.'[63] In 1914, the newspaper was intent not exactly on widening the debate concerning the slashing of *The Rokeby Venus* but rather on suggesting that there was room for debate. ' "Arty" People and a Sliced Venus: Praise and Blame for the Daring Suffragist: Views on Both Sides', ran the headlines three days after the incident. The newspaper published a letter from 'a Tottenham reader, who reverences *life* more than "Art" ': 'the outrage on *living* women by "forcible feeding" is passed over without a single word of reprobation, while an "outrage" on a dead painting is deplored as "an appalling outrage which must fill with horror all who have any feeling or reverence for art" '.[64] The *Daily Herald* transformed the discussion by insisting on the extent to which 'The latest OUTRAGE' was a construction of the press, rather than assuming that 'outrage' was a neutral and necessary term.[65]

THE GREAT WAR: ENEMIES WITHOUT AND WITHIN

Press coverage of the 'home front' during the war would almost suggest that the non-combatant was a myth. In January 1917, the *Daily Mirror* paid passing attention to 'War Table Decorations': 'even our table decorations have become militarian. At lunch yesterday I found my host's table decorated with a pot in which a cabbage was growing.'[66] Even advertisements were touched by the Zeitgeist, with slogans such as 'War Declared Against Dyspepsia'.[67] For housewives, there was a stream of 'Economy Ideas' to put into practice. 'Why not Keep Ducks or Geese: the Pond Difficulty: Duck's Eggs Plentiful: a Valuable Bird.'[68] A few days later, potentially converting the suburban garden into a farmyard, further tips followed – 'Keep Rabbits: How to Save on the Meat Bill: Pigeon and Sparrow Pie.'[69]

Such blandness on the 'home front' was disrupted by a need to combat enemies within. Under the headline 'War's "Purifying Flame" ', the *Daily Mirror* stressed the importance in planning for future peace of 'the endeavour to restore the sense of stability and quietness to private life here, the effort to reconstitute family life in itself; to calm the hysteria of the idiot flapper; to bring back some vestige of modesty to millions who seem to have lost it for ever. This will be the moral war, if you like.'[70] There were enemies within who seemed yet more menacing than 'the idiot flapper'. Photographs were published in the *Daily Mail* of 'The Coddled "Conchys" at Dartmoor', who perturbed another newspaper in Lord Northcliffe's stable, *The Times*.[71] *The Times* published a letter headed, 'Anarchic Dartmoor: a Hotbed of Malcontents'.

If the Government desire a revolution after the war they could hardly have proceeded in a more efficient manner. Eleven hundred men who have a grievance, fancied or real, against society, are assembled from all parts of

England and there have ample time and opportunity to organise resistance, armed or passive, against the existing order of affairs. Meetings are held constantly which are terminated, not by the National Anthem, but by the singing of the 'Red Flag'!

The writer advised that conscientious objectors should be removed from Devon to the east coast of England, more subject to bombing. 'The dropping of a bomb near the "Conchys" would perhaps bring about a sudden conversion; at any rate the whirr of the midnight raider might help them to a truer view of the political situation'.[72]

One way in which conscientious objectors who sang 'The Red Flag' were objectionable was in being Englishmen apparently behaving like foreigners. Not surprisingly, there was a preoccupation during the war, in poetry, fiction and journalism, with extrapolating a version of 'Englishness' which could serve as a counter-ideology to 'Prussianism' or 'Germanism', and help to establish that the war effort was just and that God was on the side of the English, if not actually an Englishman. Such a preoccupation did not necessarily slight England's allies: it could be argued, at a pinch, even or especially during the Bolshevik revolution, that the 'real' Russia was fortunate in resembling the 'real' England. Popular fiction during the war recurrently tries to compare England or Britain with Germany in terms of 'national character'. In John Buchan's *Greenmantle*, the attempt to establish reliable distinctions is a failure which may be thought a noble one, considering the crude propaganda to be expected from a novel published in 1916. Zorn, relates Richard Hannay, 'was a white man and I could have worked with him'. 'Gaudian was clearly a good fellow, a white man and a gentleman. I could have worked with him for he belonged to my own totem.' A sort of relief is provided by Stumm: 'I had struck something I had been looking for for a long time, and till that moment I wasn't sure that it existed. Here was the German of caricature, the real German, the fellow we were up against. He was as hideous as a hippopotamus, but effective.' The relief is qualified by the typically Buchanesque conjunction of 'caricature' and 'real', not usually ventured in the same breath or phrase. For journalists during the war, it was irksome trying to define 'Prussianism' or 'Germanism', or developing racial theories of Bolshevism, if Englishmen were frivolously to upset such theories and definitions by acting indistinguishably from foreigners.

Trade unionists as well as conscientious objectors were thought to be developing foreign tendencies. The former Victorian Positivist and friend of George Eliot, Frederic Harrison, wrote a letter to *The Times*, regretting that 'both abroad and at home, passionate groups of revolutionists are clamouring to divert the national war of Free Peoples against military Absolutism into a civil war of Labour against Capital'. Harrison asked, 'can it be the deliberate policy of our workmen to reduce our country to the industrial chaos of Russia, in some cloudy vision that it will raise the condition of their class and prove them to be above the greed and selfishness of wealth?'[73] To the *Daily News*, however, the constituted authorities were betraying England and the notion of 'Englishness' by acting like Prussians. 'It is a tragic irony that just as the German armies are beginning at last to stagger under the blows of the Allies the spirit of German militarism should be winning the greatest victories in this country.' The immediate example was the measure passed in the House of Commons to exclude conscientious objectors from the vote. 'If that decision is to stand we must take it that henceforth it is illegal in England to hold certain opinions and to act upon them,' commented the newspaper, envisaging streams of disenfranchised Plymouth Brethren or Anti-Vivisectionists.[74] The mystical and reactionary *Morning Post* had its own enemy within, 'aliens who camp in the Tubes', and who 'must be taught that the saving of their unsavoury skins is not the first end to which the resources of London are dedicated'. This enemy, however, though within, thanks to liberal attitudes which the *Morning Post* deplored, and representing 'the heavy price this country has paid for permitting through all these years the unrestricted immigration of aliens, however debased and degenerate', remained manifestly foreign, at least to the *Morning Post*.[75]

One attempt to encapsulate 'Englishness' was prompted by Sir Arthur and Lady Lee presenting their mansion in rural Buckinghamshire, Chequers, for the use of the prime minister and future prime ministers.

> We may be sure that Hampden, Burke, and Disraeli often mounted the hill which rises behind Chequers Court to enjoy the view, not indeed a grand or sublime one, but what is better, typically English in its characteristics and most pleasing – a well-wooded land with Church spires and mansions; great stretches of arable and pasture fields, with substantial farmsteads – cottages, tiled and thatched, the whole scene giving an extraordinarily gratifying impression of competence, comfort, and peace … Any future prime minister staying at Chequers – who follows in the footsteps of immortal statesmen along the ridge – may well have his understanding of England enlarged, may well exclaim at the view – ' A country worth undying love and tireless service!'[76]

Perhaps it was not obvious what such a vision of 'Englishness' had to offer militant trade unionists, or whether it could incorporate them. Not every Englishman could look out on 'great stretches of arable and pasture fields, with substantial farmsteads', and still less could he own them. The humble might not even inhabit cottages, whether tiled or thatched. Invoking Hampden, Burke and Disraeli, however, may have helped to broaden the appeal. Resisting absolutism, Hampden might be claimed as a founding father of modern democracy. In Young England mood, at least, Disraeli disapproved of an England divided into two nations, rich and poor. Burke proffered a corrective for such radical impulses, insisting on society as a slow organic growth, which the Buckinghamshire countryside might seem to epitomize, like Loamshire in a novel by George Eliot. For Burke, as Disraeli's poor or their modern equivalent might note, a revolution such as the French of 1789 was somehow excluded from history for not observing this principle.

If what was 'typically English' gave 'an extraordinarily gratifying impression of competence, comfort and peace', the enemy was characterized differently though variably. The use of the term 'Hun' was standard in the *Morning Post* and in the Tory popular press, though not in the Liberal *Daily News*. The *Daily Mail* published a cartoon captioned 'Out of his Apprenticeship', in which Attila was addressing the Kaiser: 'years ago you bade your soldiers gain a reputation like the Huns under Attila. I have seen the towns and villages you have burned and the wells you have poisoned. You have excelled me, and I can teach you nothing further'.[77] The Germans were liable to be depicted as subhuman. After the German evacuation, France was reported to reveal 'the general impression of desolation wrought by some bull-headed minotaur or vulture harpy'.[78] In March 1917, the *Daily Mail* published on its back page a photograph of soldiers in uniform, 'a group of youthful Germans, wearing the dull bovine expression of the average country-bred Hun'.[79] Predictably, the serpentine female of the 'Hun' species was deadlier than the male: 'Hun Women: Torture of Wounded: Food and Drink Tantalus'. 'They were extraordinarily venomous in preventing anything from reaching the prisoners, and their general display of spite, their heartless cruelty, and their profusion of gross insults were barbarous beyond all words.'[80] The *Morning Post* combined an aversion to the 'Hun' with a moralism and providentialism which might have done service in the *Quarterly Review* during the French Revolution. One article was entitled 'The Hun and His Ways: Monstrous, Therefore Ineffective'. The suggestion was to bomb German cities in retaliation for the bombing of English ones: 'there will be another prompting to think with satisfaction that monstrous wickedness bears within it the seeds of its own destruction, and that the supreme force in the world is for good'.[81]

The *Morning Post* referred to 'Germanism': the alternative was to refer to 'Prussianism'. This had different connotations. The *Daily News* was averse to a creeping 'Prussianism' in England, whereas 'Germanism' could not be exported. In February 1917, the *Daily Mirror* published a photograph headed 'Fritz Set to Work on the Land'. The caption was: 'Hoeing Huns. Removed from Prussian influence they are as docile as a spaniel.'[82] So far as these prisoners of war were concerned, the Allies might be seen virtually as liberators.

The *Times* stressed that the war effort was ultimately against 'Prussianism'. Predictably, this view was shared by the *Daily News*, not renowned for concurring with the Northcliffe press:

> This war remains what it always has been, a war to decide whether despotism and the sword or democracy and the ballot box are to rule the world. That is not the view of the *Morning Post* and our reactionaries. They think the object is only to take the sword out of Prussia's hand and use it over our own democracy. But they are wrong.[83]

The *Morning Post*, indeed, had no quarrel with 'Prussianism'. The newspaper acknowledged that Germany was a despotism, but then, it shrugged, so were all nations in wartime.

> What the world is fighting for is something that goes deeper than mere forms of government, namely, the spirit which is behind all forms and without which all forces are dead things…. . This war will decide whether those things full of life which underlie the Christian faith shall continue to serve as a model or yield place to the crass materialism that dominates modern Germany.[84]

A significant absence in either analysis is any reference to competition between Britain and Germany over empire. For a corrective, one need not invoke modern historians of the period, but may turn instead to Erskine Childers's novel, *The Riddle of the Sands*, published in 1903. Childers was already anticipating war between the two nations, and his novel was designed to warn of the inadequacy of British naval defences. Childers, himself an Irishman who was to be shot by the National Army in 1922 as an opponent of the acceptance by the Dublin parliament of a limited Dominion Status, does not quite emulate in 1903 his protagonist, Davies, in combining patriotism for Britain with having 'not a particle of racial spleen in his composition'. The British former naval officer, known as Dollmann, both is less than a man in crossing over to Germany and merely exemplifies that Britishness cannot be suppressed by a pseudonym: 'It was something in his looks and manner; you know how different we are from foreigners.' Nevertheless, Davies is allowed to adopt an impressively even-handed attitude to German imperial ambition, remarking of the Germans: 'They've got no colonies to speak of, and *must* have them, like us.' He adds: '*We* can't talk about conquest and grabbing. We've collared a fine share of the world, and they've every right to be jealous.' The perception that the German situation echoed that of the British, so that not only racially, as was touted by those proposing the French as the natural enemy, and in sharing an extended royal family were the Germans 'like us', did not yield an inspiring ethic for actually fighting the war. Thus in 1917 the Germans were imagined either as minotaurs and harpies, or at best as the benighted products of despotism.

Late in 1917, new enemies were appearing. In December, the *Daily Mail* published a report by an anonymous Englishman in Petrograd applying for a railway pass of an interview with Lenin and Trotsky, the Bolshevik leaders, 'immersed in internal disorders on the one hand and in peace negotiations on the other'. The portraits of the pair recall those of agitators in Victorian novels. Of Trotsky, the visitor wrote: 'he is in appearance Jewish, like a small

Svengali.... . He belongs to the clever, restless, scheming type; I cannot say what his motive may have been.' The writer was kinder if more condescending about Lenin: 'he is a very benevolent-looking old fellow, not really old, but the kind of man who can never have been young'. Presumably assured that the 'motive' of both was a kind of restless egoism, the Englishman posed an English question. Lenin and Trotsky were asked: 'if your country's interest required it, would you retire?' Lenin stressed that he would not hesitate. Trotsky was more laconic. 'He replied, "Sure, why not?" But at present [we] are supported by nine-tenths of the people, at any rate in the north.'[85]

The last admission is unusually frank in the British press in 1917. Friends of the Englishman in Petrograd had advised him to wait until the Bolsheviks had been overthrown to apply for his railway pass. The Englishman thought that he might be waiting a long time. Typically, the Bolshevik revolution was greeted in British newspapers by Carlylean intuitions of spuriousness and metaphors deriving from physiology. Under the headline 'Coup D'Etat in Petrograd', *The Times* commented,

> for the moment the Allies of Russia can do little but look on at this agony, getting what comfort they can from the reflection that the voice which struggles up from it is assuredly not the authentic voice of Russia. They may remember, too, that revolution works in the blood of nations like a fever, which must come to its crisis, but, if historical analogy is worth anything, is apt to leave the patient stronger than before. [86]

The insistence that the Bolsheviks did not represent the 'real' Russia relied in part on the widespread belief or assertion that they were German agents. *The Times* avowed that 'Lenin and several of his confederates are adventurers of German-Jewish blood and in German pay, whose sole object is to exploit the ignorant masses in the interest of their own employers in Berlin'.[87]

The *Daily News*, mourning Kerensky, agreed. 'The news from Petrograd is sufficiently startling, but we shall do well not to take it too tragically. Petrograd is not Russia. It is rather the headquarters of the German influences in Russia.' The newspaper's correspondent in Petrograd, however, was Arthur Ransome, future author of a classic of children's fiction, *Swallows and Amazons*. In the context of opinion in England, including the editorial line of his own newspaper, Ransome's reports are distinctive and distinguished. Ransome remarked that it was 'folly to deny the actual fact that the Bolsheviks do hold a majority of the politically active population'.[88] Bravely trying to answer the question, 'What is Bolshevism?', he dismissed the nonsense about the Bolsheviks being German agents. 'Their attitude towards the war has been dictated by their steady opposition to war in general. This attitude has not been dictated by pro-Germanism.' He also insisted that 'though the Bolsheviks will fail, Bolshevism will persist as long as there are no means for putting flesh on skeletons, and turning hunger into a patriotic citizen'.[89]

CONCLUSION

This necessarily highly selective inquiry into British newspapers in the early twentieth century may aptly draw to a close by quoting Arthur Ransome. His reports from Petrograd are a salutary reminder of the possibility of transcending the conventional wisdom of the day. Press coverage of the war period and the suffragettes, and of the cases of Crippen and Edith Thompson, was typically less enlightened. I have referred in passing to samples of contemporary popular fiction, and both Crippen, according to the *Daily News*, and certainly Edith Thompson, were avid readers, whose conceptions of reality seem to have been shaped by their reading, just as the press constructed the Crippen case in terms of a Sherlock Holmes story rather than those of Crippen's own favoured model of *The Four Just Men*. There are two distinct though potentially complementary approaches which the literary critic or theorist may adopt towards popular fiction. As a description of the first and more modest, Lady Mary Wortley Montagu on the nature of her interest in the popular fiction of the eighteenth century has hardly been bettered: 'Perhaps you will say I should not take my ideas of the manners of the times from such trifling authors; but it is more truly to be found among them than from any historian: as they write merely to get money, they always fall into the notions that are most acceptable to the present taste.'[90] An exemplary brief demonstration of the second approach is provided by Catherine Belsey's discussion of a group of Sherlock Holmes stories. Belsey contrasts the 'scientific optimism' of the stories, the faith in the method of observation, reasoning and verification to dispel enigma and doubt, which perhaps would correspond with the level of interest of Lady Mary Wortley Montagu, with the evasion and contradiction to which the stories are reduced in relation to female characters by the Victorian double standard in sexual morality.[91]

Like popular fiction, journalism will be prone to 'fall into the notions that are most acceptable to the present taste', and so will provide a record of such notions. E.J. Hobsbawm has remarked on the essentially non-revolutionary nature of the impact of the mass press, as opposed, say, to that of the cinema, entirely new in technology, mode of production and manner of presenting reality. The mass press, by contrast, while dissecting content into digestible chunks for those lacking the education and intellectual stamina of middle-class readers of *The Times*, 'was limited by its reliance on the old-fashioned printed word'; it 'transformed the environment of print, but not its content or associations – perhaps because men who founded newspapers were probably educated and certainly rich, and therefore sensitive to the values of bourgeois culture'.[92]

Newspapers, however, again like popular fiction, may be read also as implying the inadequacy of currently acceptable notions. Pretensions of journalism to be factual and objective may be merely embarrassing if the treatment in the press of the Crippen case uncannily resembles a Sherlock Holmes story. Catering to public demand may not be easily compatible with editorial missions. At a time when the public was intrigued or titillated by rumours of Freud and psychoanalysis, psychology could not be ignored in newspapers. Predictably, however, the concessions to psychology may be seen to undermine the stance on capital punishment. Thus one may conclude of early-twentieth-century newspapers, with only slightly more reservation than Catherine Belsey concludes of Sherlock Holmes stories, that the truth which they tell is liable not to coincide with what they would proffer as the truth, but will rather be 'the truth about ideology, the truth which ideology represses, its own existence as ideology itself'.[93] The applicability of this axiom in the case of the press is not confined to newspapers early in the century, but is no less perennial than at least some of the talking-points in those newspapers. In September 1922, a letter to the *Daily Mail* was published under the heading, 'Kissing Footballers'. 'Sir. I appeal to you, as an advocate of decorous behaviour on the football field, again to devote a little of your valuable space in protest against the practice of certain professional footballers of embracing and kissing when a goal is scored. This unseemly and unmanly conduct should be discouraged forthwith.'[94]

NOTES

1. Quoted in Peter Keating, *The Haunted Study* (London, 1989), p. 296.
2. Ibid., p. 297.
3. Ibid.
4. Paul Ferris, *The House of Northcliffe* (London, 1971), p. 48.
5. Tom Clarke, *My Northcliffe Diary* (London, 1931), p. 71.
6. Ibid., p. 197.
7. Ibid., p. 200.
8. Ibid., p. 278.
9. *Daily Mail*, 6 October 1917.
10. Ferris, p. 99.
11. *Daily Mail*, 12 June 1922.
12. Ferris, p. 148.
13. Robert Graves and Alan Hodge, *The Long Weekend* (Harmondsworth, 1971), p. 53.
14. *Daily Mail*, 11 August 1922.
15. Clarke, p. 251.
16. *Daily Express*, 3 October 1922.

17. *Daily Express*, 4 October 1922.
18. Clarke, p. 233. The author of *If Winter Comes* was A.S.M. Hutchinson.
19. Arthur Christiansen, *Headlines All My Life* (London, 1961), p. 145.
20. Ian A. Bell, *Literature and Crime in Augustan England* (London, 1991), p. 19.
21. *Daily Mail*, 19 October 1910.
22. *Daily Telegraph*, 2 August 1910.
23. *Daily News*, 1 August 1910.
24. *Daily Mail*, 24 October 1910.
25. *Daily News*, 24 October 1910.
26. *Daily Mail*, 18 July 1910.
27. *Daily Telegraph*, 18 July 1910.
28. *Daily Telegraph*, 19 July 1910.
29. *Daily Mail*, 1 August 1910.
30. *Daily News*, 21 July 1910.
31. *Daily Telegraph*, 2 August 1910.
32. *The Times*, 1 August 1910.
33. *Daily Mail*, 30 July 1910.
34. *Daily Telegraph*, 1 August 1910.
35. *The Times*, 1 August 1910.
36. *Daily Mail*, 1 August 1910.
37. 'The Field of Philippi', in *A Thief in the Night* (1905). See my essay, 'The Immorally Rich and the Richly Immoral: Raffles and the Plutocracy', in Clive Bloom (ed.), *Twentieth-Century Suspense* (London, 1990), pp. 1–21.
38. Clarke, p. 199.
39. *Daily Express*, 5 October 1922.
40. *Daily Mail*, 6 October 1922.
41. John Stevenson, *British Society 1914–45* (Harmondsworth, 1984), p. 170.
42. *Daily Mail*, 2 November 1922.
43. *Daily Mail*, 7 October 1922.
44. *Daily Mail*, 24 October 1922.
45. *Daily News*, 12 December 1922.
46. *Daily News*, 4 November 1922.
47. *Daily Mail*, 9 December 1922.
48. *Daily Mail*, 12 December 1922.
49. Quoted in the *Daily Mail*, 13 December 1922.
50. *The Times*, 12 December 1922.
51. *Daily News*, 11 December 1922.
52. *The Times*, 12 December 1922.
53. *Daily Express*, 12 December 1922.
54. *Daily Mail*, 13 December 1922.
55. *Daily News*, 12 December 1922.
56. *Daily News*, 13 December 1922.
57. *Daily Mail*, 11 March 1914.
58. *Daily Mail*, 24 November 1910.
59. *Daily Mail*, 11 March 1914.
60. *Daily News*, 11 March 1914.
61. *Daily Mail*, 13 March 1914.
62. *Daily Mail*, 11 March 1914.
63. Graves and Hodge, p. 56.
64. *Daily Herald*, 13 March 1914.

65. *Daily Herald*, 4 June 1913, on a suffragist invasion of the Royal Academy to hold a propaganda meeting.
66. *Daily Mirror*, 27 January 1917.
67. *Daily Mail*, 8 March 1917.
68. *Daily Mail*, 16 March 1917.
69. *Daily Mail*, 19 March 1917.
70. *Daily Mirror*, 30 January 1917.
71. *Daily Mail*, 13 October 1917.
72. *The Times*, 8 October 1917.
73. *The Times*, 9 October 1917.
74. *Daily News*, 22 November 1917.
75. *Morning Post*, 3 October 1917.
76. *The Times*, 8 October 1917.
77. *Daily Mail*, 22 March 1917.
78. *Daily Mail*, 23 March 1917.
79. *Daily Mail*, 24 March 1917.
80. *Daily Mail*, 28 December 1917.
81. *Morning Post*, 9 October 1917.
82. *Daily Mirror*, 28 February 1917.
83. *Daily News*, 10 November 1917.
84. *Morning Post*, 30 October 1917.
85. *Daily Mail*, 21 December 1917.
86. *The Times*, 9 November 1917.
87. *The Times*, 23 November 1917.
88. *Daily News*, 9 November 1917.
89. *Daily News*, 23 November 1917.
90. Quoted in Colin Watson, *Snobbery with Violence* (London, 1987), p. 15.
91. Catherine Belsey, *Critical Practice* (London, 1980), pp. 109–17.
92. E.J. Hobsbawm, *The Age of Empire 1875–1914* (London, 1987), pp. 237, 238.
93. Belsey, p. 117.
94. *Daily Mail*, 5 September 1922.

There are excellent books both on Crippen and on Edith Thompson: Tom Cullen, *Crippen: The Mild Murderer* (London, 1977); René Weis, *Criminal Justice: The True Case of Edith Thompson* (London, 1988).

CHAPTER SIX

John Reith and the Rise of Radio

Robert Giddings

THE EARLY PIONEERS

John Charles Walsham Reith, in *Broadcast over Britain* (1924), remarked,

> Broadcasting is much too big a thing to be ignored for long. Sooner or later it
> will cross all paths. It has crossed most already. It will eventually force itself on
> the attention of any who have succeeded for a time in overlooking it ... The
> responsibility weighs heavily with us. Let there be no misunderstanding on that
> score. It is realized to the full; it is apt to become an obsession. It is a burden
> such as few have been called upon to carry. Whether we are fit or not is for
> reasoned judgement only, but at any rate it is relevant and advisable that our
> recognition of the responsibility should be known. Pronouncement may be
> reserved till the proofs of the effort are established.[1]

On Christmas Eve 1906 ships within two hundred miles of Brant Rock,
Massachusetts, accustomed as they were to radio communication by means of
dots and dashes, were surprised to hear on their radios the sounds of the human
voice and music. They heard a message asking them, if they had received the
words and music, to contact Reginald Aubrey Fessenden, a Canadian engineer
working at Brant Rock. The age of radio broadcasting had begun. It had been
a long time in coming.

In 1864 James Clerk-Maxwell, the Scottish physicist, worked out the
existence of radio waves.[2] His theories were not initially accepted by other
scientists. In 1879 the Anglo–American electrician and inventor David Edward
Hughes, who had patented a type-printing telegraph instrument and who
pioneered the development of the microphone, built a crude radio transmitter
and receiver and passed signals without wires 500 yards along Great Portland
Street in London, just round the corner from where Broadcasting House now
stands.[3] Although these experiments were witnessed by several leading scientists of the day, the theories of radio broadcasting were not accepted. It was

Heinrich Rudolph Hertz who finally proved Clerk-Maxwell's theories correct when investigating the electromagnetic theory of light at the Karlsruhr Polytechnic between 1885 and 1889.[4] Hertz proved the existence of electric or electromagnetic waves in the space round a discharging Leyden jar. As Clerk-Maxwell had predicted, the waves were propagated with the velocity of the light. Hertz's experiment involved a high induction coil which built up a charge across a spark gap (in much the same manner as an induction coil in an internal combustion engine). Each terminal of this gap was connected to a metal plate. When the charge was enough to cause a spark to jump the gap, the sudden surge of electrical current round the circuit produced a radio wave which shot out into space from two metal plates. A receiver, a large loop of wire, connected to a smaller spark gap, acted as an ariel and picked up some of the wave's energy and produced a charge across the spark gap each time a radio wave reached the loop. If the transmitted energy was enough there would be a tiny spark to prove that the wave had travelled from the transmitter to the receiver. Hertz's scientific papers were translated into English by D.E. Jones and his work taken up by Chunder Bose at Calcutta University and Augusto Righi at Bologna. Righi had a pupil named Marconi. At this stage the primitive form of spark received was insensitive and could only be used to detect quite powerful signals over short distances. Hertz's work had laid the foundations of radio broadcasting by demonstrating that electromagnetic waves are in complete accordance with the waves of light and heat. The transmission and reception of signals by means of radiated electromagnetic waves was proved. Oliver Lodge, working in Liverpool (and later in Birmingham), used other developments to improve the reception and amplification of signals and in 1894 he transmitted over a distance of 150 yards. A year later Alexander Pofov in Russia transmitted three miles.

It remained for Guglielmo Marconi to establish wireless broadcasting on a commercial basis. He had been interested in physics and electrical science since boyhood and by his early twenties he was convinced that a system of telegraphy through space was possible by developing and exploiting a knowledge of electromagnetic waves. It was Marconi who conceived the means of putting together the discoveries of Clerk-Maxwell, Heinrich Hertz, Oliver Lodge, Righi and others in a practical way to achieve a totally new method of telegraphic communication. At his father's house at Pontecchio, near Bologna, Marconi began a series of experiments in the summer of 1895. He was soon able to demonstrate effective communication over a mile in distance.

He came to England and in June 1896 he took out the first patent in the world for wireless telegraphy. He established the first permanent wireless installation, the Marconi Wireless Telegraph Company Limited at The Needles, on the Isle of Wight, Hampshire. He gave demonstrations of his invention to officials from the Post Office, and representatives from the

Foreign Office and other government departments on the roof of the Post Office, St Martin's-le-Grand, later on Salisbury Plain and across the Bristol Channel from Penarth to Brean Down, near Weston-Super-Mare. His demonstrations involved distances up to nine miles. At the invitation of the Italian Government he demonstrated communication at Spezia with warships and achieved communication over twelve miles in the summer of 1897.

The Wireless Telegraph and Signal Company Limited was established in London in the same year, to acquire Marconi patents in all countries except Italy. This Company was formed to further Marconi's tests. He established permanent stations at Bournemouth, Alum Bay and Poole. By the end of the century wireless telegraphy had been used for communication between lightships and shore stations and for communication in saving life at sea – when a lightship was run down by a steamer in March 1899. The accident was reported to South Foreland by wireless. Marconi also achieved wireless communication across the Channel between England and France. During naval manoeuvres communication over seventy-four miles was demonstrated and wireless communication was used during the Boer War from 1899 to 1901. In the year in which the Boer War ended, Marconi received the first transatlantic wireless message. The letter S was tapped out in Morse code at Poldhu, Cornwall, and Marconi picked it up with a kite antenna.

He sent a wireless greeting from US president Theodore Roosevelt to King Edward VII on 19 January 1903. He had built four 250-foot wooden towers, with cement foundations, at South Wellfleet, Massachusetts; and he used electrical waves generated by a three-foot spark gap rotor, worked by an operator with a huge key which transmitted the message at the rate of seventeen words a minute. He arranged for a station at Glace Bay, Nova Scotia, to relay the message. The signal was so powerful that the wireless station at Poldhu, Cornwall (three thousand miles away) picked it up directly.

The next stage was the development of methods and technology to improve the transmission and receiving apparatus and further exploitation of the atmospheric conditions which affected the propagation of radio waves. Marconi's invaluable work had amply demonstrated the long distance over which messages could be sent by wireless telegraphy, but Marconi was still limited to sending messages in Morse code, using generators – high frequency alternators or combinations of oscillatory circuits with an arc, which produced a continuous train of waves, or with a spark generating intermittent pulses. By these means the long and short signals on which Morse was based could be transmitted and received over many miles. The final pieces which solved the problem of transmitting sounds and made possible the broadcasting and reception of words, sounds and music, were put in place between 1904 and 1906, the result of Owen Willans Richardson's work at the Cavendish Laboratory in thermionic emission, and John Ambrose Fleming's work on the thermionic valve (diode). With the development of its potential as rectifier, detector, amplifier and oscillation generator, the valve gradually replaced all other apparatus: a simple radio wave, called the carrier, delivers no intelligence apart from the fact that a transmitter is being operated. To communicate a message, changes have to be made in the wave to produce an internationally recognizable code – the dots and dashes of the Morse code. Speech or music requires a more complex process of transmission. The process developed was known as modulation, carried out by causing changes in the amplitude, frequency or phase. The earliest stage employed Amplitude Modulation (AM) used in medium, long and short wave broadcasting. The carrier amplitude was made to vary in sympathy with the electrical impulses generated by the speech or music to be transmitted. A radio transmits sounds which are converted into electrical signals by a microphone, amplified and used to modulate a carrier wave that has been generated by a transmitter. This modulated carrier is then amplified and applied to an aerial, which radiates electromagnetic waves into space at the speed of light. The receiving aerials intercept part of this radiation and feed it into a receiver where it is amplified and transformed back into its modulating signal. When these have been separated from the carrier wave they are fed into the loudspeaker and converted into sound. The stages are: microphone (radio frequency oscillator) – modulator – transmitting aerial – receiving aerial – tuned circuit – demodulator – amplifier – loudspeaker.

THE BIRTH OF COMMERCIAL RADIO IN THE UNITED STATES

Lee De Forest, the American radio pioneer, was able to broadcast music from phonograph records from the Eiffel Tower in 1908, heard within a twenty-five-mile radius in Paris. In January 1910 he broadcast live opera from the Metropolitan Opera, New York, with Enrico Caruso. These broadcasts were heard by wireless operators on ships nearby and a few reporters assembled at the De Forest works in Newark.[5]

In 1912 David Sarnoff became operator and manager of 5-KW station, at that time the most powerful in the commercial field. He was situated on the roof of Wanamaker's Store in New York. Wanamaker's in Philadelphia had a similar station, and these stations were used to link the two stores in order to promote sales. The novelty of radio connection, it was hoped, would pull in the crowds. And so it proved. Sarnoff himself was an attraction, seen busily

149

operating equipment, wearing earphones and tapping the key on telegraph equipment. He was to play a dramatic role in demonstrating how radio was to make the world a smaller place. On 4 April 1912, amidst routine dots and dashes, he picked up a message from SS *Olympic* one thousand four hundred miles away: 'SS *Titanic* ran into iceberg. Sinking fast.'

Sarnoff signalled back to the *Olympic* for details. He notified the press. Crowds gathered outside the store. The police had to be called to keep order as details came in. President Taft ordered all other radio stations to be closed down and for three days and three nights, almost without food and rest, David Sarnoff took the news and relayed it to the world. News of the survivors and the names of the 1,517 who were lost came through the airwaves. Seventy-two hours after he heard the first message, he laid down the earphones: 'Much of the time I sat there with nothing coming in. It seemed that the whole anxious world was attached by my earphones during the seventy-two hours I crouched tensely in the station ... I passed the information on to a sorrowing world, and when the messages ceased to come in, I fell down like a log at my place and slept the clock round.'[6]

But when he woke up again, the world had become a different place, a place where radio was no longer a scientific toy or technical plaything. It was a fact that, because of radio, 732 people had been rescued from a terrible disaster at sea. Congress passed a Radio Act. It was now mandatory that ships carrying more than fifty people had to have radio installed and had to keep a constant watch at sea. Radio operators were to be licensed and equipment was to be inspected regularly. Godfrey Isaacs, managing director of Marconi in Great Britain, came over to the United States to organize their American subsidiary as business boomed. He was instrumental in the establishment of powerful stations, two on the Atlantic coast and one on the Pacific coast, to enhance radio communication with Europe and the Far East. In this same year which saw the massive growth in the commercial and utilitarian use of wireless communication, another development achieved massive expansion in the entertainment potential of broadcasting – General Henry Dunwoody of the United States Army developed the crystal receiver. Dunwoody's prototype had been a carborundum detector. Others used silicone and other crystals. Crystal was cheaper than the tube detectors hitherto in use and thousands of amateurs took to listening to the dots and dashes and voices and music which could be plucked out of the ether.

Direct wireless communication began between the United States and Japan on 27 July 1915. In 1916 the world's first news broadcast was made by Lee De Forest. The following year Major Edwin Howard Armstrong of the United States Army Signal Corps developed the superheterodyne circuit, which increased the selectivity and sensitivity of radio receivers over a wide band of frequencies. This was to become the basic design for all AM radios.

By 1915 the American Telephone and Telegraph Company laboratories had utilized Armstrong's findings and installed a system at the United States Naval radio station at Arlington, Virginia, which broadcast voice programmes on an experimental basis which were heard as far away as Paris, San Francisco and Honolulu. The costs were considerable and the results erratic but the possibilities were enormous. It was David Sarnoff, by this time contracts manager at Marconi (US), who realized the revolutionary impact radio would have on domestic entertainment and cultural consumption if it could be comparatively cheaply manufactured and retailed. He set forth his ideas in a memorandum which is a landmark in the history of communication:

> I have in mind a plan of development which would make radio a 'household utility' in the same sense as the piano or phonograph. The idea is to bring music into the home by wireless. While this has been tried in the past by wires, it has been a failure because wires do not lend themselves to this scheme. With radio, however, it would be entirely feasible.
>
> For example, a radio telephone transmitter, having a range of say 25 to 50 miles can be installed at a fixed point where the instrumental or vocal music or both are produced. The problem of transmitting music has already been solved in principle and therefore all the receivers attuned to the transmitting wave length should be capable of receiving such music. The receiver can be designed in the form of a simple 'Radio Music Box' and arranged for several different wave lengths, which should be changeable with the throwing of a single switch or pressing of a single button.
>
> The 'Radio Music Box' can be supplied with amplifying tubes and a loudspeaking system, all of which can be neatly mounted in one box. The box can be placed on a table in the parlour or living room, the switch set accordingly and the music received.... .
>
> The same principle can be extended to numerous other fields as, for example, receiving lectures at home which can be made perfectly audible; also, events of national importance can be sent simultaneously and received. Baseball scores can be transmitted in the air.... . This proposition would be especially interesting to farmers and others in outlying districts removed from cities. By the purchase of a 'Radio Music Box' they could enjoy concerts, lectures, music, recitals, etc. which may be going on in the nearest city within their radius.[7]

As Sarnoff perceived, the commercial implications of this vision were considerable: there were about fifteen million families in the USA, and if only 7 per cent of the total number of families bought a radio this would gross seventy five million dollars. Over and above this, the profit to be made from advertising would be huge; products and companies would receive national and universal attention. The ideas were extraordinarily prescient but years before their time. Europe was at war; the United States would be involved in the struggle. Effort and involvement were directed elsewhere and his recommendations were not acted upon then, but this was genuine prophecy. In 1919 the Radio Corporation of America was founded. The following year the world's first radio broadcasting station began regular schedules on 2 November. The result of the Harding/Cox election was broadcast to thirty thousand listeners. In May 1921 Sarnoff became general manager of RCA and in July he engineered radio coverage of the fight between Jack Dempsey and Georges Carpentier (a share of the proceeds was donated to the American Committee for Devastated France) heard by an estimated three hundred thousand radio listeners in theatres, ballrooms and concert halls. By 1926, Americans owned three million radio sets. In 1926 RCA gave birth to NBC and soon had a network of nineteen radio stations with thirty-one affiliates. Home audiences grew throughout the twenties and thirties. By 1938 NBC owned over 142 broadcasting stations, and 88 per cent of the American public owned twenty-five million radio sets between them.[8]

The context within which radio developed in the USA, and the commercial direction and emphasis such developments began noticebly to take, were to have a severe and lasting impact on the planning and establishment of national radio broadcasting in the United Kingdom. In New York WEAF (later WNBC) began paid commercials in 1922, and the pattern of private control of the airwaves began. Radio pioneer Dr Lee De Forest complained 'What have you done with my child? You have sent him out on the street in rags and ragtime to collect money from all and sundry. You have made of him a laughing stock of intelligence, surely a stench in the nostrils of the gods of the ionosphere.'[9]

David Sarnoff acquired a half interest in Westinghouse radio station WJZ in Newark, New Jersey, in 1922, and bought the other half the following year, with spacious studios in the Waldorf-Astoria Hotel, Fifth Avenue and 34th Street. In the same year the British Broadcasting Company began broadcasting.

American broadcasting pioneers, such as David Sarnoff himself, might initially have begun with considerable ambitions not only to run the business successfully, but to provide some intellectual and cultural benefit to the consumers in addition to entertainment and information. In Sarnoff's case, it is a fact that the ambition lasted a very long time (after all Sarnoff created the NBC Symphony Orchestra for Arturo Toscanini and broadcast concerts of unquestionable quality between 1937 and 1954). In the United States the debate about the balance between public service and commercial profitability was short lived. Various schemes were aired. Was radio in America to be subject to government control as a public utility? Was a fixed percentage of wavelengths to be reserved for a federal broadcasting chain? Was there to be government control at some state or municipal level? Was the whole enterprise to be thrown open to commercial factors? The Department of Commerce favoured toll broadcasting from a very early stage. This meant that commercial radio facilities would be hired by advertisers. The result was that very soon all the radio broadcasting networks were dominated by two giants – National Broadcasting and Columbia Broadcasting, and advertising agencies produced nearly all sponsored network radio programming.

One American radio advertising pioneer summed up the way things were clearly going in 1928: 'Agencies are planning the programmes, engaging the artists, and writing the announcements, just as they prepare plans, copy, and art for printed advertisements.'[10]

BRITISH BROADCASTING AND THE BBC

It might seem rash to state it baldly in so many words, or to summarize it so briefly, but it was as a reaction to these bold free commercial experiences in America that the extraordinary empire founded by John Reith was built. It is of course true that Reith's BBC emerged at a particular socio-political juncture in Britain, but the American example was vividly before the decision makers in Britain who acted as midwife to the British system of radio broadcasting. A complex set of factors resulted in a series of decisions being made to avoid the market free-for-all and the apparent total surrender to taste of the lowest common denominator. These causes and the nature of these decisions are to be examined in a moment. The result, and it was almost immediate, was the establishment of a unique corporate monopoly of radio broadcasting which incredibly lasted nearly four decades. The essence of John Reith's stewardship and the legacy it bequeathed to the nation is the fact that although he claimed, and might well sincerely have believed, that he was reflecting Britain's national character and its manifestation in the nation's culture – he actually achieved something of a coup d'état over the nation's means of cultural production and distribution. Consequently, he actually (and actively) engaged in the construction of the nation's culture at a particular juncture of the nation's history. This is the real importance of the Reithian imperial experience.

Media imperialism required its colonists and colonial administrators. The first great stage of the BBC's development, the empire that John Reith built, has been termed a 'total institution' by Anthony Smith; within that Reith endeavoured to construct a BBC which itself

> recruited, trained and employed all those who provided the material of the broadcasts. The BBC constructed eleven house orchestras. It had its own repertory company of actors. It employed many of the major writers of the time on its staff. When confronted with problems of religious doctrine, it published its own hymn book. When looking at the problem of dialect, it established its own idiom of pure English. In the field of engineering it tried for a long time to create or modify its own technology.[11]

To understand John Reith's astonishing sense of purpose it helps if one appreciates his sense of the hand of God in these events. The sense of mission, that God had created him and sent him on earth to realize certain tasks, was inbred in him as a son of the manse, a Scottish Presbyterian strongly marked by Calvinism. The faith for him was not a matter of Sunday observances and regular thoughts of the afterlife, it was a matter of fulfilling divine purposes on earth, here and now. As he told the audience of undergraduates and academic staff at the University of Glasgow when he was installed as rector in October 1966.

> Many of us were under Christian instruction when we were young, with varying effects in after years. But we haven't begun – nor have the churches in my view – to take Christ seriously, his person and his message. In particular we haven't begun to comprehend the mystery and the magic of the indwelling Christ – therein *via*, the way, therefrom *veritas*, the truth. I know this to be true and I long for you to discover for yourselves what I have come to realize so late.[12]

His father, Dr George Reith, had told him as a boy that he should keep close to his Saviour, nothing else was worth while; we had not been born to get great things for ourselves, but to make the world a better place for others. This sense of mission gave him his characteristic inner strength to ride out crises which might have caused others to crumble. He did not do sufficiently well at Gresham's for his father to wish him to continue his studies. Though he secretly wanted to continue to university, he accepted the decision, believing God had a purpose for him somewhere else, which would be revealed to him when the time came. He bowed to the career chosen for him as a mechanical engineer even though he wanted to study the classics and philosophy. He tried to enrich his life as best he could while apprenticed to a trade he felt uncongenial, and he joined the Glasgow officers' training corps, where he became a sergeant, and was later commissioned in the 5th Scottish Rifles in February 1911. He worked at Pearson's engineering contractors on the Albert Dock at Woolwich. He served in the war from its earliest days, acting throughout as if he was convinced not only that God was on our side, but that He walked beside John Reith wherever he went. For Reith, the war was very much a matter of the cause of righteousness out to smite the hosts of the Philistines, and he clearly felt he was following his destiny right up to the time he was shot in the face by a German sniper on the morning of 7 October 1915. Even then his rock-like patience and calm belief in his purpose was not shaken.

After a period in hospital he returned to the civilian war effort, working as an engineer at a munitions factory at Gretna and then as an inspector of the supplies of small-arms production for the Ministry of Munitions at Philadelphia. He returned to Britain when the United States entered the war, and served as an officer in the Royal Engineers on various engineering and construction projects before resigning his commission in the spring of 1919.

He then took several management positions in engineering companies with varying success but with little of the deep satisfaction he believed would be his when he found the task intended for him by his destiny. He considered entering politics and he nearly became a prospective parliamentary candidate for the Labour Party in 1922. At this time he gave a talk at Gresham's, his old school, in Norfolk. It was here that he first handled the thread which was to lead him through the labyrinth to the great task of his life. Through one of Gresham's sixth-formers, Stephen Bull, he got to know Sir William Bull, the Conservative MP for Hammersmith. Reith sought his advice about a career in politics and the upshot was that Bull, impressed with Reith's variety of management experience, offered him a post as his honorary political secretary. This, he assured the 33-year-old Scot, would give him first-hand experience of insider politics. It certainly did. He now moved in circles which included Lloyd George, Austen Chamberlain and Lord Birkenhead.

Then, on the first Sunday of October 1922, John Reith had an unmistakable sign that his Creator had some Great Work for him to accomplish, and that the time for its revelation was near. He went to the service at the Presbyterian Church, Regent Square, where he heard a sermon preached by Dr Ivor Roberton, on this text from Ezekiel:

> Thus saith the Lord … I sought for a man among them, that should make up the hedge, and stand in the gap before me for the land that I should not destroy it, but I found none.

Dr Roberton assured his congregation that the Almighty was always looking for someone to fill the gap, as an example to others. Perhaps there was someone listening to him now who might have great deeds in him to fulfil for the good of the nation.

Reith took this as a direct reference to himself. He told his biographer, Andrew Boyle, that he wrote in his diary that same night: 'I still believe that there is some great work for me to do in the world.'

It was less than a week after hearing this sermon that John Reith saw the newspaper advertisements for several posts in the 'British Broadcasting Company' – among them, that of General Manager. Reith had no idea what broadcasting was, but he knew something about management. The specification that the Company were only seeking applicants with 'first class qualifications' did not apply in his, special, case. Several things helped clinch the post for Reith. Fate seemed to guide him, for after having written his application he was somehow prompted to look up the Chairman of the British Broadcasting Company, Sir William Noble, in *Who's Who* – and found he was from Aberdeen. Reith then retrieved his letter from the mail and rewrote his application, stressing his own 'Aberdonian ancestry'. Moreover, it was Bull who showed the advertisement to Reith in the first place, and Bull undoubtedly mentioned Reith to Noble. The fact is that Bull was on the board of the British Broadcasting Company, and an associate of Sir William Noble. No doubt in Reith's view this would be seen as evidence of God's providence. The result was that Reith had a very harmonious interview, several knowing winks and nods from Sir William Noble, and the job was his.

THE NEW COMPANY

The broadcasting company which the 28-year-old controlled was modest at this stage. By September 1925 forty million receivers in the United Kingdom were in uninterrupted service range of radio broadcasting for six and a half hours a day. One million had bought licences. In the history of nations and empires one often discerns a moment, an event or decision, after which things were never the same and, in the case of Reith and British broadcasting, that moment was undoubtedly his conduct during the General Strike of 1926. The significance of the watershed may be seen when comparing the nature of broadcasting before and after this crisis. The British Broadcasting Company, which John Reith now virtually controlled, had been formed by combining six radio manufacturers. The new unit was a monopoly licensed by the Post Office. It obtained its income from the ten-shilling licence paid to the Post Office by purchasers who bought the radio sets made by the British Broadcasting Company (and so stamped). Initially, news reporting was severely restricted by newspaper interests. News could be broadcast by radio between seven o'clock at night and and one in the morning – this was the so-called 'seven o'clock rule'. News was not gathered and written by the broadcasters either; it was a product of the major news agencies and these were acknowledged and attributed. Problems involved in gathering the British Broadcasting Company's revenue from the issue of licences, challenged what was perceived as the Company's 'monopoly' in broadcasting, and fears of rivalry with the newspaper industry led to the Postmaster-General's Committee of Inquiry into Broadcasting in 1923, chaired by Major-General Sir Frederick Sykes, with representatives from Parliament, the Post Office, the public and the BBC itself.[13] There was considerable resistance from the press at the Company's desire to broadcast coverage of major public events such as the King's Speech at the opening of Parliament as well as racing and football results; the Company assured the Committee that there was no intention to take the bread out of the newspaper industry's mouth. The news agencies agreed to provide the Company with a regular daily summary of world news, to be used as a broadcast message of half an hour, approximately 1,200 to 2,400 words in length. The bulletin had to be acknowledged: 'Copyright News Service from Reuter, Press Association, Exchange Telegraph and Central News'.

This was a moment of national significance in the development of radio broadcasting, for what happened was that from the very beginning British radio broadcasting established *press definitions of what was identified as news, and established news priorities*. Newspaper definitions of 'news' – the basic raw materials of the industry on which the entire edifice of the 'Fourth Estate' was built – were based on the need, established very early in newspaper history, for news to be so selected that it would cause offence to as few sections as possible of a very mixed population. Commercial pressures, the need to produce a commodity which would appeal to the several different social classes and racial groups which constituted the United Kingdom, had in large part constructed the basic formula on which news definitions functioned. Our earliest broadcast news accepted these as concepts from the beginning and, when radio began to develop its own news service, it was created on the same principles. Thus was the basic idea of 'public service' broadcasting brought into being.

The Newspaper Proprietors Association was represented on the Sykes Committee by Lord Riddell (George Allardice Riddell, Chairman of the *News of the World*). In response to a comment made by Sir Henry Bunbury, of the Post Office, about the kind of reaction which could be expected if broadcasting were ever to be controlled by the public who received it, rather than radio manufacturers, Riddell made a comment which becomes more striking in the light of events not so far distant from the deliberations of the Sykes Committee:

> You say you can conceive that the time may come when broadcasting will be controlled not by the manufacturers but by the public. Well, I gather that the fact that you gentlemen are sitting here today indicates that the public indirectly controls broadcasting, if a government can be said to represent the public, as I suppose it ought to do. The government obviously control the whole business, and if they grant a licence they do so because they think that it is the best way to make use of their powers.[14]

This statement is clearly echoed by John Reith's own famous syllogism about the people, the government and the BBC during the General Strike.

The Sykes Committee report gave detailed discussion to the implications of broadcasting as a social issue, and it came down firmly in favour of the assumption of broadcasting as 'a public utility'. The wavebands available in any country, the report stated, should be regarded as a valuable form of public property,

157

and the right to use them for any purpose should be given after full and careful consideration. Those which are assigned to any particular interest should be subject to the safeguards necessary to protect the public interest in the future.[15]

The Sykes Committee believed that because radio broadcasting was, in essence, so effective and so inexpensive a method of communication it should remain in the hands of the state and not be allowed to become an unrestricted commercial monopoly. Direct government control, the Committee felt, was undesirable, but control should be directed through the licence which by law could only be had through the Post Office. The BBC had only another two years granted to it. The long-term basis of broadcasting and its control by the state was to be decided by the Crawford Committee, set up in 1925. (The Committee's Report was published in March 1926.)

John Reith, as managing director of the British Broadcasting Company, was invited to provide a statement of his views on broadcasting policy. This memorandum is vital evidence of Reith's fundamental beliefs about the purpose and functioning of broadcasting in a pluralist democratic state.[16] Reith concentrated on the central issue of programming. Someone, or some body, would have to decide, somehow, what was to be broadcast, and when. On what basis were such programming considerations to be founded? The principles were clear to John Reith. His confidence was wholly characteristic. It was not just a matter of providing entertainment. There was a *responsibility*, vested in those who organized broadcasting, to bring the *best* from every department of human knowledge, achievement and endeavour into the nation's homes. All that was hurtful and vulgar was to be eschewed. Broadcasting was to *lead* public taste, not follow it. Radio broadcasting, as he was to say in a memorable phrase, was to be the sword which parts the clouds of ignorance. Over and above this, it had a role to play in increasing public and national harmony, bringing all classes together, reinforcing the sense of national identity and unity. It had a role to play in the functionality of our democracy. In Reith's view, the monopoly of the BBC would have to be extended, in order to develop the idea of broadcasting as a public service along the lines he envisaged, as a national service of guaranteed quality. The Company, in his view, would have to undergo a change of status, to become a corporation in the public sector, but it must stand free from direct government control. He had begun to formulate a pattern for a national system of broadcasting as yet some way in the future. As it was, the Company tried to extend their news and coverage of outside events – official functions, speeches, ceremonials – but continued to be obliged to stick to the seven o'clock rule.

BROADCASTING AND THE GENERAL STRIKE

By the beginning of 1926 it was obvious that things were heading for a showdown in the mining industry. By way of preparation for the coming conflict the miners' union formed an alliance with railwaymen and transport workers. The government began its plans, too, and England was divided into ten areas, each with a civil commissioner. A register of volunteer drivers was kept to maintain delivery of essential goods, and plans were made for the navy to control the power stations. A government commission on the mines reported in March 1926 and recommended certain improvements in the future – including pithead baths, nationalization of royalties, amalgamation of smaller pits, other improvements in working conditions – but also an immediate reduction of pay. The owners rejected all recommended improvements but accepted the idea of reducing pay, adding a recommendation of their own – longer hours. Talks between both sides and the government continued throughout April, to no avail. On 1 May the miners were locked out, and on the evening of 2 May the printers at the *Daily Mail* refused to set up an Editorial endorsing government policy vis-à-vis proposals for strike-breaking. The one and only national strike in our history began at midnight on 3 May.[17] It lasted a mere nine days, but its impact on British broadcasting was to last decades.

The Crawford Committee recommended that radio broadcasting should continue to be run as a single authority monopoly under public control. The BBC was to be established as a corporation, under a charter granted by the government; it was to be run by a governing body representing a fairly wide spectrum of the nation. The actual range represented was interesting – Sir John Gordon Nairne, formerly of the Bank of England, Dr Montagu Rendell, ex-headmaster of Winchester, Mrs Philip Snowden, wife of the Labour ex-Chancellor of the Exchequer; the chairman was George Herbert Hyde Villiers, sixth earl of Clarendon, former Lord-in-Waiting to King George and Chief Whip for the Conservatives in the House of Lords, the vice chairman was Joseph Albert Pease, the first Baron Gainford, Quaker iron and coal magnate, Liberal MP and former Postmaster-General.

Reith had always insisted that broadcasting should be reasonably free of constraints on issues of politics and controversy, and he found these recommendations tending towards restraint and caution. Nevertheless, the behaviour of the British Broadcasting Company during the General Strike fully vindicated the faith in the Company implied by the Crawford Committee Report.

Radio broadcasting suddenly had greatness thrust upon it. There were no newspapers. Stanley Baldwin, rightly perceiving in his Home Secretary,

Winston Churchill, an undoubted capacity to make this situation even worse than it was, decided to keep him far too busy to have the time to further tensions. He asked him to run a government newspaper, the *British Gazette*. The government had the power to commandeer radio broadcasting. Several powerful members of Baldwin's Cabinet wanted the government to do so, and use its control of communication to stifle the strike almost at birth. John Reith's compliance with the government's position, soon recognized by Baldwin, meant that a take-over was not necessary. The British Broadcasting Company would deliver without the embarrassment of direct government control. This was a much more gentlemanly arrangement.

Reith's actions were his own, but were no doubt driven by his fear that, if he did not toe the line, the Company would forfeit its independence. His view now seems naive. Clearly he reasoned that the government, elected in a free and democratic manner in a secret ballot, represented the British people. The Broadcasting Company should speak for the British people, too. And therefore, the British Broadcasting Company should support the government. As Reith himself wrote at the time in a memorandum (which has since achieved notoriety in broadcasting history): 'Assuming the BBC is for the people, and that the Government is for the people, it follows that the BBC must be for the Government in this crisis too.'[18]

During the strike the seven-hour rule was waived and the BBC broadcast five bulletins of news a day. In the absence of news agencies the Company had to put together its own news stories – special messages, announcements, official notices, reports of proceedings in Parliament, regular updates as to the current situation and other news items. This was the work of a specially established News Section within the BBC – a little acorn from which a mighty oak has indeed grown.

The British Broadcasting Company considered that its behaviour during the General Strike was impressively disinterested. This may well be a difficult impression to hold in the light of the fact that the Prime Minister had access to the microphone (and had BBC help in drafting his broadcast speeches) but the Leader of the Opposition, Ramsay MacDonald, was not allowed to broadcast. Nor were trade-union leaders given access to radio broadcasting, and even the Archbishop of Canterbury, who wished to broadcast a message of conciliation, was denied access to the airwaves. The government's was the sole voice to be heard during the crisis. It tried to steer a middle course between the conflicting sides of the dispute and kept at by all rumours of revolution or Bolshevism, attempting to maintain good public morale and national unity.[19] The Company's behaviour found favour with Baldwin's government after the strike, but clearly did not satisfy all quarters. Ellen Wilkinson, Labour MP for Middlesborough, wrote to *Radio Times* on 28 May 1926:

The attitude of the BBC during the Strike caused pain and indignation to many subscribers. I travelled by car over two thousand miles during the Strike and addressed very many meetings. Everywhere the complaints were bitter that a national service subscribed to by every class should have given only one side of the dispute. Personally I feel like asking the Postmaster General for my licence fee back.

At the same time, John Reith was anxious to push home the advantage he felt the BBC had achieved by its conduct, and wrote to the Post Office suggesting that the lead the Company had adopted during the crisis should be seen as a precedent on which to build future broadcasting policy:

The recent Emergency proved conclusively, if proof were required, how important a factor Broadcasting can be in the life of the community, and we have, as you know, long felt that it is much to be regretted that the influence of the Service should be so restricted ... We are anxious to take a lead in ordinary times, as we were through force of circumstances bound to take in the Emergency.[20]

Reith's ambitions for the BBC were considerable. He was very anxious to ensure that the arrangements necessary to bring the Corporation into being should not restrict the development of his dream for a broadcasting system in the UK which he made clear in a paper he drafted and sent to all Members of Parliament.

The BBC feels that the service cannot stand still. If it does not go forward, it must decline. The saturation point of productive and efficient expenditure on broadcasting is not yet within sight. Moreover, if it is desirable to make broadcasting a permanently supplementary source of public revenue, much more satisfactory results may reasonably be anticipated if the service is more fully developed, particularly in research, equipment and improved quality and variety of programmes, before its resources are curtailed.[21]

Reith's major contention was that the funding proposals – a share of gross licence income on a sliding scale – were grossly inadequate to fuel his ambitious plans. After $12\frac{1}{2}$ per cent was taken out to pay Post Office collecting expences etc., the BBC were to get 90 per cent of the first million licences, 80 per cent of the second million, 70 per cent of the third million and 60 per cent of the fourth and following millions. The BBC was also allowed to borrow up to £500,000. It is important to remember (especially in the light of some recent opinion) that Reith's opposition was considerable, and it was only after the government threatened to fire the existing board of governors and replace them with those who would be willing to sign the Charter that Reith agreed, under violent protest, to sign. Another thing which irked him was the ban on broadcasts about controversial issues.

In one respect at least the government had played its hand deftly. Instead of bringing the new BBC into official being under the Companies Act or by special statute, it had been resolved that the new corporation should be established by Royal Charter – thus creating the very interesting (and in most respects valid) impression that the British Broadcasting Corporation was by no means simply a creature of Parliament. It is fact that Reith, after expecting that funding and controversial broadcasts would be subject to further negotiation, was deeply aggravated to learn that the Postmaster-General announced in the House of Commons that the Charter was 'an agreed' document. Reith immediately wrote to the Chairman of the Governors of the BBC.

> I cannot express my opinion of the way that the Post Office has treated us. They have been unfair, arbitrary and quite dishonest. They have printed outside the document that the terms were mutually agreed ... The constitution was to be changed to admit more scope and more autonomy, but none of these has materialized.

As Asa Briggs points out, the highly upholstered ceremonial prose of the Charter gives no hint of the acrimony behind the scenes.

> Whereas it has been made to appear to us that more than two million persons in Our United Kingdom of Great Britain and Northern Ireland have applied for and taken out Licences to instal and work apparatus for ... the purpose of receiving Broadcasting programmes AND WHEREAS in view of the widespread interest which is thereby shown to be taken by Our People in the Broadcasting Service and of the great value of the Service as a means of education and entertainment, We deem it desirable that the Service should be developed and exploited to the best advantage and in the national interest ... [by] a Corporation charged with these duties ... [and] created by the exercise of Our Royal Prerogative.[22]

The British Broadcasting Company was wound up and, at a farewell dinner, Reith made a speech in which he attempted to summarize his broadcasting policies. These suggest continuity in the development of his philosophy of public-service broadcasting, which is very interesting in the light of its subsequent manifestations in the British Broadcasting Corporation:

> We have broadcast systematically and increasingly good music; we have developed educational courses for school-children and for adults; we have broadcast the Christian religion and tried to reflect the spirit of common-sense Christian ethics which we believe to be a necessary component of citizenship and culture. We have endeavoured to exclude anything which might, directly or indirectly, be harmful. We have proved, as expected, that the supply of good things creates the demand for more. We have tried to found a tradition of public service, and to dedicate the service of broadcasting to humanity in its fullest sense. We believe that a new national asset has been created; not the kind of asset which brings credit entries to the books of the Exchequer, though it happens to be that kind of asset too and to a much greater extent than we had imagined ... the asset referred to is of a moral and not the material order – that which, down the years, brings the compound interest of happier homes, broader culture and true citizenship.[23]

It seems strange, but at the very moment when it might have seemed to Reith that he was about to realize his walk with destiny, to fulfil the great task his Creator had in mind for him – running the British Broadcasting Corporation – he was beset with unexpected difficulties. The first came through tensions in the board of governors, particularly from Mrs Snowden and Lord Clarendon. The second found its source in his own personality, as he was the first to admit. The BBC which had fallen into his lap was run by committee; he was not a good committee man, being, by experience, by nature and indeed by temperament, autocratic. He wrote of himself,

> I have always functioned best when responsibility for decision rested solely on me. Every faculty is then alerted, mobilized. When, as on a committee, others are involved, it has often been otherwise. I can neither explain nor defend; it is certainly not the result of a deliberate decision to sit back and let others do the thinking and deciding. It is at least as likely to indicate respect as disrespect for other people.[24]

Other members of the board found him difficult. Mrs Snowden, for example, thought him an egoist, and utterly unable to delegate responsibility. A favourite weapon in his armoury was to threaten resignation. Clarendon likened Reith to Mussolini. Nevertheless tensions eased and mutual trust returned at the end of the decade when Lord Clarendon went to South Africa as Governor-General, and John Whitley, Liberal MP for Halifax and Speaker of the House of Commons, became Chairman of the BBC Board of Governors.

CONSOLIDATION

Reith was gradually recruiting what he regarded as a sound senior team around him, including several whom he got to know through the establishment, one of whom was Cecil Graves, nephew of Earl Grey of Faffoden, regarded for several years as the man most likely to succeed Reith as Director-General. Roger Eckersley, his Controller of Programmes, was appointed through the agency of his brother Peter, head of the BBC's Engineering Division. Roger was very useful to Reith as he was an accomplished socialite and entertained at a property in Thurloe Square maintained at BBC expense for general public relations and diplomatic purposes. (It was Eckersley who taught Reith how to tie a bow-tie.) It has been estimated that these functions cost the Corporation thirty thousand pounds a year, but the value to the BBC was considerable – a wide cross-section of the public thus met BBC personnel and it was a useful listening post for current attitudes, opinions and anxieties; it also introduced possible recruits for BBC staff. However, Peter Eckersley was compelled to leave the BBC in 1929 when he was involved in a divorce case.

In 1929 Reith promoted Val Gielgud (brother of John Gielgud) from assistant editor of *Radio Times* to Director of Productions, responsible for all productions of drama and variety. He was to build up BBC radio drama into the largest radio drama production company in the world, with an output of over a thousand productions a year. Val Gielgud was an inspired choice, for he very soon realized that radio drama was not simply West End theatre broadcast on the wireless. Radio required a new kind of drama, conceived in terms of words and sounds, and performed in a manner wholly unlike drama on the stage, but with tone and attitude suitable to broadcasting. He once employed the great stage tragedian Henry Ainley to play Othello and recalled,

> In Henry Ainley's mind the studio remained obstinately equated with a super Drury Lane and he pulled out every stop of that magnificent organ, his voice, to such effect that I had to station two 'effects' boys – one at each of his elboys – to withdraw him gently but firmly to a distance from the microphone. His performance was magnificent but it was not broadcasting.[25]

Val Gielgud fortunately knew what broadcast drama was and set about achieving it on the nation's wireless. Radio broadcasting in its initial stages of development in most countries followed a similar pattern – news and information services regularly scheduled, with what was deemed appropriate entertainment filling in the gaps. Each national culture produced its own 'appropriate' entertainment. In Italy there was a penchant for opera; in Austria, Strauss waltzes and Mozart; America's oldest surviving item of broadcast entertainment is *The Grand ol' Opery* – Country and Western music. Sometimes very local interests produced very interesting results. It is a fact that WGY players in Schenectady, New York, broadcast plays from as early as 1922. In Britain there was a manifest cultural bias towards drama, and it was here that Val Gielgud fulfilled the pioneering role Reith had assigned to him. An excerpt from Shakespeare's *Julius Caesar* was broadcast in 1922 and the first specially commissioned radio drama went on air in 1923. These endeavours were ably assisted by Charles Lewis, the first Organizer of Programmes. In 1924 he wrote a book which has become invaluable evidence in constructing our understanding of what really motivated the founding fathers of public service broadcasting – *Broadcasting From Within*. In a key passage, Lewis spoke of always attempting to 'keep on the upper side of public taste, and to cater for the majority, 75% of the time' – the remainder, he was certain, should be set apart for certain important minorities.

Certain items were to be avoided: sensational murder trials, unsavoury divorce cases, for example. Things like this, if people really wanted them, could be got from print media. Reading, he argued, was a private matter.

Radio broadcasting, Lewis realized, was a very different thing. Children might be listening. As well as that, why drag in the 'seamier side of life', he asked. The wireless might attract large numbers of listeners by doing this kind of thing, but it would not then be realizing its role as 'a permanent asset to our national life'. Moreover, radio should be free from direct political control.

> It must establish itself as an independent public body, willing to receive any point of view in debate against its adversary. Its unique position gives the public an opportunity they have never had before of hearing both sides of a question expounded by experts. This is of great general utility, for it enables the 'man in the street' to take an active interest in his country's affairs.[26]

Reith was by no means ploughing a lonely furrow. Before the decade was out, it was clear he had able hands to help him, and there was general agreement as to what should be planted and cultivated. Looking back at those early, optimistic, days, one cannot but be impressed at their belief in the fertility of the ground.

NOTES

1. John Charles Walsham Reith, *Broadcast Over Britain* (London, 1924), pp. 78ff.
2. James Clerk-Maxwell (1831–79) was elected the first Professor of Experimental Physics at Cambridge in 1871. Earlier in his career he was Fellow of Trinity College 1855, and Professor of Natural Philosophy at Aberdeen 1856–60 and at King's College, London 1860–65.
3. David Edward Hughes (1831–1900) was born in London but left with his family for the United States when he was seven. In 1850 he was Professor of Music at Bardstown College, Kentucky, and later moved into natural philosophy. He brought his telegraph-printing machine to Europe in 1867, where it was widely used and earned him several awards and prizes. He played a major role in developing telephony and the carbon-transmitting microphone. He also contributed major work on theories of magnetism. He died in London.
4. Heinrich Rudolph Hertz (1857–94) originally studied engineering but later turned to physics. He worked at Berlin, Kiel and Karlsruhr, where he became Professor of Physics. In 1889 he became professor at Bonn, where his early death interrupted his vital work which might have led to his own discovery of X-rays.
5. Eugene Lyons, *David Sarnoff: A Biography* (New York, 1966), p. 58.
6. Ibid., pp. 59–60.
7. Ibid., pp. 71–2
8. Joseph Horowitz, *Understanding Toscanini* (London, 1987), pp. 150–1.
9. Lee De Forest, quoted in James Trager, *The People's Chronology* (London, 1979), p. 813.

10. Daniel J. Czitrom, *Media and the American Mind: From Morse to McLuhan* (Chapel Hill, North Carolina, 1982), p. 81.
11. Anthony Smith, 'Licences and Liberty', in Colin MacCabe and Olivia Stewart, *The BBC and Public Service Broadcasting* (Manchester, 1986), pp. 13–14.
12. Quoted in Andrew Boyle, *Only the Wind Will Listen: Reith of the BBC* (London, 1972), pp. 17–18.
13. See Asa Briggs, *The History of Broadcasting in the United Kingdom* (Oxford, 1965), Vol. 1, pp. 174ff.
14. Boyle, p. 141.
15. *The Broadcasting Committee Report* (The Sykes Report) (London, 1923) p. 6.
16. See Paddy Scannell and David Cardiff, *A Social History of Broadcasting* (Oxford, 1991) pp. 7ff.
17. See Christopher Forman, *May 1926 The General Strike: Britain's Aborted Revolution* (London, 1944) and A.J.P. Taylor, *English History 1914–1945* (Oxford, 1965), pp. 239–52.
18. Philip Schlesinger, *Putting Reality Together: BBC News* (London, 1978), p. 18.
19. Michael Morris, *The General Strike* (Harmondsworth, 1976), p. 251.
20. Scannell and Cardiff, p. 34.
21. BBC Archives, quoted in Boyle, p. 209.
22. Briggs, vol. 1, pp. 403ff.
23. John Charles Walsham Reith, *Into the Wind* (London, 1949), pp. 108ff.
24. Ibid., pp. 118–19.
25. Val Gielgud, *Years in a Mirror* (London, 1965), p. 75.
26. Charles Lewis, *Broadcasting From Within* (London, 1924), pp. 48–50.

CHAPTER SEVEN

British Cinema: From Cottage Industry to Mass Entertainment

Lez Cooke

Cinema was barely five years old when the twentieth century dawned – a scientific novelty destined to become the first mass entertainment industry of the new century. Yet who could have envisaged the phenomenal growth of the cinema as a mass medium when, on 17 October 1894, the first Kinetoscope parlour opened in England? How many of the clientele who stooped to peer through the peep-holes of the Kinetoscope machines at 70 Oxford Street, to see films which lasted less than a minute, could have conceived of sitting in a picture palace seating hundreds or even thousands of people, to watch a film which lasted two hours or more? Yet by the end of the 1920s the latter experience had become commonplace and twenty million people were going to see films at Britain's four thousand cinemas every week.

While the opening of Edison's Kinetoscope parlour marked the first public appearance of moving pictures in Britain, it was over a year before the British public had its first opportunity to see films projected onto a screen. Following its premiere in Paris on 28 December 1895 a programme of films by Auguste and Louis Lumière was screened at the Regent Street Polytechnic on 20 February 1896, the first public performance of projected films in Britain. The programme consisted of 'actualities' like *Workers Leaving A Factory*, *Demolition Of A Wall* and *Arrival Of A Train* plus staged scenes like the one of the gardener and the hosepipe, *L'Arroseur Arrosé*, which was popular enough to be remade several times by other film makers over the next few years. Following the Regent Street screening the Lumière programme transferred to the Empire Theatre in Leicester Square where it became a fifteen-minute item in the variety programme there. Soon after, the British pioneer Robert William Paul was invited to show a programme of his films at the Alhambra Theatre, another music hall in Leicester Square, which was anxious to compete with the Empire for the record crowds which were being attracted by the Cinematographe Lumière.

By the end of 1896, films had been screened in many other parts of the country and, by the turn of the century, nightly screenings of films in 'penny gaffs' (disused shops), fairs, amusement parlours and music halls had become commonplace. But in 1900 there were still no purpose-built cinemas – film production was little more than a cottage industry and moving pictures had yet to achieve an institutional presence in British towns.

THE BEGINNINGS OF CINEMA IN BRITAIN

Although some of them had experience of photography and the optical lantern, the early British film makers were not artists but craftsmen – inventors and manufacturers like R. W. Paul who started making films in order to sell the equipment he was manufacturing. In early 1895 Paul, along with another British pioneer, Birt Acres, shot a number of Kinetoscope films including *Incident Outside Clovelly Cottage, Barnet*, 'the first successful kinetoscope film to be made in England' according to John Barnes.[1] In late 1895 Paul turned his attention to the development of a film projector – having previously manufactured copies of Edison's Kinetoscopes when he discovered that Edison had not taken out patents on them in Britain – and in April 1896, having developed a new camera, Paul began making films to be projected onto a screen. Like most of the first films these were actualities, but he gradually began to produce staged films like *Come Along Do!* (1898), possibly the first film in Britain to be made up of more than one shot.

By 1904 Paul was making longer narrative films like the seven shot *Buy Your Own Cherries* (lasting about four minutes), a scene by scene reproduction of a nineteenth-century lantern slide show about temperance. This film illustrates the evangelizing tendency evident in many magic-lantern shows of the late nineteenth century in its story of a man rescued from the degradations of drink by a Methodist preacher. After joining the Independent Order of Good Templars a miraculous transformation takes place and in the next scene he is able to resist the temptations of the gin house and instead buys cherries from a cart outside. The transformation undergone is illustrated by the *mise en scène* in the final scene, where the decor and clothing, not to mention the gifts brought home for the family by the father, suggest a comfortable middle-class household rather than the impoverished working-class one illustrated in the earlier scene. The ideological implications here are obvious. Cinema was essentially a middle-class invention – even though it soon became an entertainment for the mass working-class audience – and the fact that most of the early films were made by middle-class men like Paul is evident in the subject matter of many of the early films. The temperance films simply continued the nineteenth-century tradition of the middle classes providing moral guidance for the masses.

Unlike radio and television, whose beginnings were subject to state regulation, cinema developed in the free competitive market situation of late-Victorian capitalism. There was little or no state involvement in the early development of the cinema and it wasn't until the 1907 Patents Act that the confusion caused by the invention and manufacture of dozens of different kinds of camera and projection mechanisms began to be sorted out. Many of the early cinema showmen who were buying projectors – and the films to go with them – very soon found it expedient also to purchase a camera in order to make their own films. Getting hold of new films which were compatible with the equipment they owned could be difficult.

One such showman was William Haggar who earned a living touring the fairgrounds of Wales and the west of England with his travelling theatre company in the late nineteenth century. Having introduced a photographic business as a sideshow, he bought a projector in 1897 with the profits made after a successful season in Aberafon. The following summer he handed the theatre over to his son and went on tour with his film projector. As Michael Chanan records in his book on the early British cinema, Haggar 'opened on 5th April 1898 at the Aberafon fair, and collected £15 in twopences and threepences. The following week at Pontypridd he took nothing at all, owing to a combination of rain and a strike. Such were the tribulations of the itinerant film shows'.[2] Haggar started to make his own films in order to compete with other travelling showmen in the region after a competitor scored a big success with a film of the 1901 Wales–England football match at Cardiff. But unlike many travelling showmen who were content to film actualities in the places they stopped at (thus contributing local interest to their programme of films) Haggar staged dramatic films using his own theatre company. *The Maid Of Cefn Ydfa* (1902), one of his first films, proved how attractive dramatic films were to Haggar's working-class audience, taking £40 at the ticket office on the first screening alone, and he reputedly sold 480 prints of his 1905 film *The Salmon Poachers*, over 100 of them being exported to Europe through a distribution agreement he had with Gaumont.

The example of Haggar demonstrates clearly the link between a form of nineteenth-century popular entertainment like the travelling theatre shows, which according to Chanan featured lewd melodramas as well as Shakespeare in their repertoire, and the new entertainment form of moving pictures. Raymond Williams has discussed the different ways in which cinema drew on, and was influenced by, aspects of nineteenth-century popular culture, especially forms of melodrama.

As melodrama became popular, from the 1820s, its plots increasingly resembled events reported in the popular press: sensational crimes and seductions – though in melodrama these were eventually concluded by providential rescues and escapes – at times presented in a radical perspective. From the 1860s there existed in effect two broad kinds of melodrama: this well-remembered type, but also the earlier and always numerically more common 'costume epic', peopled by pirates, bandits, sailors and 'historical' figures of all kinds. Each type was to contribute massively to cinema: at first by direct adaptation (*Pearl White, Jane Shore, Ben Hur*); later by the cinematic adaptation of similar plots, themes and shows, and (as in Britain before 1914) by the addition of such new but congruent techniques as the close-up and the chase.[3]

Part of the popularity of Haggar's *The Salmon Poachers* was undoubtedly the fact that it was a chase film, one of the most popular forms of early cinema, but Noël Burch has commented also on the 'subversive' aspects of Haggar's films which may have appealed to a downtrodden audience.[4] In *The Salmon Poachers*, for example, the poachers, having been apprehended by the police while poaching salmon at midnight – an encounter which provokes a chase and a series of violent confrontations – outwit their pursuers and make their escape with the catch. Perhaps his experience as a travelling showman resulted in Haggar being more in touch with the desires of his working-class audience than many of his middle-class contemporaries.

George Albert Smith, one of the latter, was based in Brighton, and was thus far removed from the industrial working-class heartlands of film-makers like Haggar in South Wales, or Frank Mottershaw in Sheffield. But Smith was very important in the early development of the cinema, making a major contribution to the development of film form. He was experimenting with superimposition as early as 1897 and using close-ups in films like *Grandma's Reading Glass* and *As Seen By Telescope* (both 1900) eight years before D.W. Griffith, who is often credited in popular histories of the cinema with the 'invention' of the close-up. Smith is also credited with originating the point-of-view shot and with the idea of breaking a scene down into a number of shots taken from different positions, both innovations being evident in *Grandma's Reading Glass*. British cinema before 1905 is renowned for such innovations in film technique, to the extent that it led the world in developments in film form in the early years. Noël Burch has suggested that this precociousness may have been due to the tradition of visual storytelling in the lantern slide shows with which many of the pioneers were familiar, a tradition which was more advanced in Britain in the late nineteenth century than it was in other countries.[5]

FROM CRAFT TO INDUSTRY

During its early years film making was very much a one-person enterprise where a manufacturer like Paul or a travelling showman like Haggar would film actualities, or set up staged scenes using friends or members of the family, directing the scene, operating the camera, often processing the films themselves and, in the case of showmen like Haggar, exhibiting them too. But it did not take long for the separate branches of production, distribution and exhibition to develop and for cinema to move towards becoming a more industrial activity.

By 1898 two enterprising showmen, J. D. Walker and E. G. Turner, who had formed a company called Walterdaw, had initiated the process of film distribution by conceiving the idea of renting films from their large stock to other exhibitors. The advent of distribution undoubtedly accelerated the development of cinema as a mass medium, for it allowed exhibitors to make more frequent programme changes than in the days when they had to buy films for screening and this in turn created a demand for more films. The development of a new form of film manufacture by Eastman Kodak in 1899 also served to initiate a shift from artisanal to industrial production as it forced many manufacturer-producers to standardize their equipment for the new film stock, thus disadvantaging those producers and exhibitors whose equipment did not conform to the Eastman Kodak standard.

By the time Cecil Hepworth produced *Rescued By Rover* in 1905, he was employing actors to appear alongside himself and his family and he had his regular director, Lewin Fitzhamon, behind the camera. His hired actors were paid 10s. 6d. and although the film was longer than average and used arc flood lamps in some of the scenes it still cost only £7 13s. 6d. to make. A tremendous success, *Rescued By Rover* sold nearly 400 prints at £10 13s. 9d. each. Even allowing for the fact that the film had to be remade twice due to the negative wearing out in the printing, Hepworth clearly made a tidy profit.

Another classic example of middle-class film making, *Rescued By Rover* is interesting for its middle-class perspective on the poor, conveying what has been described as 'the privileged classes' dread of the lower depths' in its portrayal of the baby of a middle-class family who is abducted by a member of the poor, drinking classes.[6] The class divide is illustrated in the film in the distance travelled by Rover from the middle-class family home in a leafy suburb to the row of plain terraced housing in the working-class district which is the home of the alcoholic woman who has abducted the baby. The river crossed by Rover en route emphasizes the divide, both physical and meta-phorical, between the classes and, as in *Buy Your Own Cherries*, the decor and clothing also establish the class difference: the comfortable middle-class

171

household contrasted with the stark attic room – bereft of furniture, with bare rafters and crumbling plaster – where the woman lives. Similarly the ragged shawl of the woman illustrates her poverty and contrasts with the incongruous top hat and tails of the father as he follows Rover's trail to the rescue of the baby whose fine clothing is abandoned to the woman in the attic.

Rescued By Rover was an international success. In 1905 there was still a healthy market for British films abroad, but with the setting up of the Motion Picture Patents Company in America in 1908 small importers like the British companies were driven out of the American market and this was to have a drastic effect upon British film production. Yet even before this, production had begun to stagnate in Britain. The British pioneers had been very successful, but as technicians rather than businessmen. They had been instrumental in the development of cinema in Britain as a craft, a cottage industry which had its roots in the nineteenth-century magic-lantern shows, but they were unable, or unwilling, to adapt to the development of cinema as a mass industry. And from 1905, with an ever increasing demand for longer and more sophisticated films, many of the pioneers withdrew from film making as cinema underwent its own industrial revolution, making the transition from a cottage industry to an industry of mass production and mass entertainment.

THE INSTITUTIONALIZATION OF CINEMA

The reasons for the increased demand for films during the first decade of the twentieth century had much to do with a gradual increase in leisure time for the working classes during the period. Where the standard working week had been between sixty and seventy hours in the nineteenth century, it was down to fifty-three by 1910, and this increase in leisure time coincided with a change in forms of popular entertainment. The music-hall was in decline as a working-class entertainment, having been appropriated by the middle classes with the building of larger halls in town centres, and cinema had emerged to fill the gap that had opened up at the bottom end of the market. With the emergence of cinema as a mass medium there was increasing paternalistic concern about the moral effect films were having upon their working-class audiences, especially young people.

> It was partly the gloom, as well as its comparative novelty, which made the cinema in the 1900s a focus for adult anxiety about the sexual morality of youth. There were reports published by bodies such as the National Council of Public Morals deploring what these unsupervised groups of young people might be led to think in such conditions.[7]

The concern was exacerbated by the fact that there was no film censorship at this time and it was not until 1912 that the industry made moves to pre-empt state censorship by setting up its own organization – the British Board of Film Censors. Gradually, however, cinema was drawn under the umbrella of state regulation. The 1907 Patents Act had rationalized the free market entrepreneurial beginnings of British cinema, effectively ending its period of existence as a cottage industry. This was followed in 1909 by the first piece of legislation directed exclusively at the cinema. The Cinematograph Act, which became law at the beginning of 1910, was designed to regulate the exhibition of films, the ostensible purpose of the Act being 'to safeguard the public from the danger which arises from fires at cinematograph entertainments, which are especially liable to outbreaks of fire on account of the long highly inflammable films which are used in the lanterns'.[8] In a study of film censorship in the period, however, Annette Kuhn has argued that the safety issue was little more than a pretext for the extension of institutional control over the rapidly expanding medium.

> Local licensing authorities were quick to take advantage of the latitude the Act appeared to offer in the matter of determining licensing conditions. Even before the statute came into force, the LCC [London County Council] had recommended a condition prohibiting exhibition of films on Sundays. The Cinematograph Act was already being used for a purpose other than that which had supposedly inspired it.[9]

Purpose-built cinemas had already begun to appear as early as 1905 but the Cinematograph Act gave impetus to the building of more cinemas to replace the makeshift penny gaffs.[10] The rapid growth in exhibition during this period is indicated by the fact that, by 1910, there were about 1,600 cinemas in Britain, 500 of them in London, although it is likely that these figures include converted halls and other places of exhibition and do not refer to purpose-built cinemas alone.

As a result of the 1909 Act the tradition of itinerant film showmanship declined as cinemas established a permanent institutional presence in British towns and with the dying out of this tradition the industry, concerned to enhance the status and reputation of the movies, began to shake off its image of a fairground entertainment for the illiterate masses.

CINEMA WOOS THE MIDDLE CLASSES

Although middle-class intellectuals continued to despise the cinema, the new cinema owners in the early 1910s were anxious to attract a more upmarket clientele to their picture palaces, desiring to emulate the 'respectable' image of the legitimate theatre. The industry responded with a string of adaptations of stage and literary classics – *Henry VIII* (1911), *Richard III* (1911), *Hamlet* (1913), *David Copperfield* (1913) – inviting famous stage actors like Herbert Beerbohm Tree and Johnstone Forbes-Robertson to bring their celebrated Shakespearean roles to the screen. Cinema had previously been despised by the theatre as a fairground entertainment for the uncultured masses, but as cinema moved out of the fairgrounds it gradually became more 'respectable' and was able to lure stage actors with the promise of a wider audience and greater income. With the development of new film studios on the outskirts of London from 1915 actors were able to pursue a dual career, filming during the day and returning to the West End to appear on stage at night.

The film industry saw the possibility of acquiring cultural prestige in its flirtation with the stage and the theatre was content to let cinema bask in its reflected glory. But the price that cinema paid was an abandonment of the inventiveness which had characterized much of the work of the pioneers. Stage plays were transposed to the screen in a static, unimaginative manner, usually filmed straight on without any variation in camera positioning or any attempt to utilize the visual possibilities of the medium which had been explored with such enthusiasm by the likes of G.A. Smith and others in the early years.

Theatre and literature provided cinema with ready-made plots and characters, but because most of the screen adaptations were located within a tradition of nineteenth-century realism it is hardly surprising that narrative cinema also developed along these lines, rather than pursuing an alternative modernist aesthetic of anti-illusionism, suggestions of which had been glimpsed in some of the work of the early pioneers.

In an attempt to gain a middle-class audience literary classics were treated with reverence, even though they were often reduced to a skeleton of the plot as a result of running times which were often less than an hour. The 1911 version of *Richard III*, for example, was reduced to just half an hour, and half of this time was taken up with title cards! Moreover, as with many adaptations of stage plays, there was a considerable lack of visual imagination in the transposition of *Richard III* to the screen.

> The seventeen scenes which amount for the other half of the footage all last less than three minutes, several less than half a minute. This is extremely short for Shakespearean scenes, and it is obvious that the intensification of gesture has been accompanied by drastic cuts in both the speeches and the action of the play. For shots, on the other hand – and they are, in effect, both scenes and shots at the same time – they are on the average exceedingly long and more than a little tedious. Each scene is a single medium shot which takes in the whole of a small stage. There is no camera movement or change of camera angle in the whole film and the only cuts are those marked by titles between each scene.[11]

One of the early pioneers who made the transition from shorts to features did however show more awareness of the possibility of 'opening out' stage plays. Cecil Hepworth, in his 1913 production of *Hamlet*, with Forbes-Robertson, took the cast out of the studio for as many scenes as possible, reconstructing Elsinore Castle at Lulworth Cove in Dorset and filming other scenes, including the death of Ophelia, in the grounds of Hartsbourne Manor in Hertfordshire. Though not directed by Hepworth but by E. Hay Plumb, the film showed glimpses of what could be achieved in transposing Shakespeare to the screen, composing for the camera instead of framing a proscenium arch, and using occasional close-ups and reaction shots for dramatic effect.

But on the whole Shakespeare and the classics did not translate well to film. Works of popular fiction, however, elicited a less reverential approach than that which was accorded to the classics, encouraging a less stilted, more *cinematic* treatment.

> It has become a cliché that films derived from second-rate fiction are more likely to be successful *as films* than those derived from classics. The silent screen was already offering some evidence of this, as it staked out the literary territory and dug with results that reflected, not the prestige of its sources, but the varying degrees of film-makers' command of the screen's representational mode... . *David Copperfield* is a good example of primitive film – little camera movement, no scene dissection, no use of close-up – whereas *Tom Brown's Schooldays* (1916) reveals some near continuity cutting (from faces peering into a shop to their owners entering), a clear use of a point-of-view shot as a girl watches boys fighting, a move away from the tableau-like frontality of *Copperfield*, and some vestigial scene dissection. We are, that is, getting *into* the picture.[12]

'Getting into the picture' is what Noël Burch has characterized as the process by which cinema developed from a primitive mode of representation – as in the frontal tableaux of the early films – to an institutional mode of representation – the latter being essentially the development of the rhetoric of continuity editing by means of which the viewer is drawn into the narrative world of the film through the deployment of close-ups, point-of-view shots, eyeline matches, reverse angle shooting and all of the other elements of the continuity system which were in the process of being perfected at this time. As Roy Armes has noted, this process had an ideological function, serving to institutionalize the feature-length film in a form which was designed to reassure rather than provoke its audiences at a time of uncertainty and rapid social change.

> During the fifteen years of its existence the cinema's development had already been shaped in accordance with nineteenth-century models. The increasing control which film makers had by this time acquired over all aspects of production allowed them to manipulate audience response and create a totally convincing illusory world. With the establishment of the feature-length film, the

cinema used these techniques to assert itself as a medium offering its audiences a reaffirmation of traditional values and beliefs in a changing and disorienting world.[13]

Thus a form was evolved for the new cinematic medium which conformed to the realist mode of the nineteenth-century novel, rather than the anti-realist discourse of the modernist novel, and reproduced a visual equivalent of realism in painting and the theatre, rather than experimenting with the kind of anti-illusionist visual strategies which were being developed, contemporaneously, by the Cubists, Futurists, and, in England, the Vorticists, among others.

While the adaptation of the classics reflected their literary and stage origins, the adaptation of works of popular fiction were less constrained in their cinematic style, though nevertheless adhering to the conventions of the classic realist text. The crime drama was one of the most popular genres among the mass working-class audience from the early years, initially with the adaptation of serials from magazines and then, with the move towards longer films from 1912, with the adaptation of thrillers and detective novels. The narrative drive in crime and detective fiction towards an inevitable denouement accounts in part for their popularity and also for their important role in the transition towards longer films – for the popular audience would sit through a longer film if it was a crime drama or detective thriller but were less likely to tolerate a dreary adaptation of a literary 'classic'.

We can see here the beginnings of a polarization in the audience between the mass working-class audience with an appetite for comedy, crime drama and detective thrillers, and the middle-class audience which exhibitors were trying to attract to the new picture houses with programmes of more upmarket melodramas and adaptations of stage and literary classics. While this segmentation of the audience was by no means as pronounced as this generalization may suggest, it is an early indication of the attempt by the industry to move upmarket by wooing a middle-class audience while at the same time continuing to cater for the working-class audience which still comprised the bulk of its clientele.

AMERICAN HEGEMONY

The number of stage and literary adaptations rose steadily during the early 1910s as the industry shrugged off the stagnation of the previous few years in its transition from one-reelers to longer films. The transformation from 1906 to 1918 was dramatic, reflecting the passage from cottage industry to an industry of mass entertainment. Whereas in 1904 films over seven minutes long had been exceptional, by the end of the war the economic structure of the industry was based around the ninety-minute feature film and with audiences increasing from an estimated seven to eight million per week before 1914 to twenty million per week in 1917 – cinema in Britain was undergoing a boom. But while audiences were flocking to the new cinemas during the war, it was not necessarily British films they were going to see.

While there was certainly an expansion in film production in the early 1910s, the number of British films being screened during this period stayed at around the same percentage as in 1909 when 85 per cent of the films showing in British cinemas were foreign imports. From 1913, when American imports overtook European ones, the majority of films that British audiences were going to see were not adaptations of Shakespeare and Dickens but films from *Hollywood*.

In 1909, America had contributed 30 per cent of the films screened in Britain, already double the British contribution. By the outbreak of war this had increased to 60 per cent and with the depletion of the European film industries during the war Hollywood capitalized, achieving a near total hegemony which it has never lost. By the end of the war over 80 per cent of the films being shown in British cinemas were American.

Even before the war American companies had begun setting up distribution divisions in Britain and this process was extended during the war years. The British market represented surplus profits for the American companies and because of this they were able to undercut the British distributors, selling packages of films to exhibitors and thus 'block booking' the cinemas, also encouraging exhibitors to take films that they hadn't seen, or in some cases films that hadn't even been made, in the associated practice of 'blind booking'. British distributors were forced to charge higher rates because they were dependent on the home market for their income and consequently British films were squeezed out by the American product. British film production suffered as a result with producers unwilling to gamble on the production of the more ambitious films that were needed to compete with the glossy Hollywood movies and the war was followed by a slump in the production of British films.

BRITISH CINEMA IN THE 1920S

The endeavour of British cinema to court respectability and woo the middle classes by adapting literary and stage successes was continued into the 1920s, but it was a policy that was doomed to failure. Unlike the BBC, which was founded in the 1920s and which also propagated middle-class values, British cinema was not a monopoly and its main competitor, Hollywood, was capturing the mass audience hands down. Even more galling for British cinema was that it was an Englishman, Charlie Chaplin, who was helping Hollywood to achieve its hegemony.

In 1920, Famous Players-Lasky, the production arm of the most powerful of the Hollywood studios, Paramount, set up a production division in Britain with the intention of 'making films the American way' and it was here that Alfred Hitchcock got his first job in the film industry as a title card illustrator.[14] It was symptomatic of both the malaise of British film making at this time, and the professionalism and high production values of the Hollywood films, that the person who was to emerge by the late twenties as Britain's leading film director should choose to enter the industry by working for an American company based in Britain rather than going to work for a British company. And it was because of the dearth of British talent available that Famous Players-Lasky decided to give up its British base in 1924, complaining that the films they made in Britain 'failed to reach a quality comparable to those made in the States'.[15]

One of the problems for British cinema following the war was that too many producers returned to film making with prewar attitudes and failed to adapt to changed circumstances in which American companies were calling the shots by providing British audiences with entertaining films with increasingly polished production values. Cecil Hepworth was one of the few British pioneers who continued to make films in the postwar period and, while he enjoyed some commercial success with his films, the prosaic quality of a film like *Comin' Thro' The Rye* (1922) locates it firmly in the prewar tradition of middle-class literary cinema with which the industry had tried to gain prestige. As has already been seen with his 1913 production of *Hamlet*, Hepworth liked to give his films a quality of 'Englishness' by setting them in an English landscape: 'I would never work indoors if I could possibly get into the open air. It was always in the back of my mind from the very beginning that I was to make English pictures, with all the English countryside for background and with English atmosphere and English idiom throughout.'[16] But the kind of English picture Hepworth inclined towards was a middle-class view of rural England which was far removed from the kind of picture that the mass audience was going to see.

In contrast to Hepworth's middle-class values George Pearson's films were aimed at a more working-class audience. Between 1916 and 1917 Pearson had made the *Ultus* series: four films aimed at the popular audience, beginning with *Ultus: The Man From The Dead* (1916) – crime thrillers which were designed to rival the success of the popular *Fantômas* series in France. In the early twenties he embarked upon another series based upon a character called *Squibs* in which Betty Balfour was to become one of the most popular British stars of the period as the eponymous heroine. Pearson demonstrated the possibility of producing a popular British cinema that could coexist alongside Hollywood, but the conditions for the establishment of such a cinema were not favourable in the early twenties. James Park attributes Pearson's failure to his 'lack of interest in methods of play construction [which] led him towards even more unfocused ways of organizing his films, aiming for a sort of primitive naturalism'.[17] This 'failing', however, is merely symptomatic of a more basic problem in British cinema at this time. Pearson had been involved in film making when cinema in Britain was little more than a cottage industry. Hepworth, even more so, had learnt his trade in the pioneering days of the early 1900s when 'mass production' meant running off 400 prints of *Rescued By Rover*. After the war these and other British film makers continued to apply outdated criteria to the production of feature films at a time when Hollywood had already captured the mass audience with movies which exploited the universal appeal of stars like Chaplin, Pickford and Fairbanks and which were becoming increasingly sophisticated in technique as well as more extravagant in their production values. In addition the American industry was busy consolidating its worldwide hegemony by organizing itself into a highly efficient industry with the establishment of the first vertically integrated companies.

The difficulty that British cinema was having competing with Hollywood at this time was illustrated in 1922 when only six out of 422 British films found American buyers, and while 25 per cent of the films that were shown to the trade in Britain in 1923 were British, in 1924 this was down to just 5 per cent. In 'Black November' 1924, British cinema reached its lowest ebb when every British studio was dark and in the whole of 1925 only twenty-six British films went before the cameras.[18]

Despite this spectacular collapse, talented and enterprising British directors and producers were emerging onto the scene. In 1924, following the departure of Famous Players-Lasky, the studios which they had occupied in Islington were bought by an ambitious young producer, Michael Balcon, who established his own company, Gainsborough Pictures, there. After his spell with Famous Players, Hitchcock stayed on at the studios working for Balcon in a variety of roles as assistant director, screenwriter, art director and editor before being given his first opportunity to direct, in 1925. Balcon was one of three talented producers who emerged in the 1920s, the others being Victor Saville and Herbert Wilcox. But whereas Saville and Wilcox also directed, Balcon concentrated upon producing, the first of the new breed of producer who recognized that the task of producing, like that of directing, was a specialized activity.

Balcon adopted three strategies for success: firstly, following the example set by Herbert Wilcox, he imported Hollywood stars, at considerable expense; secondly, again following Wilcox's example, he developed co-productions with

Germany, recognizing the economic advantages and the technical superiority of German studios at the height of German Expressionist film making and it was as a result of this policy that Hitchcock got his first opportunities to direct, filming *The Pleasure Garden* and *The Mountain Eagle* at the Emelka studios in Munich; thirdly, Balcon combined these strategies with a continuation of the policy of adapting stage plays and novels for the screen, but ensuring that these adaptations were from successful plays and best-selling novels.

One of the early successes of this strategy was *The Rat* (1925) starring Ivor Novello – one of the most popular stage actors of the day who also became the most famous British male film star of the period. Originally written by Novello for the screen, *The Rat* became a successful stage play before it was turned into a film by Graham Cutts, who co-founded Gainsborough with Balcon in 1924 and was the leading film director there until he was usurped by his young protégé, Alfred Hitchcock. The American star Mae Marsh was added to the cast for the film which was successful enough to merit a sequel, *The Triumph Of The Rat*, in 1926. After the success of *The Rat*, Novello appeared in *The Lodger* (1926), the film that Hitchcock himself regarded as 'the first true "Hitchcock movie" '.[19] Cutts had demonstrated with *The Rat* how a successful stage play could be turned into a visually interesting film, opening it out for the screen through the judicious application of cinematic techniques. Hitchcock went even further with *The Lodger*, imbuing it, through the use of inventive camerawork and chiaroscuro lighting, with an atmosphere of menace and suspense appropriate to the subject matter – the film being about a man (Novello) who is suspected of being Jack the Ripper and is persecuted as a result. This was Hitchcock's first film in the popular genre of the thriller, a genre with which his name was to become virtually synonymous. His thorough grounding in Hollywood cinema is evident in the sophisticated technique and narrative economy of the film and this was combined with an Expressionist style derived from the German cinema of the period, with which he was equally well acquainted. As Tom Ryall has observed, this combination represented 'a confluence of entertainment and art cinema', and Hitchcock, in the mid-1920s, seemed to be straddling the two branches of the film culture, the commercial and the artistic, the world of entertainment and the world of 'film art'.[20] Indeed *The Lodger* was considered too 'highbrow' by certain industry figures and Michael Balcon encouraged Hitchcock to make some changes to the film in order to make it more commercial, bringing in Ivor Montagu to assist him in this task.

What this illustrates is a dilemma not only for Hitchcock but for British cinema at the time, caught between the desire to produce 'art' and thus elevate the status of a medium which 'still suffered from the social opprobrium of the educated classes' and the need to compete with the more popular Hollywood films at the box office.[21] The success of *The Lodger* was that it managed to do both, proving to be both a critical and commercial success. The promise that the film showed for the future of British cinema was noted by the trade paper *Kine Weekly* at the time: '*The Lodger*, and other new productions give promise of a genuine reaction against the deeply-rooted Wardour Street superstition that America will only buy pictures similar to her own.'[22] The film held out the possibility of an indigenous British cinema that was sufficiently different from Hollywood in style and content to have a character of its own, and yet was sufficiently commercial to compete with Hollywood for a popular audience.

The Lodger was adapted from the novel by Marie Belloc Lowndes, and Hitchcock's reworking of it for the screen proved more successful than his two subsequent films which were both adaptations of stage plays: *Downhill* by Ivor Novello and *Easy Virtue* by Noël Coward. Generally novels seemed to lend themselves more readily to a cinematic treatment than stage plays where a director had to work much harder to create cinema out of material which tended to be more static and verbose. *Easy Virtue* was one of two Noël Coward plays to be filmed in 1927 and while Hitchcock brought his cinematic ingenuity to bear in an attempt to free the play from its stagebound qualities he was still handicapped by the lack of sound in conveying the nuances of Coward's dialogue. Adrian Brunel had a similar struggle with his adaptation of *The Vortex* (1927) where, according to Geoff Brown, 'lack of speech proves a distinct handicap, and the facetious titles sprinkled throughout ... are poor compensation for Coward's special brand of repartee and lancing wit'.[23] Not that the arrival of talking pictures at the end of the twenties was to see a successful fusion of stage and screen – in fact the initial difficulties of recording sound saw a return to the static 'filmed theatre' of the early years. This would have suited Bernard Shaw who insisted, when he signed a contract with British International Pictures in 1930 to film a number of his plays, that BIP provide 'faithful reproductions of the play as written and designed for ordinary theatrical representation'.[24] The result, as Brown observes, was 'tedious films bogged down with talk'.[25]

EXHIBITION CONTINUES TO BOOM

While British film production had reached crisis point in the mid-twenties the exhibition sector, riding the endless wave of popular Hollywood movies, continued to expand. By the early twenties, cinema-going had become a firmly established social habit with twenty million people going to the cinema every week and, like the audience, the number of cinemas had more than doubled from the 1,600 of 1910 to 3,878 in 1925.[26] Cinemas had also grown larger and more luxurious, befitting the description of them as 'picture palaces'. The first 4,000 seat cinema in Britain opened in Glasgow in 1925, followed by another 4,000 seater in Croydon in 1928, and cinemas seating over a thousand people were becoming increasingly commonplace.

The extent to which cinema had become established in British social life by the late twenties as the pre-eminent venue of mass entertainment is indicated in this extract from Paul Wild's study of recreation in Rochdale.

> On 26 March 1928 the Victory Super Cinema was opened, making a total of nine commercially run cinemas within a one-mile radius of the Town Hall, each showing twice nightly or continuous programmes plus matinées. Six months later the Rialto (Rialto Cinema Rochdale Ltd), with directors Madigan, Close, Lord and Hoyle, was opened with a film called 'Dawn'. Full programmes started at 2.45, 6.45 and 8.45 p.m.; prices were 1s.3d. and 6d. Perhaps most significant was the fact that the Rialto offered a café and lounge plus a well-appointed cinema, with carpets and comfortable seating. The owners emphasized: 'whilst famous for their industry and thrift, Rochdale people are removed from misery, and it seems a fairly pure prophecy that not a single unit of the twenty five thousand homes will resist the appeal of the stately Rialto pleasure house'.[27]

The building of bigger and more luxurious cinemas is symptomatic of the gradual 'embourgeoisement' of cinema during this period – a cultural development comparable to the building of the larger music halls in the late nineteenth century – and the two-tier price bracket, divided between stalls and circle, is indicative of the extent to which cinemas were by this time catering not only for a working-class audience but for the middle classes as well.

A further polarization occurred at the end of the twenties with the arrival of talking pictures. Exhibitors were forced to wire their cinemas for sound at great expense, and mergers took place between cinema chains in order to share the huge costs of conversion. This left the smaller exhibitors who could not afford the conversion to continue to show silent films in the less comfortable 'flea pits' which the poorer members of society continued to patronize while the better-off went to the new super-cinemas.

THE 1927 CINEMATOGRAPH FILMS ACT

The decline in British film production was a cause for increasing concern during the 1920s, but it was not until the middle of the decade that the importance of the cinema was acknowledged by the government, and then it was in relation to film's potential for propaganda. In a speech made in Parliament in June 1925 the Conservative prime minister, Stanley Baldwin, included a mention of the film industry.

> I think the time has come when the position of that industry in this country should be examined with a view to seeing whether it be not possible, as it is desirable, on national grounds, to see that the larger proportion of the films exhibited in this country are British, having regard ... to the enormous power which the film is developing for propaganda purposes, and the danger to which we in this country and our Empire subject ourselves if we allow that method of propaganda to be entirely in the hands of foreign countries.[28]

With America at this time contributing up to 95 per cent of the films being shown in British cinemas it was clear that it was not German or Soviet propaganda that Baldwin was concerned about. Reading between the lines of his speech one can see a concern about a growing 'Americanization' of British culture and this concern was made explicit several years later by a member of the Board of Trade.

> By 1925 the depressed state of the British industry was causing general concern. Apart from the purely industrial aspect of the matter it was felt that from the point of view of British culture and ideals it was unwise to allow the United States to dominate the cinemas of this country. At that time nearly every film shown represented American ideas set in an American atmosphere, and the accessories were American houses, American materials, American manufacturers, etc. Whatever the position today, cinematograph audiences then were made up of the most impressionable sections of the *community*, and it was felt to be of the utmost importance for our prestige, for our trade and, it was asserted, for our morals, that they should see at least some proportion of British films.[29]

As with the 1909 Act we can see once again how the second Cinematograph Act, which was ostensibly designed to boost British film production, had an implicit cultural objective – the paternalistic concern to protect the masses from the consequences of overexposure to American culture.

Baldwin's 1925 speech raised the possibility of introducing a quota for British films to ensure that they were not squeezed out by Hollywood movies, as they had been since the war. The Federation of British Industries had already shown some interest in the film industry, recognizing that its decline was 'a very visible symptom of the nation's economic problems' and the government responded by giving responsibility for the film industry to the Board of Trade in July 1925.[30] Seeing the healthy state of the exhibition sector of the industry and recognizing that Britain's traditional industries were in decline the government began to see that there might be some economic sense in investing in British film production. But first the industry had to be protected from American competition and so, in 1927, legislation was introduced which was designed to encourage British film production by ensuring that a quota of the films made in Britain would be guaranteed distribution and exhibition.

183

The quota was set initially at 7½ per cent for distributors and 5 per cent for exhibitors – both were to rise to a maximum of 20 per cent by 1936. For a film to be registered as British it was stipulated that certain criteria had to be met: the film had to be produced by a British company, the author of the scenario had to be British, the studio scenes had to be filmed in a British studio and 75 per cent of the labour costs had to go to British technicians.

One of the consequences of the Act was the establishment of two vertically integrated film corporations – in fact moves had been made towards this even before the Act was passed. The Gaumont-British Picture Corporation was an amalgamation of the old Gaumont company – one of the earliest film companies, Michael Balcon's Gainsborough Pictures, several distribution companies and a chain of provincial cinemas. At about the same time John Maxwell formed the Associated British Picture Corporation, an amalgamation of his own distribution company and cinema chain with a new production company, British International Pictures.

Apart from these 'combines' a number of small companies came into existence, hoping to capitalize on the opportunities for production which had been made possible by the Act. But what these companies hadn't anticipated was the arrival of sound and, while 1928 saw a significant increase in the production of British films, the small 'quota companies' which came into existence as a result of the Act were not in a financial position to meet the huge cost of producing talking pictures, coming as they did at a time of worldwide recession. By 1931 seven of the eleven companies which had come into existence as a result of the 1927 Act had become bankrupt. The two combines survived but only British International Pictures succeeded in making a profit during the transition to sound, thanks to John Maxwell's shrewd move to equip his Elstree studios with RCA recording equipment at the earliest opportunity.

While the Quota Act, as it came to be known, had the intended effect of boosting British film production, the quality of the films being produced left much to be desired. Hollywood, in fact, had much to do with this state of affairs. The American companies undermined the Act by financing British films which were, in the words of Simon Hartog,

> cheap, awful, and just long enough to qualify as feature films under the 1927 Act. The films, which were usually financed at a rate per foot, became known as 'quota films' or 'quota quickies'. By complying only with the letter of the law, the American renters funded the production of hundreds of British films which discredited both British film production and the quota legislation.[31]

On the positive side, however, the 1927 Cinematograph Films Act did give a financial boost to an ailing industry by attracting new investors, stimulating production and encouraging new talent. Although the introduction of sound caused considerable financial problems which soon curtailed the initial production boom, sending a number of the quota companies to the wall, once these problems had been ironed out British cinema, protected by the quota, went from strength to strength. The number of films produced rose each year and by the early thirties the British film industry had become 'the most important centre of European film production and began to believe that it could beat Hollywood at its own game'.[32]

BRITISH FILM CULTURE

The struggles of British cinema in the twenties were seen mainly in relation to Hollywood which had emerged as the dominant form of cinema at this time. But there were significant alternative traditions which emerged in other countries during the twenties: the post-revolutionary cinema of Soviet Russia, the Expressionist cinema of Weimar Germany, the Impressionist cinema in France, as well as the more avant-garde work of other French and European film makers like René Clair, Man Ray, Hans Richter, Walter Ruttmann, Luis Buñuel and Salvador Dali. Because of the dominance of American films in British cinemas, there was no outlet for these films in Britain until 1925 when the Film Society was set up in London with the specific objective of showing foreign films, including experimental and avant-garde films which would not otherwise have found a distributor because of their uncommercial nature.

Ivor Montagu, a Cambridge-educated intellectual, was the driving force behind the Film Society and for him it had definite cultural and educational objectives, not least of which was to stimulate British film production at a time when the industry was at its lowest ebb. But where the cultural imperatives of the 1927 Films Act were to see an increase in the number of British films showing in British cinemas in order to counter American influence, Montagu and other members of the Film Society were concerned to see British cinema develop along artistic lines under the influence of the stylistic developments of European art cinema, rather than merely to secure the establishment of a commercial British cinema which could compete with Hollywood on its own terms. Montagu hoped that Film Society screenings would 'fertilize British film ideas' and change the nature of that cinema, encouraging film makers to experiment and develop a form of 'art' cinema in opposition to the dominant (Hollywood) cinema.[33] Because of this the Film Society met with some hostility from the established trade, despite the fact that mainstream industry figures like Michael Balcon, Victor Saville and Ivor Novello enrolled as members, and there were the inevitable accusations of communist sympathies following screenings of Soviet films like Eisenstein's *Battleship Potemkin* and Pudovkin's *The End of St Petersburg*.

The formation of the Film Society led to the establishment of an alternative exhibition network, first with the formation of other film societies around the country, and then with the opening in the late twenties and thirties of a number of 'art' cinemas such as the Shaftesbury Avenue Pavilion, the Curzon in Mayfair, the Everyman in Hampstead and the Academy in Oxford Street.

The other important cultural development in the late 1920s was the publication of a journal, *Close Up*, which shared the cultural objectives of the Film Society movement and provided a forum for debate for the mainly middle-class intellectuals who were concerned to see the development of an alternative film culture in opposition to Hollywood commercial cinema. One of the leading film critics of the time, Paul Rotha, shared the same ideals and his writings on the cinema were published in 1930 in his influential book *The Film Till Now*.

But all this activity failed to see the emergence of an alternative tradition of film making in Britain in the late twenties. While the influence of German expressionism, even Soviet montage, can be seen in Hitchcock's *The Lodger* and *Blackmail* these were on the whole mainstream *commercial* productions which incorporated some European stylistic devices. The arrival of sound was probably largely to blame for preventing the development of an alternative radical and experimental cinema because of the considerable costs of producing sound films – experimental film making has always been a marginal activity existing on shoestring budgets. Also, in Europe, political developments curtailed radical and experimental film making in Russia and Germany at the end of the twenties and during the thirties. As a result of these developments the supply of experimental and avant-garde films decreased and *Close Up*, finding itself with less to write about, eventually ceased publication in 1932.

In Britain the interest that the Film Society movement and *Close Up* had spawned in an alternative form of 'art' cinema was eventually realized in the 1930s in the documentary movement. Far from stimulating British cinema in the way that the Film Society might have hoped, 'the radical separation of "art" cinema from its commercial counterpart prevented any interaction between the two that might have helped to create a more aesthetically interesting entertainment cinema in Britain during the interwar years.'[34] What *Close Up* and the Film Society movement did help to establish was 'a minority film culture articulated in opposition to the majority film culture based upon the commercial cinema'.[35] In doing so it helped to establish a division between a dominant, commercial, mainly Hollywood-led popular cinema and an alternative middle-class minority-interest art cinema, a cultural dichotomy which exists in Britain to the present day.

By the end of the twenties, then, British cinema was struggling to establish an identity for itself in relation to the dominant cinema of the time: Hollywood. After its precocious and exciting beginnings as a small-scale cottage industry, British cinema failed to adapt to the commercial development of film as a mass entertainment industry and went into a decline, as far as production is concerned, re-emerging after 1910 with an attempt to capitalize on the cultural prestige of its literary and theatrical heritage. Preoccupied with the war, along with its European neighbours, British cinema succumbed to the dominance of Hollywood. While audiences continued to flock to the new picture palaces in ever-increasing numbers British cinema, squeezed out by the glossier Hollywood product, went into a serious decline. Rescued by government legislation British films increased in number, if not in quality, at the end of the twenties and new film combines were formed in an attempt to compete with Hollywood on its own terms. Meanwhile, an alternative, minority film culture was developing in opposition to the mainstream: commercial cinema. Both branches of this British film culture – majority 'commercial' and minority 'art' – were to bear fruit in the 1930s and beyond. With twenty million people going to the cinema every week in Britain at the end of the 1920s, cinema had established itself as the foremost medium of mass entertainment, but the golden period of British film making was yet to come.

NOTES

1. John Barnes, *The Beginnings of Cinema in England* (London, 1976), p. 202. Other historians of the early cinema have claimed that a French inventor, Augustin Le Prince, filmed moving pictures – which he was also able to project onto a screen – in Leeds as early as 1888. See Christopher Rawlence, *The Missing Reel: The Untold Story of the Lost Inventor of Moving Pictures* (London, 1991).
2. Michael Chanan, *The Dream That Kicks* (London, 1980), p. 233.
3. Raymond Williams, 'British Film History: New Perspectives', in James Curran and Vincent Porter (eds), *British Cinema History* (London, 1983), p. 16.
4. Noël Burch, *Life To Those Shadows* (London, 1990), pp. 99–102.
5. Ibid., pp. 85–91.
6. *What Do Those Old Films Mean?: Great Britain 1900–1912*, directed by Noël Burch and transmitted on Channel 4 in 1985.
7. Paul Thompson, *The Edwardians* (London, 1975), p. 296.
8. Herbert Samuel, House of Commons debates, 21 April 1909, quoted in Annette Kuhn, *Cinema, Censorship and Sexuality, 1909–1925* (London, 1988), p. 16.
9. Kuhn, p. 17.
10. David Atwell dates the first purpose-built cinema in Britain as the Bioscope in Wilton Road, Victoria, London. *Cathedrals of the Movies* (London, 1980), p. 5.

11. Rachel Low, *The History of British Film, 1906–1914* (London, 1949), p. 226.
12. Brian McFarlane, 'A Literary Cinema? British films and British novels', in Charles Barr (ed.), *All Our Yesterdays: 90 Years of British Cinema* (London, 1986), p. 124.
13. Roy Armes, *A Critical History of British Cinema* (London, 1978), p. 53.
14. James Park, *British Cinema: The Lights That Failed* (London, 1990), p. 26.
15. The Bioscope, 7 February 1924, quoted in Tom Ryall, *Alfred Hitchcock and the British Cinema* (London, 1986), p. 39.
16. Quoted in Armes, p. 30.
17. Park, p. 33.
18. Ibid., pp. 28–38.
19. François Truffaut, *Hitchcock* (London, 1984), p. 45.
20. Ryall, p. 88.
21. Ibid., p. 89.
22. Quoted in Ryall, p. 24.
23. Geoff Brown, ' "Sister of the Stage": British Film and British Theatre', *All Our Yesterdays*, p. 150.
24. Quoted in Brown, p. 152.
25. Ibid.
26. Curran and Porter, p. 375.
27. Paul Wild, 'Recreation in Rochdale, 1900–1914', in John Clarke, Chas Critcher and Richard Johnson (eds), *Working Class Culture* (London, 1979), pp. 155–6.
28. Quoted in Simon Hartog, 'State Protection of a Beleaguered Industry', *British Cinema History*, p. 60.
29. Ibid., p. 73.
30. Ibid., p. 61.
31. Ibid., p. 68.
32. Ibid., p. 65.
33. Quoted in Ryall, p. 11.
34. Ibid., p. 21.
35. Ibid., p. 13.

CHAPTER EIGHT

The Visual Arts: Change and Continuity

Robert Chaplin

WHISTLER AND THE AESTHETIC MOVEMENT

It may seem odd to begin any survey of a century some twenty years before its opening, but in England in 1877 a single event brought into direct legal conflict two opposing forces which still persist in Britain. The event was the Ruskin versus Whistler trial in an action brought by James Abott McNeill Whistler (1834–1903) against the pontifical Slade Professor of Fine Art at Oxford, John Ruskin (1819–1900). What had prompted the extreme action by the artist was a comment made by Ruskin in his magazine *Fors Clavigera*, within which Ruskin had accused Whistler of 'conceit' and of 'flinging a pot of paint in the public's face'. Both these comments, though undoubtedly true of Whistler's attitude to the public and of his own estimate of the artist's worth, brought to a timely pass the tensions of a middle-aged Victorianism.

Ruskin, by sheer force of opinion and a greater voice, had established a reputation and a position as the arbiter of taste and the purveyor of all that was good and true in matters of art and culture. Part of his project was the return to former glories, whether this was the paintings of the early Italian masters or the virtues of the Middle Ages. He would not simply exalt the beauty of the past, of architecture or art or manufacture, without demanding the reason why it all seemed so beyond modern society. In 1875 he established the St Georges Guild along the lines of the medieval crafts guilds as a vehicle for his scheme of 'practical improvement'. The repair of the Hinksey Road, part of the Back to the Land campaign, was more enthusiastic than effective in the restoration of a stretch of road to everybody's benefit – not least, supposedly, the assorted collection of landowners and undergraduate 'navvies' who undertook the task. In all his actions, lectures and writings Ruskin presented a utopian vision of a chivalrous socialism bent not to the whim of the profiteers but to honest work producing beautiful things for the good of all. And in the shadowy regions beyond the clear light of the *Lamp of Truth* the foreigner Whistler painted his *Nocturne in Black and Gold – Falling Rocket* (1874), which so outraged Ruskin among the Alma-Tademas, Millaises and Burne-Joneses at Sir Coutts Lindsay's Grosvenor Gallery.[1]

Whistler won a farthing damages from the case against Ruskin as the 'butterfly' showed his sting.[2] Repeatedly from the witness box the artist would loose some barb, more wounding and spiteful in its precision, as the Attorney-General pursued his case. The exchanges in the court, somewhat polished to his own advantage by Whistler in *The Gentle Art of Making Enemies*, effectively ended Ruskin's hegemony over public taste and ruined Whistler financially.[3] Most hurtfully, his bankruptcy in 1879 forced the sale of the White House in Tite Street, Chelsea, to Harry Quilter, the successor to Tom Taylor, *The Times's* art critic who appeared for Ruskin in the trial. Whistler's reputation too was in tatters and his sharp tongue and untimely remarks continued to lose him friends and supporters – denigrating his patron, the shipping magnate and self-made man Francis Leyland, as a parvenu, within his hearing and in his own house. As the self-appointed 'Enemy' of the 'Islanders', as he disparagingly called the English, he continued to attack all that he thought petty, foolish and plain philistine, and all those who promulgated it. His own background was indeed as a 'foreigner'; an American by birth, he had spent part of his childhood in St Petersburg, a spell in London, some years in the United States Military Academy at West Point – his was a soldiering family – before finally coming to live in Paris in 1855. In Paris he immediately assumed a Bohemian style and existence; attempting to create for himself the fictional world of Henri Murger's *Scènes de la Vie de Bohème*.

Whistler's enthusiasm for the Bohemian life, and his easy manner, took him to the centre of things. The most advanced French writers – Théophile Gautier and Charles Baudelaire – had established a new aesthetic of Art for Art's Sake which broke with the tradition of the subject and tore down the doctrine of the utility of art, its moral purpose, its literary reference and, particularly in England, its passion for narrative. What the artist should deal with was form and its perfectibility; the material may be drawn from everyday life but its treatment and any beauty it may possess is given to it by the artist. The foolish sunset is to be displaced by the dingiest slum and, by the eye and hand of the artist, is to be transformed and made beautiful as a work of art. 'Art', said Théophile Gautier, 'is not a means but an end in itself.' While his English companions toiled diligently at their easels, exercised energetically, ate mutton and drank bottled beer, Whistler became the intimate of the leaders of the new movements, of Impressionism, Art for Art's Sake and Symbolism – Monet, Baudelaire and Stéphane Mallarmé.[4] What he learnt here formed and informed his style, stated as a doctrine in the *Ten O'Clock Lecture*, first given at the Prince's Hall, London in 1885.[5] Even before Pater's celebrated declaration that 'All art constantly aspires to the condition of music', Whistler had expanded the title of his first major success, *The White Girl*, to *Symphony in White, No. 2* (1865).[6]

After Whistler returned to England in 1863 he maintained a regular contact with Paris, travelling there frequently, not least to visit 'La Porte chinoise' where he had been first introduced to the arts of the East – most notably the 'blue and white' porcelain which he collected. However, he was not the envoy of Impressionism – which was coming to prominence in France – as might have been supposed of a friend of Degas and Monet. Both his technique and philosophy ran against the grain of Impressionism; while his concerns were with atmosphere and the evanescent effects of light he did not employ the impressionist technique of dabs of pure colour painted to fuse optically; nor did he valorize Nature as the final referent, declining to paint outdoors in some foolish pursuit of 'the moment'. He would collect notes and sensations and later, in the studio, assemble and reorder these into his paintings or etchings. The Impressionist project was not carried into Britain in Whistler's knapsack, and even if it had been, his reputation was so tarnished at that time it would have fared no better than in its eventual slow and confusing entry.

RUSKIN'S LEGACY – WILLIAM MORRIS, THE ARTS AND CRAFTS MOVEMENT AND THE DEVELOPMENT OF MODERNISM

The fate of the two men who had almost faced each other across the courtroom – Ruskin, because of ill-health, never attended the trial – was one of waning stature. Ruskin continued to write from his sanctuary in the Lake District, though notably less pungently as his mental powers became ever more clouded and weakened.[7] Whistler and aestheticism had, it seemed, won the day in his claims for artists to practise as they will. There was, though, one man in whom the influence of Ruskin and the noble cause of a humanist aesthetic and honourable labour ran strongly – William Morris (1834–96).

Morris had read Ruskin at Oxford when, with Edward Burne-Jones (1833–98), he was searching for the vehicle in which to carry forward their holy war against the age. They found this in Ruskin's writings, particularly in the influential *Stones of Venice* and most especially the chapter 'On the Nature of Gothic'. Here was their creed, and Morris made open acknowledgement of this in his preface to the Kelmscott edition of 1892, declaring it 'one of the most important things written by the author', and that it pointed out, at least to Morris, 'the road on which the world should travel'. The road which Morris travelled however was not smooth; personal, emotional, social, political and business problems beset him, but with an inexhaustible energy and indomitable zest and enthusiasm his was an astonishing achievement.[8] At Exeter College, in the eager company of the 'Birmingham Group', Burne-Jones, Charles Faulkner, R. W. Dixon, William Fulford and Cornell Price, he turned away from ecclesiastical history – both he and Burne-Jones were to have taken holy orders – and toward the poetry of Keats and Tennyson, to Dickens and Kingsley and to Ruskin. They took from these writers a love of the past, a horror of the present and a fear for the future. They immersed themselves in this romantic history; they sought out the medieval where it was to be found; they toured in France and Belgium, pored over old books and visited old churches. They revelled in the paintings and poetry which revived that age, all the time holding it up in comparison to the hellish cities of the industrial age. The lamp that was lit at Oxford was not to be extinguished – despite so many disappointments to come – and Morris took his idealism firstly into the office of the architect G. E. Street, where he met Philip Webb who was to design the Red House for Morris. After nine months, and under the inspiration of Dante Gabriel Rossetti (1828–82), he took premises with Burne-Jones at Red Lion Square in London to pursue a career as painter. It was through Rossetti they came to meet and know Ruskin who would regularly visit them there.

After his marriage to Jane Burden – the enigmatic 'stunner' who held Rossetti in thrall throughout their friendship – the Morrises moved into the Red House within whose medieval echo was found the focus and inspiration for the formation of the Firm. The collaboration in the decoration and furnishing of the Red House was done in the aftermath of the dismal showing of British manufacture in the Great Exhibition of 1851. Design reform was a controversial issue which circulated around the exquisite claims of academic art and the needs and demands of industry. Morris saw no controversy; like Ruskin before him he saw only evil in machines, and the start that was made at the Red House – the sturdy furniture and hand-painted decoration – was to remain a feature of his work. The paradox in his project was that his serious attempt to elevate man through an improvement in his surroundings – and the eventual goal to restore to all men the opportunity and desire to effect that improvement themselves, to make an artist of everybody ('Art made by the people and for the people, a joy to the maker and the user') was only affordable and perhaps only attractive to the wealthy and the educated: the 'swinish rich'. However, what Morris had to say about design was to influence the whole Arts and Crafts Movement and this was to spread across continents and inform the very essence of modernism.

The prime principle of design as given by Morris, and which he resolutely adhered to, was that of personal knowledge of the materials used. This was not some mere technical know-how but a first-hand and thorough understanding of the capabilities and the limitations of the material in the hands of the craftsman. Morris himself was to dedicate many hours to the mastering of crafts and materials, at the loom or up to his elbows in the dye vats at Merton.[9] The same applied in his decorative work, the design of wallpapers, carpets and chintzes, where a knowledge of past achievements and a familiarity with the elements which comprised the design – drawn from but not imitating nature – were the principles which would give 'meaning in your patterns'. This going back to the source was an integral part of Morris's approach; whether translating the Norse sagas or manufacturing the dyes for his cloth, he always made exhaustive practical researches, trekking across Iceland or seeking out medieval trade secrets in obscure French texts.[10] In furniture design the maxims were simplicity and splendour for the two types of 'workaday' and 'state' use. The sturdy and uncluttered design of the workaday recalled again the medieval and is reflected in the chairs and tables made for the Red House. The splendid was made so by the ornamentation of inlays, carving and most spectacularly in painting. Morris, Rossetti, and most especially Edward Burne-Jones, were the principal artists of the painted pieces. Burne-Jones – a friend of Whistler who nonetheless felt unable to support him in the trial, and perversely appeared for Ruskin – brought an ethereal wistfulness to his knights and maidens while Morris, characteristically, lent a more robust edge to the mawkish sentimentality of the pictures. The principles of furniture design, and certainly those most readily exported, were those expressed in the Firm's production of a variation of the Sussex rush-seated chair. Here were the ideals of simplicity and fitness for function which underpinned good design. The heavy overbearing stoutness of the medieval style – chairs 'such as Barbarossa might have sat in' – gave way to a more eclectic vision taking in the Japanese influence initially derived from Whistler's 'blue and white' and which, while occasionally straying into fancifulness and even decadence in Art Nouveau, refined those simple ideals.

This vision was enlarged in the numerous groups and societies which were established in the last years of the century in some emulation of the Firm and Morris & Co.; many small independent presses also sprang up which sought to continue the revival in fine printing begun by Morris at the Kelmscott Press. Mackmurdo's Century Guild, the Art Workers' Guild of Walter Crane and Lewis Day, Ashbee's Guild and School of Handicraft, as well as the Rural Industries Bureau under the auspices of the Ministry of Agriculture, were the offshoots of Morris's initiatives. All shared some dedication to the cause theorized by Ruskin and mobilized by Morris, complete with its socialist idealism which saw once and for all the yoke of capitalism lifted from the neck of the working man and his being released to a future free from the oppression of the machine. The Arts and Crafts Movement retained, even in some part in its last practitioners, Charles Ashbee (1863–1942) and W.R. Lethaby (1857–1931), the horror of the machine, but it was these men who confronted the beast and, while not proposing some machine aesthetic, acknowledged the inevitable supremacy of mechanical production. However, it was not to be in Britain, nor with the Arts and Crafts Movement itself, that the ideals of Ruskin were to be matched to the demands of the twentieth century. Lethaby's innovations at the Central School, which he founded in 1896, were to set something of the pattern which was to be taken up more enthusiastically and to better purpose in Europe, in Austria, Denmark, Sweden and most notably in Germany. The Central School was dedicated to the principle of good design and training in craftsmanship, and all things; drawing and painting, too, were means to these ends. However, the impetus which inspired Arts and Crafts, and which ran from Ruskin through Morris and to Ashbee, was lost in an Edwardian age which inherited the wealth of the Victorian Empire and dissipated it in high living and laissez-faire economics. The decline of British industries and the loss of its markets brought to an end the attempts to link art to industry and the torch passed to Germany, to the Werkbund, Walter Gropius and the Bauhaus.

THE ROYAL ACADEMY AND THE PERSISTENCE OF VICTORIANISM

As the dramas of the Aesthetic Movement and the good sense and purpose of Arts and Crafts pulled this way and that across the face of the crumbling empire, shoring up the sentiment and complacency of Victorianism was the Royal Academy of Arts. The Academy held what now seems a dead hand over the exhibition, appreciation and acquisition of works of the 'modern movement'. The dissolution and waning powers of the pre-Raphaelite brotherhood left a vacuum in British painting only partly filled by the efforts of their second generation: Rossetti, Burne-Jones, Holman Hunt (1827–1910) and even to some extent Morris himself. The continuing contacts between English and French painters of the time, though convivial, were marginal to the establishment art of the Academy. Morris and Burne-Jones had been well received in France for their symbolist style; Rossetti, though more profoundly symbolist, was less well known. In the other direction Alphonse Legros had arrived, Manet visited in 1868, Fantin-Latour a year after; Monet, Pissarro and Alfred Sisley spent long periods here; later visitors were Degas, Renoir and Gauguin.[11] The critic Frank Rutter, alive to their importance, had agreed with the dealer Durand-Ruel a price of £160 to secure Monet's *Véthueil: Sunshine and Snow* for the nation. The National Gallery however considered it 'too advanced' and settled for Boudin's *Harbour at Trouville* as a safe purchase from the French Impressionist Fund raised by Rutter from public subscription. Durand-Ruel's gallery in New Bond Street, and later his exhibition at the Grafton Galleries in 1905, had been the first major introduction of the modern movement to England and almost all his efforts were met with controversy followed by indifference. While across the Channel there was a rigorous concern with the formal problems of painting and a close observation from life, the Academy had slipped into a habit of coy moralizing and sentimentality.

The authority of the Academy rested partly in its venerability, but mostly in its monopoly of the power of pronouncement on matters of aesthetic or artistic concern. The Academy – which means of course the Academicians – had, in effect, *been charged to secure the past against the future*. Its very organization ensured that its links to the past were reforged in its election of members to both Associate and full Academician status. Election was by the full membership, which in 1900 comprised forty Academicians and thirty Associate members in three categories of painters, sculptors and architects, while progress was determined only by the Academicians. Membership had certain privileges, perhaps the greatest being the right to the best and proportionally largest hanging space in the Academy Summer Show. The shows were a tour de force by the Academicians; non-members' work was quite literally edged out while the 'costume piece and the anecdote', the 'vice of the subject', continued in pride of place. Academicism, in the shape of Sir Lawrence Alma-Tadema's coy maidens in painstakingly rendered surroundings, or Lord Leighton's earnest interpretations of classical themes, were enormously popular and their paintings sold for prices far in excess of Whistler's 200 guineas for 'the knowledge of a life time'.[12] Alongside these august pieces were those which appealed to the other side of the Academy's clientele: the simpering or stoical anecdote, of Frank Bramley's *A Hopeless Dawn* or Millais's *An idyll*. The Academy in so controlling its membership effectively controlled the public taste and established a dominant aesthetic by the limitations it imposed on exhibition. Its power in this respect was extended, and abused, in its handling of the Chantrey Bequest, a fund derived from the estate of the sculptor Sir Francis Chantrey which became available after the death of his wife in 1875. The monies were to purchase for a national collection works wholly executed in the British Isles, and in 1897 the collection was transferred to the Tate Gallery's care. However, the narrowness and partisan choice of the Academicians, regularly selecting paintings for the collection from the walls of the Summer Show, and the jealousy of its authority, were the subject of a growing tide of criticism against the Academy. Change though was slow and came only in the face of increasing frustration and anger from those within, and competition and a growing disenchantment from those outside its walls. In 1903, reforms led to a revision of the hanging policy for the Summer Show reducing the number of works which a member could submit with the guarantee of hanging. More seriously for the Academy, a year later a select committee in the House of Lords was set up to inquire into the administration of the Academy and its selection policies which drew a concession from the Academy in establishing selection sub-committees to whom they would refer. Formal relations between the Tate and the Academy in the administration of the Chantrey Bequest were established in 1917, when it was agreed to make proper consultation on proposed purchases from the fund. However, a more serious challenge to the Academy's authority was to come, at least for a time, from new exhibition societies and galleries, the forerunner of which was the Grosvenor Gallery where Whistler's *Nocturne in Black and Gold: the Falling Rocket* had so enraged Ruskin.

THE NEW ENGLISH ART CLUB – THE PROGRESS AND INFLUENCE OF SICKERT

Opposition to the Academy's authority and its means of maintaining it crystallized with the formation of the New English Art Club which was established in 1886. An alternative title offered for the group's adoption had been 'The Society of Anglo-French Painters' which declared the unifying experience of its founders, that they had all studied in Paris. The Academy, of course, frowned upon this sort of influence and sought always to reward its own methods of teaching. This had remained a lengthy programme of drawing from the antique – working from plaster casts – to perfect modelling almost to the exclusion of colour. In the schools and studios of Paris, the Académie Julian or Gleyre's studio, English painters from Whistler and before had enjoyed and benefited from the French method of drawing and painting the live model from the outset – not obtaining access as some reward for diligent study. The benefits had not been lost on the Academicians but their praise of it – even from its president in 1871, Sir Edward Poynter (1836–1919), who had been an early student with Whistler at Gleyre's – did not translate into any action. Without any change within the Royal Academy, except for a steady deterioration of standards, a group of French-trained mostly English painters came, by a roundabout route, to storm its walls.

The Club modestly declared itself in the catalogue of its first exhibition to be of some fifty in number whose quiet mission was no more than to 'display ... their works' in the hope that they would be 'of interest to the public' and also to help 'explain the aim and method of their art'. The selection of works for exhibition, in a departure from Academy practice, was to be made by a jury elected by both members and exhibitors – which would often include French painters encouraged by the Club to submit works. The original group were united by more than a shared experience of the French system and an awareness of modern French painting, with Newlyn School painters forming the sizeable nucleus. This earlier group took its name from the Cornish town of Newlyn which had been colonized by artists, primarily Stanhope Forbes (1857–1947), after the lead given by the practice of the Frenchman Jules Bastien-Lepage. The tradition of *plein air* realism in England can be traced to Bastien-Lepage's insistence that integrity to one's subject can only be gained by living amongst it, the people and their surroundings. There was some appeal in this suggestion and artists' colonies sprang up in Britain from Brig O'Turk in Scotland to Newlyn in Cornwall. George Clausen (1852–1944) was, until disillusionment with his French mentor crept in, a champion of this style of impressionism tempered with a sort of moralizing realism and worthiness of subject. The general ruggedness of the subjects and the brisker treatment of the surface, which still, however, did not partake fully of the French method of broken colour, distinguishes these painters from the academicism of their fellow exhibitors at the Royal Academy. The Club, after a nervous start – salvaged by the largesse of one of its wealthier members and surviving a coup by others to use it as a platform to launch a National Exhibition of Art – established a reputation and a formidable membership to challenge the Academy.[13]

The New English Art Club was seldom free from internal struggles between its conservative wing – Clausen, Stanhope Forbes, Frank Bramley – (1857–1915) – and those grouped, though not united, in the Glasgow School – John Lavery (1856–1941), James Guthrie (1859–1930) – and the London Impressionists led by Walter Sickert (1860–1942). Sickert was a friend and supporter of Whistler and through him had come to know Degas – both men of often cruel wit and strong views – and this association perhaps, along with his own colourful background, made him entertainingly irascible. However, after organizing the first and only London Impressionists exhibition at the Goupil Gallery, Sickert left for Europe in 1899, to Venice and then Dieppe, and was not to return until 1905. In the years of his self-imposed exile he became the king over the water, continuing to send pictures to the Club's exhibitions but moving within the quicker pace of European developments.

This is not to say that on his return he was to bring a quicker rhythm to British painting, for like Whistler before him, Sickert, though he would shun the epithet, was a man of a very particular taste. Sickert's palette was one of peculiar dullness or subtlety depending on taste, and his subjects were taken from what surrounded him at the time; the momentary glance was taken in the manner of Degas who was to so influence him. The music-hall, dingy London streets or St Marks in Venice were all treated with the same enthusiasm. He applied his paint in broad areas with a nod toward impressionist technique but without their brilliance of colour or density of marks. The later London pictures witnessed some tightening of his technique, the 'solid, thick mosaic' of paint which was to distinguish this phase of English post-impressionism, but his later work was to fluctuate in quality. While Sickert remains a major figure in English painting, his activities as a painter were always mixed with his role as leader and guide to the next generation – even, it may be said, to the point where his efforts to lead necessitated the hasty overhauling of his erstwhile followers.

NORTH LONDON FROM FITZROY STREET TO THE LONDON GROUP

Sickert's departure in 1899 had left the New English Art Club already divided, and during his absence it grew ever closer to the academicism it had originally eschewed. Its pioneering liberalism, sapped perhaps by disputes and wrangles, had withered and been supplanted by a much less tolerant regime which rejected from its exhibitions much which originally had made its reputation. As its earliest members were drawn from the ranks of Academy painters they seemed now set to rejoin them. Sickert's return was to re-ignite some of the old antagonisms and eventually lead to a greater diversity of groupings and a more open, even democratic, establishment.

Sickert found lodgings in Mornington Crescent, Camden Town, a once salubrious neighbourhood now brought low in the expansion of London. It was from here he organized the Saturday morning sessions at his studio in Fitzroy Street where friends and invitees would show their pictures in an informal atmosphere where tea was served. His wish was to attract a mixed clientele, 'rich or poor, refined or ... vulgar', much perhaps as Morris had hoped for his venture. The meetings though became more a forum for debate amongst their regular membership: Sickert, Spencer Gore (1878–1914), Walter Russell (1867–1948), Harold Gilman (1876–1919), William Rothenstein (1872–1945) and Albert Rothenstein (later Rutherston, 1881–1953), Nan Hudson (1869–1957), Ethel Sands (1873–1962) and, from 1907,

Lucien Pissarro. In 1911 the group formalized its activities – after discussions which had entertained the idea of snatching control of the New English Art Club which they perceived as having abrogated its finer principles of liberalism – as the Camden Town Group. This breakaway group actually did little damage to the Club or its standing, with many members remaining loyal. The Camden Town Group shared a common perception and developed a certain aesthetic which owed something to their common impressionist tendency – and it was never much more than this – and something to post-impressionist technique which gave their paintings a firmer structure. Sickert's conversion to a more overtly post-impressionist method was partly in response to the keen interest shown by his younger associates. His paintings made in this period thus obtained a higher key, a more broken surface and a keener use of colour, especially in the shadows. The subjects chosen exalted the local, the mundane and even the risqué as testimony to Sickert's declaration that art – and painting too perhaps, 'a rough and racy wench' – would 'fade at a breath from the drawing room'.[14]

The Camden Town Group was but one of a flurry of exhibition societies which were formed partly, at least, in defence of the gains first won by the New English Art Club. The Club's apparent loss of nerve and reactionary rather than revolutionary spirit meant that the torch passed to a new generation of artists. This small community, in a period of startling innovation and change which had its faint echo in Britain – as Harold Gilman painted the lugubrious Mrs Mounter, Picasso and Matisse had already accomplished their great advances – shifted position and changed allegiance with the tempo of the age. The Camden Town Group was one of the shorter-lived groups; the Society of Twelve – which had George Clausen, William Nicholson (1872–1949) and the two Charleses, Ricketts and Shannon, among its members – held eight exhibitions from 1904 to 1915. In 1908 Frank Rutter, familiar with the Fitzroy Street gatherings, proposed an annual exhibition of the work of progressive contemporary artists – the first, of over three thousand works, was held in the Albert Hall – and from his proposal grew the Allied Artists' Association. The society of Twenty-Five English Artists, including Anning Bell, which held exhibitions from 1905, and the Fitzroy Street Group itself, were just some of the transient arrangements made by artists seeking their own direction.

The same people were members of these societies and none was more ubiquitous than Walter Sickert, now something of an elder statesman of the modern movement, but both his powers as painter and personality were diminished. Within the Camden Town Group internal differences were to lead to its break-up. An 'inner circle' of neo-realists, led by Charles Ginner (1878–1952), were concerned to represent their times, most properly but following more devotedly a path first broken by one or other continental master: Spencer Gore following Cézanne and Harold Gilman following Van Gogh. Paradoxically, Sickert – whose dictum was that art evolves gradually from one generation to the next in the development of an idea – saw his own conservative influence wane as the younger generation moved on under the influence of impressionism and post-impressionism.[15] Sickert's status, however, was sufficient for others to call him to preside over a meeting at Fitzroy Street which was to bring together the most radical wings of English art at the time. On 15 November 1913 Harold Gilman was elected president of a group which, however temporarily, comprised the neorealist core of the Camden Town Group, the rump of the Fitzroy Street Group, the Cumberland Market Group, the Vorticists under Wyndham Lewis (1882–1956) and the English Futurists with their assumptive leader C.R.W. Nevinson (1889–1946). Though this grouping was not to last long – the death of the mollifying Spencer Gore, the onset of war, disagreement and antagonism were to splinter it further – it survived long enough to gain a titular identity as the London Group. Its principal aim by which it gained its continued importance was to offer exhibition to 'serious emerging talent', and 'hospitality to all manner of artistic expression'.[16] The very instability of its composition led inevitably to disputes, and failures of leadership, and a susceptibility to influence, opened the way for the critic and writer Roger Fry (1866–1934) to exert his control.

SOUTH LONDON: THE END OF SWINBURNE

It would be a mistake to assume from the account so far that England was experiencing some radical recasting of its sensibilities. Throughout late Victorianism, and the stuffy Edwardian period of even greater polarities of wealth and deprivation, the country remained beguiled by the trivial, the anecdotal and the whimsical classicism of the worst of the Academy. While North London seemed in constant fervour of change and experiment, in South London, in a modest Victorian villa, one of the Aesthetic Movement's wildest characters was having the last of his teeth pulled. In the care of Theodore Watts-Dunton, Algernon Charles Swinburne, the flame-haired poet of genius was slowly brought to dull sobriety from the stupefying edge of outrageous fury. Swinburne had been the vanguard of Art for Art's Sake; a disciple of Baudelaire and friend of Whistler, he shocked and outraged the British public with his poems of passion and sin and romance in a heady mix of the unspoken, if not the unspeakable. His fitful enthusiasm likewise astonished his friends, as he worked himself into a frenzy of excitement over something or other before falling unconscious. Swinburne subjected his frail frame and fierce intellect to excesses of liquor and stimulation bringing himself to the point of physical and mental collapse. It was here that Watts-Dunton – the gardener to Swinburne's wilderness of exotica and parasites – stepped in and would clear the weeds, restore the light to suffocating genius and tend its proper growth. To restore Swinburne's health a regimen of rest and exercise was established; walks across the common became routine; the destructive scourge of brandy was diluted through port to burgundy to beer. His eyes brightened, the colour flowed into his cheeks – but the job was only half done. Watts-Dunton pointed out to the libertarian poet the ill-advisedness of the choice of certain words, phrases, subjects, friends – with a surgeon's skill, using the knife of innuendo, he cut Swinburne off from old associations and deftly turned him against them. But even yet his work was incomplete and behind the lace curtains of The Pines the drone of Watts-Dunton's own prejudices and opinions became the rhythm of Swinburne's life, and little by little he recanted his former views. By the end, he had remade his coat in the shape of 'hearty Toryism', denigrated Whistler, scorned the French, out-Tennysoned the Poet Laureate in patriotic verse and earned for himself the reported praise of the old queen. His death in 1909 was of a man, who, in his youth, he would have reviled and ridiculed for a philistinism masquerading as moral restraint. The heavy blanket of Victorian propriety still hung heavily over a society which was soon to be rudely shaken by the outrage of war.

BLOOMSBURY AND THE INFLUENCE OF ROGER FRY

Some thirty years after the modern movement began to undermine the salon in France, it pierced the aesthetic mists and sombre fogs of Edwardian England. The lamp which was to disperse those vapours was lit by Roger Fry in the exhibitions of post-impressionist paintings at the Grafton Gallery in 1910 and 1912. This was, however, a belated and somewhat circuitous route to influence, for even in 1905, and at the age of 39, Fry had already won sufficient status as a scholar to be considered as the next director of the National Gallery. However, the slight hesitation in appointing one so young was pause enough for Fry to feel slighted and in his own haste he accepted the position of Curator of Paintings at the Metropolitan Museum, New York in January 1906. Fry had aspired to being a painter; at Cambridge he was a member of the Fine Art Society; in the rooms of the Slade Professor, John Henry Middleton, he was awoken to the bounty of art, but the narrowness of his experience barely fitted him to live the life of a painter. Thus by 1891 he was travelling in Italy, to Rome and Florence, revelling in and absorbing the works of the masters: Raphael, Botticelli, Michelangelo. After the now almost obligatory period spent working at the Académie Julian in Paris, Fry returned to London, to fashionable Chelsea and the company of Charles Ricketts and Charles Shannon. These two men lived the 'Life Aesthetic'; in their house in the Vale, Chelsea, they surrounded themselves with the objects, people and thoughts which together formed a haven of devotion to and refined appreciation of the Arts. Here Fry heard the critical estimation of the Old Masters whose greatness he had only recently himself seen and to whom he was now redirected. In his own 'earnest endeavours to paint' – landscapes and watercolours mostly – and in the contemporary work around him, at the New English Art Club as well as the Academy, he saw a falling short of those qualities which distinguished those paintings – and indeed the paintings of Hokusai or the primitive sculptures which he had seen at the Vale. Fry began to write; partly to offset his own disappointments as an artist but also out of a sense of frustration with much of contemporary English art. As he railed at the superficiality of Sargent (1856–1925) and the provincialism of English 'impressionism' – with but the smallest note of praise for Augustus John (1878–1961) – there emerged in his writing a search for the key to what makes art. His was an almost Ruskinian crusade to re-educate the English philistine with a combination of praise (but mostly condemnation) of what passed for art. In 1903 he helped found the *Burlington Magazine* partly as the vehicle for this crusade. However, even as he groped toward it, his was still a crusade without a grail and it was not until 1906 that the shape of that elusive vessel was at least partly revealed in the work of Cézanne. From Cézanne's clumsy hands there was being built an art which seized the daring of the Impressionists while holding firm to the discipline of the Old Masters. Here perhaps, in post-Impressionism, in the work of Gauguin, Van Gogh and Matisse, was the structure, the form, the key to art.

In 1906, after the disappointment of failing to secure either the Slade chair or the directorship of the National Gallery, Fry accepted the invitation of the American millionaire Pierpoint Morgan to go to America and to the Metropolitan Museum. For several years until 1910, Fry and Morgan spent almost half their time raiding Europe. They travelled widely and richly; Morgan bought prodigally while Fry with equal enthusiasm pored over riches barely imagined. As they plundered, an insistent enquiry pricked Fry's sensibilities: why are all these varied objects, from different societies, cultures and beliefs, good? What universal element unites them? And why is it not to be found in English art? In 1910, after an unseemly wrangle over his already inflated salary, Fry abruptly returned to England. In 1909, in an *Essay on Aesthetics*, Fry adumbrated his theory of 'significant form', a term borrowed from Clive Bell and used in the same way to describe that common element of all art.[17] Significant form, though, was not an element in nature – a sentiment which Whistler would have endorsed – but was wholly the product of earnest disinterest. It was an art separated from the myriad distractions of incident, anecdote and association; it was art for art's sake, but now stiffened with a classical backbone of form, profundity and significance. It was an art purged of the excesses of aestheticism; the decadence and sordidness of Beardsley and the facileness of Whistler, expunging even representation. Fry's doctrine of 'significant form' fitted into a scheme which divided life into the 'actual' – the mundane sphere of recognition – and the 'imaginative' – the 'freer and fuller life'. Meaning – 'significant form' – flowed from the 'imaginative life' and informed the mundane world of the 'actual life'. This is Whistler in philosopher's raiment; nature is endowed by art, fogs become visible. The appreciation of form is a hard-won and personal experience and one not readily enjoyed by all those who first viewed Fry's post-impressionist exhibitions.

Fry left London for Paris in 1910 to assemble the pictures which made up the first of his exhibitions, 'Manet and the Post-Impressionists'. Of the 200 or so works in the exhibition, there were paintings by Manet, Cézanne, Gauguin, Van Gogh, Seurat, Matisse, Derain, Signac, Maurice Denis, Vlaminck, Rouault and Picasso. The scope of the exhibit was almost too broad and probably reflected Fry's own confusion and enthusiasm for this work as the exposition of his still developing theories. When the exhibition opened in London it won almost universal condemnation; Charles Ricketts denigrated it as 'a pornographic show'; *The Times* critic called it 'a rejection of all that civilisation has done'. The outrage was compared by Fry himself to that inspired by Whistler. The criticism though was not all from the conservative wing, as those who had barely assimilated the palette of the impressionists or the vision of Degas seemed caught in a cul-de-sac of provincialism. The presence of much expressionist work and the savage colours of the Fauve artists leant the exhibition the flavour of violence and revolt at best; at worst the evidence of a simple lack of skill. For Sickert the smooth progress of art would have seemed to have fallen back on its evolutionary path and regressed to a coarser age. The first large show of post-impressionism was almost too large and took in so wide an ambit that it lost focus, covering developments in France which had taken decades to mature; the English public were now asked to digest this in one gulp. The scattering directions of the modern movement demanded a more thoughtful map than the jumble of sensation and changing signposts that this first exhibition offered.

The second exhibition, also held at the Grafton Gallery, opened in October 1912 and was altogether a more coherent show. Fry's admiration for Cézanne dominated his selection of paintings: in the exhibition which reopened in

January 1913, the number of Cézanne paintings was increased from the eleven shown in 1912 to thirty-three, along with many other changes. Complementing the Cézannes were a large number of works by Matisse and a small group of Braques, some Fauves and one Cubist, which bridged the two paths. In both, however, whether the novel space of the Cubist or the brilliant colour and design of the Fauves, there was a new vision which drew upon the resources of man and not nature; not an imitation but an equivalent for life. These were not the slick and clever paintings so loved by Edwardian England, the smooth surface and illusionistic skill; these were rough and unfinished paintings, brash and even ugly. The artists who made them were dealing with the very stuff of painting: colour, line, form and shape and by doing so were discovering the elusive vessel sought by Fry. The exhibition also showed contemporary and current work of English artists selected by Clive Bell, as well as a Russian section chosen by Boris Anrep. Of the English artists represented there was Spencer Gore and Wyndham Lewis; the Bloomsbury group – Duncan Grant (1885–1978), Fry, Vanessa Bell (1879–1961) and Henry Lamb (1883–1960); Stanley Spencer (1891–1959), who had three paintings in the show, and Eric Gill (1882–1940), who had eight sculptures. The exhibition, despite its more structured arrangement and its attempt at educating rather than simply stunning, met with almost equal derision and shock to the first. However, Fry's efforts had at last brought English art into the twentieth century, in confusion and uproar to be sure, and with barely time to assimilate it before the country was engulfed in the confusion and uproar of world war.

Fry's campaign, his vision, was made in the image of those pursued by Ruskin and Morris and his own close experience of Ashbee's guild. In the manner of the time – and as early as Vanessa Bell's 'Friday Club' first organized in 1905 as a sort of parlour-café society – Fry, so often thwarted in his own attempts at leadership or control, became a member of the loose-knit 'Bloomsbury' circle whose centre was Lady Ottoline Morrell.[18] This coruscating group of artists, writers, politicians and intellectuals included Vanessa and Clive Bell, Henry Lamb, James and Lytton Strachey and John Maynard Keynes. However, Fry's contribution to that tradition of 'artist–social reformers' was in the formation, in 1913, of the Omega Workshops at 33 Fitzroy Square. The purpose of the Workshops was to bring 'significant form' into the decorative arts and into manufacture – and here the echoes of Ruskin and Morris are strongest. Fry disliked the smooth finish of machine-made goods, much preferring the texture of hand-crafted products. Unfortunately he brought neither the force of Ruskin nor the expertise of Morris to his enterprise, and often the products were an unhappy mixture of enthusiasm and ineptitude. Nonetheless, much was made of the Workshops in the name of style, and while it may appear as ill-matched and garish, they at least addressed the question of what modern design may look like. In 1919 the Workshops were closed, though some of their personnel, in particular Duncan Grant, continued to practise successfully as designers long after the company was wound up.

VORTICISM – WYNDHAM LEWIS AND ENGLAND'S MODERN MOVEMENT

Though their life had been short the Omega Workshops had attracted many younger artists into the sort of association which seemed an anachronism. The medievalism of Morris and the social purpose of Ruskin were perhaps only dormant and not dead – but the modern movement had not yet been exhausted and a new 'Enemy' was waiting in the wings to pick up Whistler's baton. In 1913 a clash over the disputed disposal of a commission from the *Daily Mail* for the Ideal Home Exhibition developed between Omega members Fry and Wyndham Lewis. Lewis claimed that Fry, in an abuse of his position, gave the commission to the anonymous staff of the Workshops when it had been directed to Lewis and Spencer Gore. Other differences resurfaced and the two men settled into a relation of dislike and distrust. Lewis, almost in pique, set up the Rebel Art Centre. The Centre lasted barely four months before Lewis's distrust and jealousy brought it to an end. Among his associates in the venture were the poet Ezra Pound, the philosopher T. E. Hulme, and the artists Gaudier-Brzeska (1891–1915), Jacob Epstein (1880–1959) C.R. Nevinson and David Bomberg (1890–1957). Lewis, despite assuming the epithet of 'The Enemy', was without Whistler's wit, substituting instead an aggressive and explosive verbal and printed assault. However, and often for the worse, his anger and suspicion were directed as much against friends and supporters as against the great complacent body of lingering Victorianism. From Tottenham Court Road to the London Group, the Omega Workshops and the Rebel Art Centre; from 'English Cubist' to futurism, vorticism and *Blast*, Wyndham Lewis had been seeking a platform for his views and expression of his ideas, but finally he was left virtually a one-man movement.

In 1910 the Italian futurist, Marinetti visited London in a whirlwind of lectures and promotion of Futurism – whose manifestos had appeared the previous year – extolling the virtue of the machine age, exalting speed, youth, destruction and the 'hygiene' of war. The Futurists' exhibition arrived in London in March 1912, with Marinetti's return in 1913 and again in 1914 to rally support for the cause. The Italians were modern, they spoke of today, they were not the belated recognition of yesterday's achievements, and so proved attractive to the young people they addressed. Lewis, though impressed with the energy and aggressive style of the Futurists remained, like Fry, unconvinced of their project – partly in Lewis's case we might suspect because of his own egotistic longings. Indeed, a loose band of anti-Futurists, lead by Lewis and including Hulme, Epstein and Gaudier-Brzeska, invaded a Marinetti lecture, disrupting it with their presence and invective. C.R. Nevinson, in the excitement of the moment perhaps, joined with Marinetti in publishing a manifesto of 'Vital English Art' in the *Observer* newspaper of 7 June 1914. Much in the nature of the Italian manifestos, it praised the modern and condemned the past, taking pot shots at Maypoles, medievalism and Oscar Wilde, and celebrating strength, virility and sport as an 'essential element in art' – a bizarre reconstruction of the trapeze-swinging English gentlemen Whistler found in the ateliers of Paris. Nevinson appended the names of Lewis, Epstein and Bomberg amongst others supporting the cause, only omitting to ask their permission and giving the address of the Rebel Art Centre as the home of this venture. Lewis was furious, but this outrage precipitated Vorticism as he rallied his 'Rebels' against the 'Italian intruder'. He hastily repudiated Nevinson's claims with his own letter to the *Observer* – with bona fide signatories – but the real assault came with the publication of *Blast* in July 1914, containing Lewis's own Vorticist Manifesto. *Blast* was a typographical blitz; a catalogue of 'blasts' of condemnation and 'blesses' of favour; poems, stories, plays – including Lewis's own *The Enemy of the Stars* – charges and declarations burst upon its pages. Pound, Ford Madox Ford and Rebecca West contributed to the first edition; T.S. Eliot to the second and last in 1914.

Vorticism was to be more a phenomenon than a movement, though for a year there persisted a vorticist style and a group which practised it – even if they were to deny it later. T.E. Hulme was a refusee of the Vorticist Manifesto but had a profound influence on its development. In 1914 he had written several articles for *New Age* magazine on modern art. He argued a return to classicism; not the classicism of the academy but that of Greece and the ancient world – hard, angular, synthetic, non-vital. Lewis's anti-naturalism, his regard for the machine's 'reality', and a paradoxical primitivism – 'crude energy' – borrowed from Pound, combined to form an aesthetic which though it initially leaned toward abstraction maintained a humanistic element. The vortex was the still centre in the confusion of life and in many of Lewis's vorticist paintings this image is found. The vorticist style – an architectonic arrangement of broken angular lines, blocks of colour which overlap, interpenetrate and disrupt each other as they fall toward a central point or area, the vortex; or the paring down of forms to a hard-edged abstraction – survived until 1915. Vorticism, though, remains as perhaps the first home-grown modern movement which eagerly took up radical ideas, reformulated them in the spirit of their original conception, and shook English art from its provincialism. Lewis's thin skin, restless energies and intellectual appetite impelled a steady outpouring of plays, novels, poems, paintings and polemic; but Vorticism could not withstand the progress of war.

THE WAR ARTISTS

The war thwarted whatever ambition the Vorticist revolution may have had, and took an early toll in the death in 1915 of Henri Gaudier-Brzeska, the gifted young sculptor whose work held such promise in its fusing of the primitive and the modern. Poets, painters and writers were dispersed in the various theatres of war, but in 1916 the British, and later the Canadian, Government commissioned the Official War Artists scheme. Under this scheme artists as diverse as John Singer Sargent and C.R. Nevinson were given extraordinary licence to record the war, its events and effects. From the witnessing and recording of scenes of devastation, moral and physical collapse and man's grosser follies, many of those artists surpassed themselves with the depth of feeling and technical virtuosity they brought to the task – for example, in Sargent's *Gassed*, Paul Nash's smashed landscapes and Nevinson's images of furious movement and enervating fatigue. The developments in painting made over the previous decades now seemed bleak, hollow and horribly prophetic as society was fractured, splintered and crushed in a mechanistic onslaught which reduced men to 'mere cogs in the mechanism'. Now, after the struggle to free art from the onus of representation and overturning tradition to gain the high ground of pure form, artists were confronted with the bare and blasted terrain of man without humanity. For many the effect was at least a temporary pause in the rush toward abstraction in a gathering of images expressive of man's resilience, fortitude and vitality.

One who entered the war with a rather more specialized knowledge and experience of its horrors was Henry Tonks (1862–1937). Tonks began his career in medicine and in 1887 had been house-surgeon to Sir Frederick Treves at the London Hospital. A year later he began to study with Fred Brown at the Westminster School and in 1892 was appointed assistant to Brown at the Slade School. From 1892 until 1930, as Assistant Professor and Professor, his towering figure dominated the school, if less its formidable roll-call of students. The Slade under Tonks employed the full rigour of the

Academy schools: drawing from plaster casts until 'promoted' to the life room, an emphasis on drawing and the 'line', 'sight-size' techniques and the use of plumb-lines for measurement and accuracy. Students began by painting from the Antique before passing onto painting from life. The discipline was severe and Tonks's own technique was 'dry' and quite austere. His anatomical pastels, made in the service of the pioneer plastic surgeon Sir Harold Gillies, and his satirical drawings and caricatures reveal, however, quite another side to him. Tonks is something of an éminence grise in English art; friend of Steer and Sickert, acquaintance of Whistler and Sargent, teacher to Harold Gilman, Augustus and Gwen John, Wyndham Lewis, Vanessa Bell, Duncan Grant, Matthew Smith, David Bomberg, Paul Nash, C.R. Nevinson, Leon Underwood, William Coldstream and Roger Hilton among many others.

THE INTER-WAR YEARS AND THE RETURN TO LANDSCAPE

The quickening pace, and the increasing factionalism, of the immediate prewar years were slowed and largely stilled after 1918, as life, distinctly different from before, came to terms with a new world. Those who served as war artists or soldiers returned from a harrowing experience which had, nonetheless, and in many cases, added another dimension to their work, now finding themselves 'without a war' and without the spirit which had previously informed their work. The effect, superficially, was reactionary: to look for the stability which so many craved after such devastation. A certain looking-inward was inevitable and to some extent this gaze fell upon the past, to old forms and old ways. The seeming headlong rush into abstraction which Fry's formalism suggested and Lewis promoted was halted as the human and the vital were reaffirmed. However, the seeds blown across the Channel had taken root and continued to nourish a native art in its recuperation. There were not the same vociferous and often combative groupings which had pursued theories and manifestos, and these postwar years are characterized by artists in loose association or independently working out a vision commensurate with their hopes and experience.

The London Group remained largely unaltered in its ambitions, if not wholly in its composition, and in this period continued to provide support and a venue for new artists and new ideas. The dominant force in the Group during the twenties was Roger Fry and the 'Bloomsbury' set – Bell, Grant, Anrep – which filled its ranks under Fry's patronage. The large retrospective

held in the New Burlington Galleries in 1928 was a testament to his influence
– and was to become, as the character and personnel of the Group changed,
something of a finale. Fry's views, though well publicized in his many articles
– and those of the more polemical and audacious Clive Bell – were also to be
modified in the shape of new hopes and old desires. In a catalogue note to
the 1928 show, Fry commented upon the reversion to 'construction in depth'
and the return of 'light and shade', but also noted the 'increased coherence of
design'. The precepts of his formalism – the grammar and syntax of line, shape,
colour and rhythm – continued to influence artists but more in the way of
sharpening design than defining ends, certainly with the more established
painters.

Duncan Grant was such a painter, with a substantial body of work and
estimable reputation. Fry admired Grant as a painter but typically and
inevitably sought some influence in the direction of his work, and this is
reflected in later work. The painting *The Tub*, made in 1912, calls up several
of Fry's themes – the integrity of primitive art, defined formal structure,
strength of design – and presages the development of Art Deco in its bold
chevrons and zig zag patterns which became so much a part of the Omega
style. While Grant, Vanessa Bell and others took up Fry's banner, it was as a
control in their work – and one which Fry on occasion felt was not all for the
better. Younger artists pursued it more thoroughly as a style in itself. Grant
continued in Fry's path, assimilating the achievements of Cézanne into his
work as the grip of formalism was loosened and light and space re-entered the
artist's perception. The paintings made in France in the 1920s by Grant most
clearly reflect this development, while later work revives an older admiration
for Matisse.

It is Matthew Smith (1879–1959), however, who most emphatically and
all but singly maintains a link with that other branch of post-impressionism
which dominated Fry's second show in 1912: Fauvism. Smith had been a
follower of Matisse and had, for a brief period in 1910, studied under him at
his school in Paris after a period in Brittany at Pont-Aven. His life was an
almost perpetual torment of painful shyness, emotional strife and real and
imagined physical distress barely relieved throughout the twenties. In 1916
he produced the *Fitzroy Street Nudes* which mark the fulfilment of the catharsis
of 1913 when the difference and timidity of his earlier work was thrown off.
The two *Nudes*, each a single figures seated on a simple chair, show a striking
boldness of design and an almost savage Fauvist colouring. From these Smith
found his own way through to a mature style, more intuitive and expressive,
toward which the Cornish landscapes, from his exile there, first point. His
first one-man exhibition of 1926 at the Mayor Gallery in Sackville Street
established his reputation and began a new cycle of, this time, professional
anguish and bitterness. Fry, detecting in Smith a functional rather than

decorative use of colour and denying him its expressive use, was encouraged to invite him to join the London Artists Association – formed in 1925 by John Maynard Keynes and Samuel Courtauld to help support and exhibit young artists. Smith, ever wary, considered Fry a 'crafty politician' manipulating public and painters alike in his tenacious and agile control of taste and style. Smith refused and Fry 'cut him in the street'.

One, perhaps, who would have benefited from such attention from Fry was Mark Gertler (1891–1939) who, along with Jacob Epstein and Jacob Kramer, belonged to that refugee community which had fled a tide of anti-semitism in Europe. Large Jewish communities grew up, in London particularly, around these groups and, once again strangers in a strange land, they held fast to their own traditions and culture – despite the attempts at 'educating' them into the ways of their adopted country in a programme of anglicization. Under the influence of Fry, Gertler was diverted from the very stuff which inspired his activity – the intense life of the ghetto, the closeness, the atavism, the binding faith of that community. Gertler's work became formally stronger but lost its cohesive energy, and his progress became fitful, exploring folk art, sculpture, a Picasso-inspired classicism, before illness and depression brought him to suicide. The painting *The Merry-Go-Round* (1916) remains his best-remembered piece, but Gertler may have been the missing English expressionist.

David Bomberg too came from London's East End and was associated with the frantic activities of Vorticism – though he later denied any Vorticist tendency. Indeed his work seems to bear this out as, though he moved decisively into abstraction, it was informed more by a pared-down vision than one enlarged by theory. His *The Mudbath* (1914) shows this clearly with the forms of the bathers at Schevzik's Steam Baths reduced to simple angular forms which, though flattened themselves, give some relief to the picture plane. After the war, and like so many others, Bomberg seemed disenchanted with the modern world and moved to the country. Perhaps, as with Lewis, the spare and stark prewar paintings now seemed hollow and wanting, but it was not until he left for Palestine in 1923 that a full break was to be made. Here, for four years, his painting took in a broader and more colourful vision. He worked in two quite distinct ways from landscape: in one he captured the harsh brilliance of the light which held everything in a sharp and precise intensity; the other was more expressionistic – rugged landscapes were treated with rich colour and bravura brushwork, close-toned and high-keyed passages described the grandeur and majesty of his subject.

Wyndham Lewis's experience of the trenches, 'those miles of hideous desert', led him to seek a greater naturalism in his work. The work he did as a war artist in some way forced this change and to some extent may have given his drawing an acuity and sureness perhaps even undemanded in earlier work.

He maintained a concern with design, with structure, but now in the service of rendering the 'flux of nature' with a classical simplicity of order, of planes and angles. This was not, however, some late adoption of cubist practice – which he anyhow denigrated as lacking in invention – but the apprehension of vitality in a precise discipline. His drawing of this period was a consummate exercise of line and form, made with breathtaking assurance. The paintings, though, are less animated; they suffer a little from a certain over construction and become in some cases – the portrait of Edith Sitwell, for example – lifeless in comparison. Increasingly, too, Lewis was dedicating time to writing; both criticism – which was often cruel and bitingly accurate – and novels, plays and poetry.

In the unpeopled landscapes of Paul Nash's war paintings, such as the bitterly titled *We Are Making a New World*, the desolation and havoc wrought by man on the earth is confronted. The recovery of that landscape, indeed of Nash himself, the victim of a breakdown, becomes the subject of much of his work in the twenties. A period of convalescence at Dymchurch brought before him the smooth and unmarked surfaces of sea and sand and the endless rhythm of the breakwaters along the sweep of the shore. The pictures made here, though bleak and sparely painted, do contain some gleam of hope, of a distant but inevitable renewal.

A major figure of this time, who also continued to be outside and beyond it, was the eccentric Stanley Spencer. It is almost impossible to place him within contemporary movements, so completely does he depart from them. In his bizarre vision, which like William Blake's was of a new Jerusalem in Albion's shores – or more precisely for Spencer in Cookham, Berkshire – there was a kind of sunset medievalism in contrast to Blake's dread torments and golden pleasures. The closeness of the spiritual world and the pulsing reality of the Bible – attributed to his father's assiduous reciting of its stories to his children – were the stuff of his life, just as the closeness of neighbours and their lives were real to him. This period of grace extended until the outbreak of war which ruptured the idyll forever but was the spur to perhaps his greatest achievement – the Burghclere Chapel.[19] At the war's end Spencer had begun to plan a chapel, to commemorate not the war but those who fought it, not the horrors of war but the deep-seated, unchanging, even mundane, and God-given goodness of humanity. It was a chance occasion which brought the plans from a wish to a reality, when a Mr and Mrs Behrend, seeking a memorial to Mrs Behrend's brother killed in the war, saw Spencer's cartoons for the side walls at the home of Henry Lamb where Spencer had been staying. After some initial difficulties Spencer's requirements for the building were met and he began, single-handedly, to paint the panels, in 1927 completing them, including the great resurrection for the end wall, some seven years later.

In 1919 a small group of painters and sculptors came together to form the Seven and Five Society – seven painters and five sculptors. They did not form a movement, but marked a distance from the aesthetic empire of Roger Fry. They placed a greater importance on subject and imagery rather than form and design; but really clung together for comfort, and only one of the original membership, Ivon Hitchens (1893–1979), was to rise above those small ambitions and remain with the group until its demise in 1935. However, in 1924 Ben Nicholson (1894–1982) on the invitation of Hitchens joined the group. Nicholson, the son of the painter Sir William Nicholson, had for years, and despite himself, sought to avoid a commitment to painting, travelling abroad and producing little. In 1920 he married the painter Winifred Dacre (1893–1981), who was to prove an inspiration to him. Even work produced as early as 1922 was to indicate an analytical and reductive eye, which though exercised upon landscape and still-life in this year, were to become concerned exclusively with colour and line, shape, surface and texture. In 1924, Nicholson, in the Seven and Five's fifth exhibition, showed *Abstraction, November* and hoisted the banner under which the society was to recruit Christopher Wood, Winifred Nicholson, Cedric Morris and Frances Hodgkins and revive the modern movement in Britain.

NOTES

1. The two terms 'lamp' and 'truth' are central metaphors of Ruskin's project – in 1849 he published *The Seven Lamps of Architecture* where, in arguing in fervent support and advocacy of Gothic architecture, he affirmed its 'truth' in both spiritual and material terms: the very stones were honest.
2. The butterfly, originally designed for him by Rossetti, was Whistler's 'signature' and became his symbol and, with a sting added to its tail, a 'badge of war'.
3. *The Gentle Art of Making Enemies* was a collection of letters, quotes, epigrams and barbs wrapped around the text of the *Ten O'Clock Lecture*, which charted Whistler's skirmishes with his adversaries – which were always increasing in number it seemed. The period it covered, and it was subject to review and addition, was from the time of the Ruskin trial to 1890. No one was safe from Whistler's fury and his wit, and more spiteful attacks cut this way and that across the establishment ranks – but all, really, to little point or effect.
4. Whistler's companions in Paris were indeed a mixed group, though all in Whistler's terms were 'shirts'. The most eminent-to-be perhaps was Edward John Poynter, the future president of the Royal Academy. George du Maurier was to immortalize the characters and events of that time in the barely fictionalized account of *Trilby*. Two others, Thomas Lamont and Thomas Armstrong, later to become a Commander of the Bath, completed the group.

5. *The Ten O'Clock Lecture* was Whistler's statement of the doctrine of 'Art for Art's Sake'. It was first given at the fashionable hour of ten o'clock in February 1885 at London's Prince's Hall. It was repeated at Oxford and Cambridge Universities and was widely disseminated thereafter with translation into, at least, French and German.

6. Walter Pater seems an unspectacular man of indifferent achievement and a peevish nature. His early life had been dominated by a religious fervour which when it was thrown over was done so with peculiar malice. His life at Oxford was one governed by the aesthetic – he took to High Church or Roman Catholic services but only for the sensual experience; he could be oppressed by the smell of flowers, even to the point of pain. Experience, he seemed to say, could, without loss, be emptied of all but the beautiful and good and retain its worth. He was the counterpoint to the 'dangerous' Swinburne: a pernicious and enervated aesthete.

7. After the trial, which he was unable to attend because of ill-health, Ruskin withdrew more completely from life. He resigned the Slade professorship and all but retired to his Lake District home at Brantwood. He made one or two appearances in his later years, but illness and waning mental powers kept him at Brantwood, where he seemed content to 'muse over the pretty water-colour drawings' of Kate Greenaway, who was enormously and perversely in his favour.

8. It is virtually impossible to paraphrase Morris's extraordinary life and achievements and I direct the reader to J.W. Mackail's book *Life of William Morris* (London, 1901) or Philip Henderson's *William Morris – His Life, Work and Friends* (London, 1967; 1986).

9. The move to Merton Abbey was the realization of a Ruskinian dream for Morris – at last, and under one roof as it were, all the Firm's activities would be together in the ideal 'factory'. It was sited on the clear waters of the River Wandle not seven miles from Charing Cross. Morris would often make the journey from Hammersmith to Merton by foot, avoiding the tedious railway trip. The river, the buildings, indeed the whole place captivated Morris, as businessman – the waters of the Wandle were ideal for dyeing – and as an idealist – the orchard, the kitchen garden and its age. The move from the sites at Hammersmith and Queen Square took place in November 1881.

10. Typically for Morris, his involvement with the Icelandic sagas was a complete intellectual and physical one. After his own lilting and watery versions of the tales, the translations he embarked upon, with the assistance of Eirikr Magnusson, were of a very different character. Morris kept closely to the originals, often making their interpretation difficult, but his poetic facility rendered them accessible. The pace of the work was breathless, often only weeks were spent on each translation and weeks again before it was in print. Morris went to Iceland twice, in 1871 and 1873 to visit the sites of the sagas.

11. Alphonse Legros (1837–1911) was persuaded by Whistler to visit, then settle in England. He was no Anglophile and never mastered the language but had reputation enough to gain the professorship at the Slade School in 1876.

12. In Whistler's account this was his infamous response to the Attorney-General's question: 'The labour of two days then is that for which you ask two hundred guineas?' Whistler embroiders the exchange to his advantage in *The Gentle Art of Making Enemies*, with the Attorney-General stumbling into the carefully-laid trap.

13. A founder member of the NEAC, W.J. Laidlay, was to be the guarantor to the Club in the early days of its difficult beginnings. A serious threat to its continued vitality was a concerted effort by certain of its members to use the Club as the

base from which to launch a National Exhibition of Art to challenge the Academy on its own ground. The scheme over-reached the resources of the Club and foundered, which probably saved the infant institution. The most eminent signatory to the proposal was George Clausen, while Walter Crane and Holman Hunt supported the scheme.

14. Quoted in John Rothenstein, *Modern English Painters* (London, 1976) from an article by Sickert on 'Idealism' in the May 1910 issue of *The Art News*.

15. This was a persistent theme of Sickert's which he never perhaps explained more colourfully than when criticizing the critics who praised the new with the same enthusiasm as they condemned the old. He declared that their actions and opinions were those which would see the admiration of a 'fascinating child' inevitably accompanied by the murder of its mother and grandmother.

16. Sir John Rothenstein, *British Art since 1900* (London, 1962), p. 11.

17. Significant form, as a theory, was first proposed by Bell in his book *Art*, published in 1914. Bell was more the popularizer than the deep-thinking theorizer, a position taken by Fry, and his development of 'significant form' as that elusive element in all art was part of a general campaign against the persistent philistinism of Edwardian England.

18. Lady Ottoline Morrell was hostess and patron to the 'Bloomsbury' set and to many artists in its orbit. Hers was an 'imperious and extravagant personality' which found some outlet in the company of intellectuals and artists whom she repaid in support and patronage and not least at Garsington Manor, the forum for their debate. Augustus John's portrait of her captures the somewhat haughty but irrepressibly vigorous character of the woman.

19. The chapel, known as the Sandham Memorial Chapel at the Oratory of All Souls, is in Burghclere, Hampshire. The building designed by Lionel Pearson stands at the centre of a group of almshouses.

The World of Popular Music

Brian Morton

> Strange how potent cheap music is.
>
> Noël Coward, *Private Lives*

The 1898 edition of *Grove's Dictionary of Music and Musicians* gives no entry for 'popular music'. The idea that there was such a thing is a much later construction, one which paralleled the most notable development of the period: the professionalization and industrialization of music making. There was, of course, already a tacit and by no means absolute split between art music (which was encoded in formal scores) and a music that was transmitted orally and, in the conventional wisdom, performed and passed along by itinerant players. However, there is now considerable resistance to the sentimentalization of 'folk' music as a pure, rural tradition gradually undermined by the Industrial Revolution and the centripetal pull of the cities.

Henry Mayhew's image of the lone Highland piper, displaced by the Clearances, and slowly drowned out by the background roar of the Victorian metropolis is a misleading icon. If 'folk music' is anything at all, it is also an urban phenomenon, and the newly professionalized class of musicians was heavily dependent on immigrants – first from Europe, but also from America – and displaced provincials. Nor does the shift from country to city, and from an orally transmitted and primarily spontaneous music to one that was increasingly systematized and commercially promoted, mark the end of a popular music imbued with a sense of community. Quite the reverse. Where Benjamin Disraeli had used the music-hall 'Temple of the Muses' as one of the ironic symbols of a divided nation, no less a man than T.S. Eliot – who had notorious difficulties with the idea of 'popular culture', but who nonetheless understood its mechanisms – identified the music-hall star Marie Lloyd as 'the expressive figure of the lower classes', whose performances were marked by a high level of intimacy and identity with her audience.[1]

That identity was, of course, partially belied by the growing physical and economic distance between 'star' performers and their public, but it also helps refute the notion that the professionalization of popular music also marked an end to the spontaneity and participatory democracy of 'folk' music. Just as it is possible to demonstrate, by reference to cultures where itinerant musicians are still the main transmitters of 'folk' forms that their performance involves sufficient artifice to alienate (in the neutral sense) the audience, so it is clear that 'popular' or 'mass' music in the more modern sense involved a high level of collective participation, mostly obviously in the music-hall sing-along. And it is also significant that the most popular (new) music form, jazz, placed particular emphasis on spontaneity and improvization.

The notion of a conflict between 'folk' and 'commercial' music, though, persists. It was given its most polemical and sentimental expression in 1899 by the recently knighted Sir Hubert Parry (a composer who represents triumphalist Edwardianism far more than the much maligned Edward Elgar) in his Inaugural Address to the Folk Song Society. It is significant that Parry locates the point of maximum tension between 'old' and 'new' cultures at 'the *outer circumference* of our terribly overgrown towns', among 'people who are always struggling for existence' – as if that were in itself an offence – 'who think that the commonest rowdyism is the highest expression of human emotion; it is for them that modern popular music is made, and it is made with a commercial intention out of snippets of musical slang'.[2]

Unconsciously, and with some far from innocent agenda, Parry sets out very exactly the difficulties of studying popular music. People who are 'always struggling for existence' expend notoriously little effort in documenting that struggle, and at the beginning of the period journeyman musicians endured very poor social conditions. Even when unionization began to take hold in the early years of the century, as Cyril Ehrlich has shown in *The Music Profession in Britain Since the Eighteenth Century: a Social History*, the origins of union activity remain 'inevitably obscure. Participants probably kept few records, virtually none of which have survived'.[3] In a much later edition of *Grove's*, where popular music is given a deservedly larger place, the tone is still one of uncertainty. Andrew Lamb declares that the subject, less than a century old, has nonetheless become 'vast and diffuse, and its documentation at a serious level is poor',[4] indicating by the qualification how little 'serious' analysis has been winnowed out of a dense chaff of often misleading ephemera. Most of the 'serious' attempts to document and investigate popular music making in Britain date from the 1980s, though E. Lee's excellent *Music of the People* was published in 1970, and there were other earlier attempts. Cyril Ehrlich is currently perhaps the only historian who has investigated the economics and social role of music and musicians in an exactly quantified way, and his work has made a huge impact on more recent study, even if younger researchers have tended to take issue with some of Ehrlich's conclusions and inferences.

There were other serious obstacles to understanding, beyond the sheer intractability of the surviving evidence. Just as Parry compared modern commercial music unfavourably with the undiluted purity of folk song, so toward the end of a century increasingly dominated by the international dispersal of popular music there has developed what Barbara Cohen-Stratyner in her American-slanted *Popular Music, 1900–1919* calls a 'profound nostalgia' for the imaginary simplicities and transparent values of earlier popular music.[5] Without offering any real indication of how such documents might be 'read' or their arbitrations adjudged, Cohen-Stratyner blithely declares popular songwriters the 'arbiters and documenters of social value'.[6]

There is no doubt, though, that popular music is more than usually responsive to social change, almost barometrically anticipating shifts higher up the cultural and social hierarchy. In the period between the death of Queen Victoria and the onset of the Depression, there were four main strands to the development of popular music making in Britain. First, there were enormous changes in the social organization and self-awareness (to avoid saying class-consciousness) of musicians. Then, there were significant technological changes in the dispersal of music, with a shift away from amateur music making in the home and collectivized theatre-going with its participatory overtones to the consumption of music on gramophone records, radio and in the equally 'private' cinema. Thirdly, there was a gradual shift away from forms borrowed from Europe and towards the dominance of American popular music which persisted until the beginning of the first British counter-'invasion', led by Herman's Hermits and then the Beatles in the early 1960s.

MUSIC FOR THE PEOPLE

In 1900, as Kurt Ganzl demonstrates in his compendious *The British Musical Theatre*, almost every kind of musical show was available and cheaply accessible in London's West End and the provinces.[7] There were comic operas and Continental-style operettas, there were musical comedies of the Gaiety variety, there were plays with songs, and, increasingly, there were American-style variety musicals. The American 'invasion' had not yet fully taken hold. In 1901, *The Times* noted that 'the genre of Savoy opera has not yet become assimilated to the type of American variety operetta', a usage that slightly muddies a more commonly accepted distinction between genres, but which is nonetheless telling.[8]

There was in popular theatre the same ambivalence about the 'correct' balance between entertainment and education which was inscribed into the working ethos of the British Broadcasting Corporation under John Reith.* For the most part, popular theatre was escapist entertainment, but there was still a hangover of late-Victorian didacticism and the even earlier tradition of using popular theatre to comment on current affairs, which persisted in pantomime until that branch of popular theatre was almost entirely taken over by television stars and formulaic references to television shows. It was a common complaint that stage shows were 'too serious'. A reviewer in the *Illustrated Sporting and Dramatic News* complained that 'the journalistic standard for this sort of piece is always very spasmodic and is sometimes placed altogether too high ... the critics ask for more than the playgoer does and the playgoer after all does not want to be educated, but to be amused.'[9] The same point was made, rather more satirically, in a comic song in W.H. Risque's and Edward Jones's highly successful *The Thirty Thieves*, which opened in 1901:

> Sing a song of nonsense, everything in turn
> Four and twenty verses, what a lot to learn!
> One for every subject underneath the sun.
> Won't you all be joyful when it's done-done-done![10]

Such didacticism, though, was gradually pushed out by what became known as the logic of 'bums on seats' (in other words, what the playgoer wants) and by American-style production values, which put greater emphasis on spectacle.

Seriousness was welcomed only when it came wrapped in (not necessarily satirical) humour. *The Better 'Ole*, 'a fragment from France in two explosions, seven splinters and a gas attack', and based on the Bruce Bairnsfather cartoon, ran for an impressive 811 performances after the war. Nothing, though, could top the long-standing record of 2,235 performances set by the 'evergreen' (as it was routinely described)*Chu Chin Chow*, which opened in the West End on 31 August 1916 and only closed on 22 July 1921. Frederick Lonsdale's and Harold Fraser-Simson's *Maid of the Mountains* had only a marginally less impressive pulling power, clocking up 1,352 performances between 10 February 1917 and 1 May 1920.

Music-hall was cheap (6d. a seat before the First World War) and resolutely cheerful. The days of the great parks and pleasure gardens, such as those at Vauxhall visited by Matt Bramble and his ménage in Tobias Smollett's *Humphry Clinker*, were gone. With the exception of the still-popular band concert and the occasional parade (though for reasons climatic or cultural this

---

*For a detailed analysis of John Reith's ethical interests see Chapter 6.

is not a substantial British tradition), music had largely come indoors, to the (relative) comfort of the music-hall theatre. Music-hall songs precisely reflect Andrew Lamb's working definition of popular music as consisting largely of 'pieces of modest length with a prominent melodic line (often vocal) and a simple and unrestricted harmonic accompaniment'.[11]

There were essentially three types of song: the plotted (narrative) or unplotted ballad; the romantic song, which could be anything from the near-*Liebestods* of the swooners to cheeky flirting songs to the mildly suggestive to carefully worded *double entendre*; and finally, novelty songs, which were often written for or by comedians. Songs were often taken from European and American materials, and adapted with a speed of naturalization that reflected the cosmopolitan and relatively tolerant atmosphere that prevailed in popular entertainment. The 'evergreen' 'Down at the Old Bull and Bush' was adapted from Harry Von Tilzen's 'Down at the Anheuser Bush', and patriotic songs of the Spanish-American War were quickly imported for half-propagandistic use in the Boer War. 'When They Play "God Save the King" ' by Vincent Bryan and Theodore Morse was a 1901 attempt to unite the British National Anthem with 'My Country, 'Tis of Thee'. Ivor Novello's 'Keep the Home Fires Burning', given maximum publicity at the exact point when the First World War began to bog down into the spring mud of Flanders, became an important symbol of Home Front stoicism and resolve. It makes an interesting comparison with the equally ubiquitous American chant of 'Over There!', which expressed a much more sanguine and less battle-hardened approach to the war. Charles K. Harris's rather self-satisfied *How to Write a Popular Song*, published in 1906, was little more than a rationalization of Harris's own highly successful method, but it was remarkably influential.

Parry's snobbish comment about musical 'slang' is to some extent justified. Just as nowadays classical music is widely communicated in advertising themes, so music-hall and popular song was to a degree parasitic on (or, less often, parodic of) canonical classical music. Whereas music-hall comedians and lyricists peppered their material with Shakespeare references (which most elements of the audience were expected to pick up) popular composers would adapt themes from Beethoven (in particular), Brahms and Mendelssohn with no such expectation. Lawrence Wright's 'Mignonette' was 'adapted' from Beethoven's Minuet in G. This had the sterling and lucrative effect of allowing free performance, publication and, in due course, recording of non-copyright material.

After the First World War, music-hall – which was still marked by socially mobile Edwardianisms – steadily gave way to 'variety', holding out longest in London itself. In the provinces, privately owned theatres were increasingly bought out by larger conglomerates which took their cue from Moss Empires Ltd, founded in 1900 and one of the most significant counter-pressures in the unionization and regularization of popular music making. The 'variety' theatres took hold first in Manchester, Birmingham, Leeds, Glasgow and Edinburgh, catering not just for the traditional music-hall audience, but for a potentially larger and increasingly consumerist constituency whose musical tastes were now conditioned – if not determined – by radio and gramophone records; this is in keeping with Andrew Lamb's attempt to define a true popular (as opposed to folkish) music which has 'begun to develop distinctive characteristics in line with the tastes and interests of the expanding urban middle classes'.[12]

Variety also had its roots in the seaside show, which has remained an important aspect of working- and lower-middle-class entertainment to the present day, enjoying a current revival on the back of 'staged' television shows – mostly sitcoms – which transfer to seaside repertoire between series. 'Placing' a song in a seaside show was a virtual guarantee of good sales for the sheet music, which was the publisher's main concern. It is clear from the continuing stress placed on sheet music sales that domestic amateur music making still flourished; according to Ehrlich, 'many publishers, including some who were highly alert to market trends, continued to regard sales of sheet music as central to their business, even when this conflicted directly with performing fees. Blackpool, an obvious focus of attention for show business, was a significant test case for their priorities. Its intensive season concentrated demand for music into a few hectic weeks, and there were later spin-off effects when people returned home wanting to rekindle holiday pleasures.'[13] One of those pleasures would certainly have been a visit to a palais de danse. After the First World War, with the influx of American dance styles, there began a huge vogue for public dancing which lasted until the effective demise of 'social' as opposed to noncompetitive dance with the start of the television era, and the gradual conversion of public dance-rooms into bingo palaces. A more sophisticated version of the public dance-hall was the thé-dansant or, more racily, the 'tango tea', where drunkenness and knife-fights were rare and flirtation and seduction carried on in an altogether more stylized way. Most of the large hotels and tea-rooms began to carry not just the traditional light-classical string trio, but an additional saxophonist, banjo player and percussionist. Groups like the Savoy Havana Band and the better known Savoy Orpheans cultivated a music that owned some mild cousinage to jazz, but in a typically 'cool' and prettified way.

The BBC made a categorical distinction between 'light' and 'dance' music, largely based on instrumentation – strings for 'light' music, horns and percussion added for strict tempo 'dance' – and it was the BBC, together with the Prince of Wales's enthusiastic patronage of bandleader Bert Ambrose, that really launched the dance-band era in Britain, giving top-flight bands like Roy Fox's, Lew Stone's, Jack Jackson's, Sidney Lipton's and Harry Roy's nationwide appeal (enshrined in series after series of cigarette cards) through their tea-time and late-night broadcasts from such clubs as the Kit Kat, the Mayfair, the Monseigneur Restaurant and the Dorchester Hotel, a kind of broadcasting known in the United States as 'remote'. The bands were not yet conceived as packaged variety shows – that came later, and Billy Cotton's band and show was perhaps the only one to survive the onset of the television era – and the main emphasis was on smoothly professional musicianship. There was very little sign of the American practice of allowing a small group within the overall orchestra to play an interlude of 'hot' numbers, and jazz strictly conceived only really took root in Britain (other than through the medium of records) at the end of the Second World War when the competing ideologies of bebop, mainstream and Dixieland revitalized popular music.

CONCERTED ACTION

Music making before the era of 'piped' or taped accompaniment was a labour-intensive business. It has been determined that there were two thousand professional musicians in the United Kingdom in 1799, the majority of them in London (though the figure presumably does not account for the large number of itinerant musicians still active in the countryside).[14] By 1901, this had risen to nearly forty thousand, peaking for the first time in 1911 (at the height of the era of music-hall and musical theatre). The figure dipped in 1921 (partly due to natural wastage, war, and the 'rationalization' of the theatres), sparking a comment from E. Evans in an article on 'Music and Cinema' in *Music and Letters* in January 1929 to the effect that there was now talk of a 'shortage'. But the figure rose again (with some dramatic but largely inexplicable regional variations) to nearly fifty thousand in 1931, an increase accounted for largely by the enormous take-up of silent cinemas and picture houses. The 1921 census revealed that there were nearly twenty-five thousand music teachers in Britain, with more than seven-eighths of that number working in England and Wales. Around three-quarters of the total were women, for the most part scratching a marginal living.

Ehrlich points out that 'extensive use of almost unlimited supplies of cheap labour was the fundamental basis of the industry at almost every level of entertainment'.[15] The 'downside' of plentiful labour was, of course, depressed wages, and a buyer's market in a climate peculiarly unresponsive to calls for better working conditions. The average pit musician at the turn of the century worked for poorer than average wages (though this was mitigated by 'day-work'), often teaching the daughters of middle-class families the elements of pianoforte and harmony. Platform 'stars' did, of course, earn very large amounts by the standards of the day; one manager angrily rebutted the charge of slave labour by stating that his leading artiste earned more than a cabinet minister, which was a less dramatic differential than immediately appears because politics and government were then still in the era of the amateur with independent means. Musicians worked in cramped, uncomfortable pits, changed and ate in overcrowded and often unhygienic dressing rooms and were occupationally prone to respiratory ailments (including tuberculosis), rheumatism and arthritis. 'Conditions', as Ehrlich rather redundantly adds, 'were evidently ripe for the formation of trade unions', once the 'pusillanimity' afflicting musicians when it came to self-organization could be overcome.[16]

The Amalgamated Musicians Union came into being in 1893, founded by the enterprising young Mancunian Joseph Bevir Williams and his indomitable mother. The union, and other less successful groupings, directed their attention to the inevitable issue (given the uncertainties of a theatrical life) of a minimum wage, graduated according to skill and status. They also touched on such issues as competition from army musicians, who could be called upon to give public concerts without further remuneration, thus putting professional musicians out of much needed work; and also the issue of 'barring', by which a cartel of theatre managers, eventually confederated as the London Entertainments Protection Association, could contractually block the time-honoured system of 'turns', the practice of performing essentially the same routine at a number of adjoining theatres on the same evening. Within London, with its thriving Drury Lane and Shaftesbury Avenue 'theatreland', this was perfectly practicable, but the larger manager put prohibitive mileage and appearance restrictions on the more bill-able players. In due time, this, and the issue of entertainments licences, sparked off the bloodless, but cheerfully histrionic and historically significant 'Music-Hall War', which ended in reasonable compromise and some significant advances for theatre musicians, raising them an average weekly wage of not less than £1.10s. with bonuses for matinée performances.

Surprisingly, the Battersea MP John Burns had taken up the musicians' cause in 1901, the year of the important Taff Vale test case, and written it into a broad programme of industrial liberalization which was eventually swept to victory in the general election of 1906, which put Burns (less effectively than he had promised) in the Cabinet. The 'Music-Hall War' was certainly a great deal less significant and less reliably documented than the Taff Vale case, but it did represent a significant step in industrial relations; more important, it reflected the fact that popular music making had become a part of contemporary industrial society, subject to the same pressure and jeopardies as any modern industry in which the means of production and of distribution had been separated.

222

Music publishing was changing rapidly. The British equivalent of 'Tin Pan Alley' had sprung up in and around Denmark Street, just off the Charing Cross Road in London. British publishers were increasingly adopting the American system of 'free' songs. Whereas in the past, songs had been the property of individual performers, who bought exclusive rights, rather than of the original composer or publisher, now songs were written on spec and had to be 'plugged'. Having a song performed in a prominent revue or musical (and songs were inserted into most non-narrative shows rather haphazardly) was a guarantee of success, shifting the publisher's emphasis from performance fees to royalties on sheet music.

Perhaps the most significant addition to the scene in this respect was the Performing Rights Society,[17] Founded in 1914, as a direct consequence of the British Copyright Act of 1911, it served to collect fees for the use of all music registered with it. After an initial period of resistance, most of the major publishers signed up and the PRS became a significant presence on Tin Pan Alley. One of Denmark Street's more exotic denizens was also responsible for another of the period's most significant forums. Lawrence Wright had graduated, via a series of spectacular publicity coups, from a market stall in Leicester to control of a significant slice of music publishing in London. As 'Horatio Nicholls', he was also known as the composer of 'Don't Go Down the Mine, Daddy', which to modern ears recalls Oscar Wilde's comment about Little Nell's death: that it would require a heart of stone not to laugh uproariously. However, Wright's business acumen was very considerable and in 1926 (a year of enormous significance for popular music in every direction) he began publication of *Melody Maker*, which was to become one of the most important arbiters of popular musical taste in Britain. Wright originally intended the magazine to be a professional forum for musicians and their publishers, 'A Monthly Magazine for All Directly or Indirectly Interested in the Production of Popular Music'. *Melody Maker's* first editor was one Edgar Jackson, née Edgar Cohen, whose views fell some way short of progressiveness, but who nonetheless used the magazine as brilliantly as his owner-proprietor to air every kind of music-related issue, and not merely aesthetic ones. It was the beginning of serious popular music journalism in Britain.

TECHNOLOGICAL CHANGE

Popular music was subject to enormous technological change in the first quarter of the century. In comparison, the carefully stage-managed technological 'revolutions' that introduced videos and compact discs were rather trivial. Ehrlich has patiently traced the progress of one of the Victorian's favourite class-icons in *The Piano*.[18] Elsewhere, he writes, 'The ubiquitous "piano in the parlour" was eventually driven out by alternative status symbols and forms of entertainment, a social revolution already perceptible immediately after the [First World] war.'[19] *The Illustrated London News* for 3 February 1900 had contained an advertisement for the Edison phonograph, which promised anyone with two disposable guineas (no mean sum at that time) 'the HUMAN VOICE, the NOISE OF THE CATARACT, the BOOM OF THE GUN, the VOICES OF BIRDS AND ANIMALS', an improbable menu that underlined the shortcomings of pre-shellac recordings for music. Only with the introduction of electrical recording in 1926 was it possible to make acceptable recordings of popular forms like close harmony and ballad-crooning, which distorted horribly on the original wax cylinder recordings, restricting the earliest commercial recordings to operatic arias of limited range, and orchestral and instrumental music.

Radio and (silent) cinema, though, had a far greater impact on the consumption of popular music. Also in 1926, the BBC was incorporated under Royal Charter. Broadcasting of light and dance music had begun in 1923, not quite over the dead body of John Reith, and by 1930 more or less dominated music broadcasting, light music taking up around 30 per cent of broadcast time, dance music (which was considered a separate entity) nearly 20 per cent.[20] By this time, the vast majority of Britons had at least access to a 'wireless' set.

A singer like Gracie Fields who matched astonishing vocal range with a personable demeanour was well suited to both theatre and radio. Fields ranged from novelty singing – 'Walter, lead me to the altar' and 'The biggest aspidistra in the world' – to much more mainstream repertoire, including the curiously gendered 'Sally'. In 1922, her career in London broke with hugely successful runs at the Alhambra, later at the Coliseum and Café Royal, and she appeared in her first Royal Command performance at the age of thirty in 1928. What really consolidated her reputation, though, was the series of films she made in the 1930s.[21] Thus, cinema exerted an extremely important influence on popular music of the time.

Cinema-going was still short of its prewar peak, but twice-weekly attendance at a local picture house was by no means unusual, and admission prices were pegged at a rate significantly below that of variety theatres or classical concerts.* By 1928, it should be noted that nearly 75 per cent of all paid musical employment was in picture houses. Many cinemas employed a single pianist, but string quartets and even small chamber orchestras were also common, a situation that prevailed until the vogue for American-style theatre

---

*For further discussion of cinema and its audiences see Chapter 7.

organs in the 1930s, by which time, of course, cinema itself had been taken over by the 'talkie', which required no 'live' accompaniment. Cinema music was to some extent an extension of the onomatopoeic effects or 'business' produced by pit musicians in music-hall and popular theatre to accompany (mostly) comedy acts. Cymbal clashes or a vulgar tuba note might underline a prat-fall, a wah-wahed trombone could suggest a drunk's walk. The narrative pace and rapid transition of scenes in cinema called for the musician(s) to segue confidently between dramatic and impressionistic sequences (conductor and pianist André Previn recalls once absent-mindedly having played 'Tiger Rag' during the Crucifixion scene in D.W. Griffiths's epic *Intolerance*).[22] Indeed Erno Rapee's 1925 *Encyclopaedia of Music for Pictures* offered a staggering 20,000 pieces cross-coded to cover almost any change of mood.

The advent of 'talking pictures' and their logical extension, the big-budget American musical brought cinema music (except as an additional diversion) to an end, only to be revived with a new interest in the silent classics in the 1980s, and the film musical, with its exotic locations, rapid transitions of scene and enormously scaled-up production numbers exerted further pressure on stage musicals.

THE AMERICAN 'INVASION'

A *Punch* cartoon from 1913 shows 'Music' stopping her ears against an explosion of raucous sound from a transatlantic cabin trunk.[23] Among the offensive sounds are 'Hitchy Koo', 'Alexander's Ragtime Band', 'I want to be down in Dixie', and 'Yiddle on your fiddle'. The 'invasion' had begun much earlier. In 1901, John Philip Sousa's band visited Britain, bringing with them innovations like the 'cake-walk' (a syncopated hybrid of the two-step and polka, and a forerunner of the soon-to-be-dominant ragtime) and the two-step march. Close behind were the fashionable *valse 'boston'* a slower-tempoed waltz than the Viennese original (and thus considerably more amenable to amateur dance-hall use), the tango and the ubiquitous foxtrot.

American music, though, only really began to take dominant hold in Britain after the First World War. The brief presence of American troops – including segregated black divisions – on the Western Front made a considerable impact on the music and night-life of postwar Paris. There was some inevitable osmosis across the Channel, but jazz and ragtime took off much more slowly than they had in France, and were subject as we shall see to greater suspicion, dismissal and outright hostility.

American cultural dominance was in a sense the last chapter of Manifest Destiny. The immediate postwar period saw the United States poised on the brink of international cultural hegemony. The process was accelerated by the postwar dismantlement of the Austro-Hungarian Empire and of the Viennese society that had fostered the classical waltz and the romantic operetta. Starved of their original context, these gradually, then more rapidly, withered away.

Though the music and theatre world had been notably racially tolerant (with the obvious and ironic exception of a little classic English anti-semitism) and cosmopolitan, there was an inevitable backlash against Austro-German operetta, identifiably German themes and against German names, whether or not the owners were naturalized. (Having said that, anti-German feeling did not appear to militate significantly against the decidedly Teutonic-sounding Oscar Asche, who had master-minded *Chu Chin Chow*.) The postwar Aliens Order effectively ratified hypothetical racism in the profession, and those musicians who did not hide behind an anglicized name or could not disguise a *Mitteleuropa* accent were often the subject of passive prejudice in the form of non-recruitment. Sadly but inevitably, the nonradical, pragmatic populism of early unionization tended to encourage racism (which was, however, directed primarily against Jews and Germans, rather than more 'exotic' foreigners like the first generations of jazz men, and may thus claim some very partial mitigation on recent historical grounds).

There was though, by no means complete acceptance of American 'Negro' musicians. In the last year of the First World War, the magazine *Performer* published a cartoon of a black man which would only have been slightly too mild for *Der Stürmer* a decade or two later, and with the caption:

First he brings us his slave ditties,
Then he charms us with his Coon songs,
Now he's sending us barmy with jazz
What's his next stunt?[24]

Unfortunately, Edgar Jackson, editor of the quickly influential *Melody Maker*, set his face soon and hard against 'Negro jazz', tolerating only the prettified white version.

Though Jim Godbolt has surprisingly little to say on the subject in his history of jazz in Britain, the music arrived more or less on the back of an extraordinary vogue for ragtime. The show *Hallo, Ragtime!* was brought across to Britain in 1912, along with the American Ragtime Octette, and Richard Middleton quotes an *Era* article of 1913 that claims no less than *130* American ragtime troupes which were currently touring Britain[25] the figure is also testimony to the vigour and extent of the provincial theatre industry. The first 'true' jazz musicians to visit Britain were the members of the Original Dixieland Jazz Band, who came over 'all the way from New Orleans, where the crocodiles [sic] come from' to appear in the Hippodrome revue *Joy Bells*.[26] The band received a huge ovation (largely, it is assumed, from a claque of American GIs in the audience) but the influential comedian George Robey was incensed and gave manager Albert De Courville an ultimatum. Either the band went, or he went. In the event, predictably, it was the band whose services were dispensed with. Fortunately, there is no overtone of racism to Robey's outburst, for the ODJB were white-skinned to a man, thereby rather setting the pattern for jazz in Britain. However, there was continuing resistance to foreign musicians; only (rather briefly) in the late 1950s and once again in the middle to late 1980s has home-produced jazz in Britain been the province of black musicians. *Era* contented itself with a rather bland rationalization: 'There is much to be said for the anti-jazzers, and it is impossible to deny that jazz music is impertinent and hath no respect for persons.'[27]

British moral panics are apt to be milder than elsewhere, and jazz was greeted with no more than a sour grimace and the comment of Dr Farnell, rector of Exeter College, 'Nigger music comes from the Devil', was mercifully untypical. There was a far greater outcry about the early days of rock and roll, but, then, rock music was essentially propagated by records and was thus far more pervasive.[28] Jazz in Britain was suppressed by simple neglect and by the long-term dominance of non-improvising hotel orchestras and dance bands.

There is still considerable controversy – definitional, aesthetic and pseudo-political – about 'popular music'. Some historians have preferred to talk about 'mass music' or 'people's music', others to obliterate any distinction between high and low forms. But there is, surely, a case to be made for the simplest and most honest. Noël Coward's comment 'strange how potent cheap music is', echoed in the title of Sir George Grove's *A Short History of Cheap Music* seems also curiously potent.[29] There is a particularly democratic slant to popular music in Britain, fostered by the country's vanguard industrialism and the technological developments (notably broadcasting) that sprang from it. Only the United States, and, more recently, ex-colonial 'Third World' countries like India have a more highly developed or pervasive popular music sector. In the early years of the century, musical entertainment was, relative to wages and other prices, genuinely cheap, an ethos that prevailed until public performance began to fall victim to 'free' (that is, at point of use) television. The long-standing notion of Britain as *das Land ohne Musik* was also countered by European travellers' marvelling that the British were all singers and that instrumental expertise was far more widespread and at a far lower social stratum than anywhere else in the developed world. That is a complex and rather fragile heritage, and understanding of it is still only in its infancy.

NOTES

1. T.S. Eliot, 'Marie Lloyd', *Selected Essays* (London, 1951), p. 457.
2. Sir Hubert Parry, 'Inaugural Address', *Journal of the Folk Song Society*, vol. I, 1899, p. 2 (emphasis mine).
3. Cyril Ehrlich, *The Music Profession in Britain Since the Eighteenth Century: a Social History* (Oxford, 1985), p. 143.
4. Andrew Lamb, 'Popular Music', in Stanley Sadie (ed.), *New Grove Dictionary of Music and Musicians* (London, 1980), vol. 15, p. 87.
5. Barbara Cohen-Stratyner, *Popular Music, 1900–1919* (Detroit, 1985) p. xv.
6. Ibid., p. xxx.
7. Kurt Ganzl, *The British Musical Theatre*, 2 vols: 1865–1914 and 1915–1984 (London, 1986).
8. Quoted in Ganzl, vol. 1, p. 750.
9. Quoted in Ganzl, vol. 1, p. 759.
10. Quoted in Ganzl, vol. 1, p. 763.
11. Andrew Lamb, 'Popular Music', in Stanley Sadie (ed.), *New Grove Dictionary of Music and Musicians* (London, 1980), vol. 15, p. 87.
12. Ibid.
13. Cyril Ehrlich, *Harmonious Alliance: a History of the Performing Right Society* (Oxford, 1989), p. 44.
14. Cyril Ehrlich, *The Music Profession in Britain Since the Eighteenth Century: a Social History* (Oxford, 1985).
15. Ibid., p. 143.
16. Ehrlich, *Harmonious Alliance*.
17. Ibid., p. 44.
18. Cyril Ehrlich, *The Piano: a History* (Oxford, 1976).
19. Ehrlich, *Harmonious Alliance* p. 46.
20. Wilfred Mellers and Rupert Hildyard, 'The Culture and Social Setting', in Boris Ford (ed.), *The Cambridge Guide to the Arts in Britain*, vol. 8, *The Edwardian Age and the Inter-War Years* (Cambridge, 1989), p. 34.
21. Gracie Fields, *Sing as We Go! – her Autobiography* (London, 1960).
22. Interview material, 6 August 1974.
23. Reproduced in Cyril Ehrlich, *The Music Profession in Britain since the Eighteenth Century* (Oxford, 1986).
24. Cited in Jim Godbolt, *A History of Jazz in Britain, 1919–50* (London, 1984), p. 7.
25. Richard Middleton, 'Popular Music of the Lower Classes', in Nicholas Temperley (ed.), *The Blackwell History of Music in Britain: The Romantic Age, 1800–1914* (Oxford, 1981; 1988), p. 88.
26. *Era* notice of 19 February 1919, cited in Godbolt, p. 7.
27. *Era* editorial of 29 April 1919, cited in Godbolt, p. 9.
28. 'Paras from the Press', *Melody Maker*, cited (without date) in Godbolt, p. 29.
29. George Grove, *A Short History of Cheap Music* (London, 1887).

CHAPTER TEN

The New Technological Age

John Morris

THE SCENE

The kitchen is a good place to start. In 1900, in almost any British household, the kitchen would have appeared to us extraordinarily old-fashioned: no different in essentials from an Elizabethan kitchen. Washday, for example, represented a dire chore even when piped water was available. In the scullery would be a copper which had to be filled with water and then a fire lit underneath it. Every garment needed to be individually scrubbed or worked up and down in a tub by a 'dolly' – an instrument with a long handle. After rinsing, white garments were put into the copper and boiled, so the fire needed constant attention (and all this in addition to other chores like cooking and cleaning). Later the clothes would be lifted out with a wooden stick as the room filled with steam. If it was fine the clothes would be mangled and hung out to dry; if it was wet, clothes were dried by the fire. Ironing by a flat-iron heated in the fire would need to be left for the following day or days. Every week the housewife, or in a richer household a servant, repeated the ritual.[1] No wonder servants were still so much an 'essential' part of life for the better-off. Similarly, cooking was a messy arduous affair involving the stoking of fires, scrubbing of wooden floors and tables and the black-leading of grates – to say nothing of the difficulties of preserving food before domestic refrigerators became available.

Yet what is described here does not mean that there was no 'new technology'. Electric irons and kettles were being advertised by the mid-1890s. The telephone was invented in the late 1870s. In 1899 Marconi sent radio signals over the English Channel.* Refrigeration started in the 1850s and the vacuum cleaner was invented in London in 1901.[2] The problem was

---

*For further information on the invention of radio, see Chapter 6.

in the social distribution and acceptance of the gadgetry and appliances which became increasingly available. In a real sense there existed a vicious circle in that until wide acceptance and distribution were obtained prices remained too high for ordinary family households, yet while prices were too high it was impossible for a sufficient number of appliances to be sold for the manufacturer to bring the prices down. The water closet, for example, had been devised in the late sixteenth century yet it was still common, even the norm, in many working-class and rural areas, for there to be no flush toilet to a household or for one to be shared by twenty or more people living in a terrace.[3]

Similarly, the motor car, initially an ornate carriage powered by the fledgling internal-combustion engine, was to take another three decades before it really began to revolutionize public travel and despoil the country-side. H.G. Wells, advocate of scientific futures, has Mr Polly in 1910 walking through idyllic pastures and woodlands in which the motor car is still essentially an irrelevance. Even the proud boast of William Morris (later Lord Nuffield) in 1914 that his cars could offer '50 miles an hour, 50 miles a gallon' had little significance for most British families.[4] In the first decade of the century the image of the 'horse-less carriage' for all but a tiny percentage of citizens would have been of an aristocrat or a member of the royal family posing self-consciously in what even they clearly regarded as an impressive but new-fangled contraption of uncertain future.[5] Even more dubious was the concept of flying, despite the success of the Wright brothers in 1903 and of Blériot's flight across the Channel in 1909. 'If we were meant to fly, God would have given us wings' dated from this time.

Yet a more dispassionate and objective observer would have realized that yesterday's imaginings repeatedly had become, or were to become, today's realities – whether or not the social or cultural effects could be seen as desirable. The coal-furnace and the steam-engine had increasingly revolution-ized work and productivity during the nineteenth century, creating the huge industrial conurbations of the North and the Midlands, crowding people into cramped and dirty habitations and reducing the working lives of many into little more than machine-appendages. Indeed, a whole genre of 'Condition of England' novels like Dickens's *Hard Times* (1854) and Elizabeth Gaskell's *North and South* (1854–55) was developed in response to these developments. William Morris, the writer, pre-Raphaelite artist and furniture-maker, in *News from Nowhere* (1891) pictured a better, cleaner, more civilized Britain in the twenty-first century, in which all industry and mechanization had been abolished. Yet literature, of course, changed nothing and the 'new technology' continued remorselessly to advance and transform lives.

By 1900, a vast and growing network of railways and industrial canals linked towns and cities with major ports. Clearly, though individual technical developments such as the washing machine or the family car would take decades before becoming available, affordable and ultimately 'essential', the forces at work at the beginning of the century meant that whatever the setbacks, short of a total breakdown of society, these things *would happen* irrespective of ethical or cultural reservations.

THE TECHNOLOGY

What I have said so far does not gainsay that a clash between the development of the new technologies and the ability of society to sustain that development would occur. There are areas where technology contains within itself the seeds of its own destruction in the sense that no conceivable society can handle that technology with safety and continuity. Nuclear technology (or even the petrol-driven car?) may be a case in point relevant to our own time. The war accelerated enormously the development of weapons, toxic gases, the internal-combustion engine, the refining of petro-chemical fossil fuels and many other innovations, but at the price of bringing European civilization to near collapse. Indeed the critical nature of the evolution of new technology was more serious than even those words suggest, for the war itself was one of industry and technology taking most observers by surprise in that it revealed for the first time and on an alarming scale 'the enormous war-making power of industrial societies'. J.M. Roberts has spoken too of 'the industrial effects' and the 'degeneration of standards of behaviour' which characterized 'the first war of the internal combustion engine'. He continues,

> This technical expansion also made the war more frightful. This was not only because machine-guns and high explosives made possible such terrible slaughter. It was not even because of new weapons such as poison gas, flame-throwers or tanks, all of which made their appearance as soldiers strove to find a way out of the deadlock of the battlefield. It was also because the fact that whole societies were engaged in warfare brought with it the realization that whole societies could be targets for war-like operations.[6]

Roberts also draws attention to the multiplicity of industrial and technical developments which the war accelerated and which to a large extent had accelerated the war – for example the propaganda machine which grew from new developments in printing, dissemination and photographic and cinematic techniques. Another example was the race to build more submarines, itself indicative of a type of war impossible before modern explosives and guidance systems. Even more sinister perhaps is the evidence that the war, sold to the public in Britain and Europe as a struggle to preserve the freedoms and

231

standards of nationhood and empire, was to a large extent about gaining the upper hand in the development of the all-important chemical and synthetics industries – an area in which Germany had made an extraordinary advance in the two decades before 1914.[7]

There are two deductions to be made from an examination of the Great War relevant to this essay. The first is that in a time of emergency the development of new technology would not only accelerate but come to dominate every aspect of social activity. The second related conclusion is that a similar, much slower but equally inevitable process was active in peace-time society. The old-fashioned, technologically undeveloped nature of so much of British social life in the first two decades of the twentieth century, the apparently slow adoption of new technological appliances and apparatus in the homes and streets, towns and villages of Britain, was only apparent. War revealed the true nature of the future in that it threw into sharp relief society's already deep commitment to and indeed dependence upon the industrial and applied scientific and technical developments already well established by the time of the Great Exhibition of 1851.

Yet, paradoxically, throughout the second half of the nineteenth century the impression we get is not one of confidence in the future: upwards and ever upwards with empire and industry. The doubts and malaise, reflected in the writing of Tennyson and Arnold, were widespread and suggest doubts not only of the possibility of continued expansion of British industry, but of the wisdom of that expansion. In fact the evidence is that, in the last two or three decades of the nineteenth century, stagnation occurred in certain key areas of industry: textiles, mining and agriculture for example. There was lack of capital investment and a failure of nerve to take up new inventions and processes.[8] (A recurrent problem that, of course, has continued to our own times, and indeed has repeatedly characterized the patchy development in Britain of innovation, of scientific and technical knowledge, throughout the entire period of the industrial era since its earliest days in the 1730s and 1740s.)[9] Moreover, C. F. G. Masterman's, *The Condition of England* published in 1909 suggested a profound schism in thought in Britain which had earlier shown itself in the great debate of religion vs. science that characterized the 1850s and 1860s.[10] What was the true purpose of life? What was the reality: the life of the mind and spirit or the life of money, industry and power? To some the horrors of war when they came were only a confirmation that the real battlefield was not only Ypres and Passchendaele but Glasgow, Tyneside and the Black Country. The 'pity of war' immortalized by Wilfred Owen was to be translated and transferred by left-wing writers – many would say mistakenly – to those on the dole in the North and the Midlands in the 20s and 30s. Though it might have been fanciful to be surprised that 'the Revolution' when it came, came to Russia and not Britain, it is certainly true that the development of British industry in the late nineteenth century and the early decades of the twentieth century was often haphazard, disorganized and arbitrary, heightening class tensions and frequently exacerbating rather than improving poor living standards. Indeed the overall picture of the development of the 'new technology' was one of inevitability, yes, but also one of a lack of social and political control of that development.

POWER SOURCES AND THEIR APPLICATIONS

During the eighteenth and nineteenth centuries Britain's progressive development of wood, coal and steam had made her by 1870 an industrial power without parallel or precedent in the world. Because of Britain's coal resources, effective transport conditions and subsequently her unrivalled railway communications network, her industrial expansion became phenomenal. For example in 1750 Britain imported twice as much iron as she made yet by 1814 her exports alone amounted to five times her purchases. In the 1780s Britain's output of iron was smaller than that of France but by 1848 Britain was smelting almost two million tons, that is more than the rest of the world put together.[11]

I think it worth keeping such facts in mind when attempting to understand Britain's subsequent development of more modern power sources: gas, petrol, oil, electricity and finally nuclear energy. Circumstances would tend to drive development in two directions: to delay as well as to encourage. (An analogy could be made with Britain's ability to compete in the long term with Japan and West Germany after the Second World War: Britain had too much of a stake in the industrial past – in outmoded ideas, organization, infrastructure, all outdated yet seemingly impossible to eliminate.) In 1900 it was clear that for an industrial power to lead she had to be in the forefront of developing the use of gas, petrol, oil and electricity, and for any country to do this the chemical industry was absolutely crucial. We have seen how Britain fell behind Germany and the United States in this all-important area during the twenty years prior to 1914. Such considerations confirm the interdependence of different branches of science and technology in the development of 'new technology' as a whole.

By 1900, the manufacture of gas from coal by carbonization was a well-established industry. However, the use of this fuel began rapidly to change. The main use of gas had been for lighting, but towards the end of the nineteenth century electric lighting appeared, superceding gas lighting within a few decades. Gas became more and more used for heating both in the home

233

and in industry and, of course, for cooking – the introduction of the gas cooker in the second decade of the twentieth century considerably reducing the burden of kitchen chores. The market for gas rose phenomenally so that in Britain demand increased eightfold between 1890 and 1950.[12] From the 1920s, coal-fired ranges and old black cast-iron stoves, which needed to be black-leaded, rapidly gave way to enamelled models that could be wiped clean with a damp cloth and scouring powder. Automatic temperature–control devices (thermostats) enabled cooking without constant attention. The first such cooker was the Davis New World of 1923 fitted with a Regulo – similarly equipped electric cookers following a decade later.[13] The gas-fired geyser, invented as early as 1868, really came into the house as an affordable luxury only in the 1920s and by the 1930s the advent of heaters fitted with aerated burners, German in origin, became commonplace in the home and known as 'Ascots'.[14]

Even more than gas, however, it was to be the supply of electricity which transformed domestic life. Appliance after appliance was electrically powered, either displacing coal or gas as the fuel or making an appliance feasible for the first time (for example, the vacuum cleaner). It is true that in the whole area of the application of fuel and power, the 'medium is the message': that is that the power source and the technology it engendered in turn effectively dictated the type of appliance thus made possible, subsequently desirable and ultimately 'essential'. The extraordinary applicability of electric power was the key to its impact. David S. Landers has expressed memorably the essence of electric power and its irresistible appeal to man:

the significance of electricity lay in its unique combinations of two characteristics: transmissibility and flexibility. By the first we mean its ability to move energy through space without serious loss. And by the second we mean its easy and efficient conversion into other forms of energy – heat, light or motion. An electric current can be used to produce any or all of these, separately or together, and the user can switch from one to other at will ...

From these characteristics two major consequences emerge. On one hand, electricity freed the machine and the tool from the bondage of place, on the other, it made power ubiquitous and placed it within reach of everyone.[15]

Nevertheless the application of electricity still had its problems. The most important was its loss of power in transmission for when supplying electricity through a conductor, for example, it was rather like supplying water through a leaky main. The best conductors, copper and silver, were expensive metals, and even aluminium became corroded. It is characteristic of the development of the new technology, however, that ways round the problem were found: aluminium was alloyed with magnesium and silicon to form 'Aldrey', while any lack of mechanical strength was overcome by wrapping Aldrey wire round a steel core.[16] What was, and of course still is, impossible to decide is the long-term effects of this and other power forms and their ramifications, for it was as if each new development created the next. Each problem created its solution; each solution its new problem. And as the twentieth century continued, the problems could be increasingly social and cultural as opposed to technical.

Other problems concerning the transmission of electric power were, however, steadily overcome by increasing voltages, using new materials for cables (including, ultimately, specially made plastics), the building of pylons and in the 1930s the advent of the national grid. In any case, utilization of electricity was impossible without control via transformers and switches, and of course, the electric motor itself, which was to allow a whole range of applications. By the 1890s a variety of early motors, dynamos and transformers were under production and in the early twentieth century were to become available to those who could afford them. The first British electric drill was produced in 1914. Initially, of course, it was industry which benefited, but, in due course, domestic appliances – not only the more obvious, such as vacuum cleaners and electric cookers, but others containing tiny motors, such as razors and clocks – were produced.[17] With the introduction, in the early years of the century, of the Leclanché type of common primary battery with zinc and carbon electrodes, the use and availability of small appliances widened, while accumulator batteries of the lead–acid type increasingly became available for use in moving vehicles: cars, railway carriages, aircraft.[18]

Of all applications of electric power, it was of course lighting which had the most revolutionary effect both in the home and at work. By 1900 electric lighting was widely established in urban areas but still regarded as a novelty or curiosity elsewhere. This writer can remember that as a boy during the 1940s it was not uncommon to find country cottages and bungalows that still relied on gas or oil lighting. Yet at the turn of the century there were already two and a half million electric lamps in London alone, largely of the carbon-filament type. Here is a further example of how the social application of technology was at the mercy of economic and organizational considerations which human aspirations could often do little to influence. The spread of electric lighting was inevitable but not *controlled* by man. Moreover, although the incandescent filament lamp is still in use, largely in the home, it is an underdeveloped and inefficient use of electricity. It was much more efficient to discharge electricity through gas, as in the Cooper-Hewitt mercury discharge lamp (1901) which gave a bluish green light, or the sodium vapour lamp which gave a yellow light. The domestic 'strip-lighting', using a mercury vapour lamp, did not appear until the late 1940s. But the revolution in electric lighting through the use of incandescent filament bulbs and the application of other substances like tungsten enabled the production of lamps for special purposes such as lighthouses, torches, bicycle lamps, cinema projectors and so on. In fact, the rapid advance of cinematography in the first three decades of the twentieth century is an indication of the ability of a technology to expand phenomenally once circumstances are made favourable by particular innovations, for example, the camera, the projector, the required lamps and so on. By 1900 one person in ten in Britain owned a camera, yet the concept of presenting what appeared to be *moving* pictures must have offered an attraction difficult to resist. Following the first showing of a motion picture to a paying audience in Paris in 1895, it was another ten years before Britain had a public cinema (in Bishopsgate). Yet by 1914 there were over three thousand in Britain alone.* The greatest expansion of the cinema industry in Britain and America and in other European countries occurred between the wars. By the 1930s, world investment was in the region of $2,500 million. It took another between-wars technical innovation, television, to reverse the trend.

Although, in the period under discussion, a high percentage of public transport in Britain continued to be powered by steam on the railways, and the petrol-driven engine on the roads – the diesel engine and electrification of rail transport coming late to Britain in the 1950s – electrically powered forms of transport became widespread in the early twentieth century, especially in towns and cities. They fell into two distinct categories: those which drew their power from an outside source and those with a self-contained source of energy. In the first category came the tramcar and the trolley bus, the first trams appearing well before the beginning of the century. In general, trams were single-deck vehicles with an arm drawing power from an overhead cable. However, such a system was unsightly, and in some cities, such as London, an underground conduit was used for the cable. Britain was virtually unique in producing double-decker trams. Trolley-buses, which of course did not run on rails, had the advantage of manoeuvrability but rapidly declined in popularity once roads became too congested for them to be used conveniently. Together, however, in the period, these types of electric transport generally provided a cheap and efficient service for work and leisure and are still remembered with affection and nostalgia by many. The second category of electric vehicles, those which are battery-operated, have been in use since the 1890s but have always tended to be slow and restricted in distance because of the need for recharging. They did, however, revolutionize the nature of delivery vehicles, especially of milk and bread, and provided – as they still do – a quiet, efficient and safe service that soon spread to every town and city in the land.[19]

Now, although at the turn of the century electricity could be seen as an important new form of energy, it had its origin in more conventional sources: fossil fuels or, occasionally, water power. And the use of one fossil fuel in

---

*For a detailed analysis of cinema development and expansion see Chapter 7.

236

particular – petroleum – was to accelerate with remarkable rapidity in the early decades of the twentieth century. In 1900, world production was 150 million barrels, by 1919, 550 million barrels, 1,100 million by 1926 and 2,200 million by 1937. (By 1950 it had risen to more than 4,000 million barrels.) During this period conventional coal production remained static.[20] The reasons for the extraordinary increase in the use of petrol are not hard to find. In 1900, the internal-combustion engine was already twenty years old but had originally been designed (by the German N.A. Otto) to run on coal gas. It was adapted by Gottlieb Daimler to run on petrol and, by 1900, some nine thousand petrol-driven motor cars had been built worldwide. Although powered flight had not yet been achieved it was clearly only a matter of time, since a study of aerodynamic principles indicated that the internal-combustion engine, unlike its steam counterpart, had, potentially at least, a low enough weight–power ratio to make flight feasible. Virtually all the early running in the development of petrol-driven engines was German inspired: Wilhelm Maybach devising a float-feed carburettor in 1893 and Karl Benz introducing a spark-plug essentially similar to those in use today.[21]

Once the principles were established, though, the production and then mass production of motor cars in Britain, the United States and other 'advanced' countries rapidly followed (for example the Morris 'Oxford' in Britain and the 'Model T' Ford, in the United States, sixteen million of the latter being built between 1908 and 1927).[22] Yet, as indicated earlier, the social effects of motoring were comparatively gradual except in the larger urban areas where, in any case, the already developed industrial economies had caused an enormous increase in horse-powered traffic as can be seen from contemporary photographs and postcards. Rural areas, country roads, even moorland tracks, were still largely incapable of coping with motorized interlopers, and it was not until the late 1920s and early 1930s that the enormous increase in the production of family cars and the related drop in purchase price really began to show itself in the need for wider roads, more garages, ribbon development and so on. In southern Britain we are perhaps now nearing the end of this, now quite old, development of saturation, a concept still unthinkable in 1930 to any other than dreamers like H.G. Wells. Similarly, though conversely, fossil fuels were finite but the increase in their use geometric. Here is another example of how technology inevitably creates problems while it 'solves' others. Yet this was a problem which appears not to have become obvious until the 1970s.

The development of the aircraft industry is another case in point. Its early days were characterized by accidents and ridicule rather than any promise of success, and even Wells had his doubts as to the ultimate viability of powered flight. Moreover, although it is true that the petrol-driven engine made heavier-than-air flight possible, the fact that it occurred at all perhaps owed as much to man's centuries-old aspirations to imitate bird-flight. Indeed, the full complex of influence that was to bring about the tenuous successes of heavier-than-air powered flight in the first decade of the twentieth century would include, if not Icarus, then certainly the experiments, drawings and speculations of Leonardo da Vinci, the gas-filled airship of the Montgolfiers in the late eighteenth century, Henri Giffard's 'controlled balloon' or 'dirigible' of 1852, Sir George Cayley's man-carrying glider or 'governable parachute' of the same year, and Henson, Stringfellow and Sir Hiram Maxim's steam-powered planes which never quite had lift-off despite the production in 1894 of a model which, on paper, was technically capable of flight.[23] Yet perhaps the most decisive event to influence the development of the aeroplane was the publication in 1889 of *Bird-flight as the Basis of Aviation* by the Lilienthal brothers of Germany. What they had discovered was crucial: if man could not have beating wings like a bird, he *could*, with the right weight–power ratio, get lift by flying with a fixed-wing plane into a headwind. Even in 1914, flying was still considered by most people to be 'nothing but sport-races, stunts [and] looping-the-loop demonstrations indulged in by dashing young madmen'.[24] Within a decade the aircraft had become something which was clearly going to not only revolutionize international travel and transport but also terrorize civilian populations in time of war. For example in May 1916, only seven years after Blériot's historic flight, a Bristol 'Scout' was being launched from another plane in mid-air, while in America a radio-guided flying-bomb was developed which could be automatically directed on to its target. And in Russia, Igor Sikorsky (later of helicopter fame) successfully developed the giant Ilya Mourametz bomber, powered by four engines each of 100 horse-power, carrying a bomb-load of 600 pounds and needing a crew of up to sixteen men who carried out minor repairs while the plane was in flight.[25]

Aircraft thus really proved themselves in the First World War. The speed of wartime advances in aeronautical technology almost defies belief. In 1914, there were perhaps no more than five thousand aircraft worldwide, of very mixed design, performance and efficiency. By 1918, two hundred thousand aeroplanes had been built, while experience in construction and flying considerably and correspondingly increased. To begin with, wartime aircraft were mostly two-seaters with pilot and observer, but soon the observer became a gunner, and then later pilot and gunner were combined, as single-seater fighters fitted with machine-guns appeared. These were used both for aerial combat and attacking troops on the ground. It is indicative of the technological ingenuity fostered by emergency that the need for fighter aircraft to fire through their propellers necessitated the invention of an interrupter mechanism that allowed the gun to fire only when the propeller blades were not in line with emerging bullets. First used by the German Fokkers, it gave them temporary superiority.[26]

So successful were fighter aircraft that the phenomenon created its own heroes such as the Red Baron who flew the Fokker Triplane while Britain's Sopwith Camel – like the Spitfire in the Second World War – became a celebrity in its own right and the favourite plane of British fighter pilots. The power of technology to create celebrities both human and mechanical, though in its infancy between 1914 and 1918, was to become a rapidly increasing phenomenon in the twentieth century. Of course, we now relate this phenomenon particularly to the entertainments industry but, in the 1920s, Mussolini and Hitler were to grasp its significance as essential to the achievement of political success, especially when systematically backed by the resources of radio, cinema, lighting, amplifiers and so on.

During the war, bomber aircraft were also developed by both sides (though the Germans made great use of Zeppelin airships) and increasingly the aircraft became multi-engined types for night attacks on relatively distant targets. Such aircraft (one of the most successful being the British de Havilland DH4 introduced in 1917) became the forerunners of postwar commercial transports.

Civil aviation, therefore, grew from war. Before the war aircraft were too unreliable and uncomfortable for anything other than casual goods and mail carriers. But, by 1919, aviation had developed so spectacularly that the first international flight could be inaugurated between London and Paris. In that same year, Alcock and Brown gave a clear glimpse of the future potential of civil (and indeed military) aircraft by making the first Atlantic crossing by air, while R. and K. Smith made the first flight from England to Australia. In 1924 a United States Army Air Force team flew right round the world. The economics of successful civil aviation was made viable by the setting up of government-sponsored national airlines in the 1920s like KLM, Sabena, Lufthansa, and Imperial Airways.[27] The 'metal bird' had come a remarkably long way in a short time, but how sociably desirable were the developments, how much under any kind of democratic control, was extremely doubtful. As Siegfried Sassoon remarked in 1932 after looking up at a group of planes in peacetime,

> In years to come
> Poor panic-stricken hordes will hear that hum,
> And Fear will be synonymous with Flight.[28]

A recent book, lavishly illustrated in colour, a sort of coffee-table book for children and adults, lists inventions through the ages.[29] The vast bulk of them date from the late nineteenth and early twentieth centuries, at least in their recognizably modern form: the camera, the battery, the record player, the telephone, the radio, the internal-combustion engine, the electric iron, the electric cooker, the electric kettle, the electric hairdryer, the cathode ray tube, the aeroplane, medical instrumentation, plastics, synthetics, polymers... . Some of these I have tried to place in the social and historical context of technological development. But the list is, if not endless, remarkably extensive. To cut off this discussion, as we must in this book, at 1929, is as arbitrary as all cuts are – particularly when we are dealing with what is essentially a *process*, one which, of course, still continues.*

Even more remarkable than the number of inventions is the staggering acceleration of social, cultural and indeed political influence of the applications of the new technology, symbolized most suitably, perhaps, by the aeroplane which went, one might say, from nowhere to everywhere in two decades. It would be churlish not draw attention to the immense benefits, particularly in the home but also at work and in the street and in the hospital, of so many of these applications in the first twenty years of our century. Life in 'advanced countries' was transformed and the transformation would clearly become, if not totally global, certainly one which spread its influence to all parts of the world.

Yet the 'two-edged' influence of the spread of the new technology in Britain (as somewhat later in Europe, North America and parts of the old British Empire), which had shown itself in the destruction of the quality of life and work in the industrial areas during the nineteenth century, was still thought by many to be avoidable until the Great War occurred. Indeed, even before a shot was fired in anger, or a tank crushed a body or an aircraft strafed defenceless people, the revolution in colour printing and the 'art' of propaganda had ensured that – as before – truth was the first casualty of the war. The difference was that such lying could now be systematized and disseminated at the level of mesmerism and brain-washing.[30]

More disturbingly, however, than such obvious two-edged qualities of technology mentioned in the previous paragraph was the haphazard, uncontrolled and essentially irrational nature of its spread. Indeed its spread appears to have been due to the technology itself dictating what developments were possible rather than to human decision. Moreover each 'advance', whether desirable as in much medicine or corrosive of humanity as in most warfare, has impinged on man and his way of life even where demonstrably antisocial. Our dependence, even by 1929, was becoming total: possibilities became probabilities and then 'necessities'. Limits in development would be for economic, commercial or political considerations rather than there being human and cultural benefits in mind – nor would environmental considerations restrict development. Ways would always be found to build new roads, more cars, more airfields and more factories. Two-edged, technology clearly was, but for many ordinary people living in Britain in 1929 it was the gentle

---

*See Volume II and Volume III of Literature and Culture in Modern Britain for developments between 1930 and 1992.

edge they felt – even when on the dole. Such was the ambiguous nature of the technology and its social effects.

NOTES

1. E.N. Nash and A.M. Newth, *Britain in the Modern World: the Twentieth Century* (Harmondsworth, 1967), p. 194.
2. Trevor I. Williams, *A Short History of Twentieth-Century Technology* (Oxford 1982), pp. 387–95.
3. Nash and Newth, pp. 20–1.
4. See Leslie Bailey, *B.B.C. Scrapbook for 1914*, (London, 1964), p. 2.
5. See Nash and Newth, p. 10.
6. J.M. Roberts, *The Pelican History of the World* (Harmondsworth, 1980), pp. 829–34.
7. David S. Landers, *The Unbound Prometheus: Technological Change and Industrial Development in Western Europe from 1750 to the Present* (Cambridge, 1972), pp. 273–4 and pp. 326–30.
8. H. Pelling, *Modern Britain: 1885–1955* (London, 1974), pp. 47–9.
9. R.K. Webb, *Modern England* (London, 1980), p. 112.
10. See C.F.G. Masterman, (London, 1960). *The Condition of England.*
11. Landers, p. 95.
12. Williams, pp. 30–1.
13. Ibid., pp. 388–9.
14. Ibid., pp. 389–90.
15. Landers, pp. 281–2.
16. Williams, p. 70.
17. Ibid., pp. 73–5.
18. Ibid., pp. 77–8.
19. Ibid., pp. 76–7.
20. Ibid., p. 24, pp. 324–40 and pp. 242–3.
21. Ibid., pp. 157–8.
22. Ibid., p. 159.
23. Ronald W. Clark, *The Scientific Breakthrough* (London, 1974), pp. 49–57.
24. Ibid., pp. 58–60. See also Bailey, p. 2.
25. Ibid., p. 74.
26. Williams, pp. 261–3.
27. Ibid., pp. 263–5.
28. From Siegfried Sassoon, 'Thoughts in 1932', in *The Collected Poems of Siegfried Sassoon 1908–1956* (London, 1984), pp. 231–2.
29. L. Bender, *Invention* (London, 1991).
30. See W. Sargant, *Battle for the Mind* (London, 1957), especially chs 1 and 7.

Index